MW00697677

Our Boys

A Team, A Town, A History, A Way of Life

by

David Pierce

ISBN: 978-1-935802-34-1

Cover design by Graphic Edge

PUBLISHING, INC.
4909 N. Monroe Street
Tallahassee, Florida 32303-7015
www.fatherson.com
800-741-2712

Dedication

To every man alive or departed who was ever an Ace, Orphan, Terrapin or Indian, who spilt his blood, sweat and tears on the field of gridiron battle for the greater good of the Ocilla community.

Acknowledgments

To the Ocilla *Star* for its wonderful articles discovered on microfilm at the Irwin County Library; to the ladies of the library for kindly allowing me repeated access to the genealogy room; to my wife, Lucy, for her valuable work photo-scanning and proofreading; to the countless faithful from near and far for kindly sharing many golden memories of football in Ocilla, Irwin County, Georgia.

Preface

High school football has been a part of our culture here for a lot of years. It still matters if the boys win. Winning lifts a little town, and we, the folks of Ocilla, Irwin County, Georgia, need all the uplift and cure we can get.

There's no action here, no place to go, nothing to do and it's hard to make a dollar. And unless you're into cotton and peanuts, there's isn't much to cheer for, either. You can pass through the city limits and wonder where the town went.

But rural life does have its advantages and, somehow, while a case could be made that Ocilla's best days are a thing of the past, football at Irwin County High is going strong, thank God. It remains a source of pride, entertainment and social enrichment for the good people of this old farming community.

"They'd rather had that than church," cracks Pat Hodnett,

the former chief of Ocilla's public works, speaking of the natives back when he was an Indian.

Some things never change. Football keeps us connected. Of course, we have not always won a large number of games. That's not what this book is about at all. We've hoed some hard rows and never were dynasty. It's just that football, like farming, is a pillar of what's left of our local heritage, and we like to observe it by whooping and hollering when our boys play, by decorating our store fronts when they're doing good and sticking Indian signs in our yards to show that we support their efforts.

Not everybody in this country town goes to the games and commits suicide if the boys lose. That is a myth. The streets don't fold up on game night any more than usual at dark. But, you can bet, the bigger the game the bigger the turnout and hoopla and you can expect to see Billy Spicer, an Ocilla man with Down's Syndrome, helping lead the band, and Sandy McClurd will be out there when the fun starts with her camera, making a pictorial record of the gridiron proceedings.

Maybe you heard of a law we have around here that says all able-bodied boys must play football or risk being thrown into the clink and a school rule that requires boys to win a letter in football or risk not getting their diploma. Those are a pack of lies. But, yes, any growing, well-made lad of the Ocilla vicinity is expected to be an Indian when he comes of age; we need all the help we can get out there. Besides, it'll do him good to play, and football here is like a civic duty, a rite of passage, sort of an unspoken law that boys down through the years have unselfishly honored. With many a boy, reporting for duty is just instinct.

"I started in the seventh grade," says Cartavion Benyard, a member of the 2015 squad that played in the Georgia Dome. Football, he points out, "is just a tradition down here in Irwin

County. When you're young, you look up to the football players, and you just want to become one."

As for myself, when I was ten, I saw the great Indian, Walter Sumner, elude tacklers with his shifty hips. To watch my older brother and his buddy—the Indian monster, Big Daddy—come out on game night and terrorize opposing lines was better than the movies.

I gave up on football until my brother advised me to finish. Wayne said to me, "When the Indians take the field, you be with them." I shrugged and said, "all right." And so, from 1969 through 1971, I was an Indian, first under Buzzy McMillan and then Conrad Nix. Before that, I had played football in Fitzgerald for a couple of years, first for Joe Compton and then Jesse Dyess, when my mother was working in Fitzgerald at a garment plant. My little brother, Danny Ray, was Indian, too, and his boy, Cam, was an Indian so I guess you could say it's in our family the way football tends to run in your blood.

Most of my boyhood I spent in Ocilla, which, if you didn't know, is pronounced "O-Silla." People around here like pickup trucks, cornbread and their tea sweet. You find a good deal of those preferences in this part of old Dixie, or what is called "God's Country." You might've heard it called "Peanut Country," and in the autumn time when the lights come on, this section of Georgia is "Football Country."

By chance have you heard of the Georgia Sweet Potato Festival? We have that in Ocilla. It happens in the fall. People drive in for "Tater Day" from as far away as Pennsylvania, and their money's as good as anybody's.

Specifically, Ocilla is the seat of Irwin County in south central Georgia and at last count, the population of our town, which probably took its name from an Indian—no doubt a great warrior—was roughly 3,400 with maybe a few thousand more spread out in the reaches of the county. To drive the distance at normal speed, we're about a three-hour ride, and worlds apart, from Atlanta. You can find us on the map roughly west of Douglas, easterly of Tifton and north of Valdosta. Or you can just say we're nine miles from Fitzgerald, Georgia. Hasn't everybody heard of Fitzgerald?

When I was growing up I can remember when Fitzgerald with its economic energy and grand dwellings, its stores and those famous brick streets, was like a big city to us folks. They had the jobs, the prestige. They also had the athletes. I think that is how God meant it to be, and it's made for some good football over the years between the two teams, although Fitzgerald has us by the throat in the record.

This work explores the history of football in Ocilla in chronological order, year by year, from its roots prior to the Great Depression to 1975 and takes a broad view of later seasons. All chapters except for a couple are preceded by a piece taken from newspapers of that period; no attempt to change the wording was made. Also, I realized that no history of football in a town is any good without some history of the town itself, which I have included, and Ocilla's history cannot be told without a dose of Fitzgerald's.

To put this book together, in addition to my own recollection, I combed through an eight-inch-high stack of old newspaper clippings that I copied from slow-chugging microfilm at the Irwin County Library and other libraries. Furthermore, I mined the Georgia High School Football Historians Association on the Web for data and relied on the knowledge of many, primarily old players and coaches, as to throw sufficient light on the subject of football as it has been played in Ocilla over the decades beginning in the 1920s.

Sadly, a few sources I called on have died since granting me an interview. Some I hoped to speak with about football could not be located or had departed before I could reach them.

At any rate, I have tried to make this book as clean and polite as possible, and I hope anyone who celebrates high school football the way we do finds something in it that they like.

David Pierce, Ocilla, Georgia

Table of contents

Part I

1

Hustle

Fitzgerald High School fast foot ball team went the way of all the other school teams (except Ashburn) Friday afternoon when they took a drubbing at the hands of our boys to the tune of 15 to 6.

At the first of the season, Fitzgerald were a bit chesty, and for a while it appeared that the Ocilla team could not attract their attention sufficiently to get a game with them. Now they probably consider Ocilla High School worthy of the best of school teams.

It was a thrilling game from start to finish and both teams played good ball.

—*Ocilla Star*, October 25, 1923

It came up fast like a summer storm—one of those swift-moving tree-benders that go *bam, bam, bam*—and blew the natives away. How they marveled at all the strangers and the speed of their axes, hammers, saws. It was all really mind-boggling—a sight to behold if you had a date, say, or were just curious to know what a boom town looked like.

By the droves and from every direction, by every mode you could imagine, people rode in on the storm to make a town. It wasn't gold but the promise of a land of milk and honey that led legions of settlers to hew a colony in the piney woods of old Dixie in the year of 1895.

You can believe that the great majority of the newcomers to Irwin County, Georgia, were Yankees. That was not a coincidence. They had a good team and a solid plan for growing a colony in this territory rich with farmable land, good space for grazing, tall timber, wild game and water fresh and clean as in the Holy Bible.

Just say that name, "Fitzgerald," and everybody'd heard about it.

But you did not say "Fitzgerald." You got away from home, maybe to find a brother or see about a mule, and told somebody that you were from "Ocilla" and got the strangest look.

It was like, *Ocilla? What, where, is Ocilla?*

Nobody knew. And let's be frank; nobody ever really gave a damn for Ocilla except for the people here and some who used to live here but who had moved away for some reason or died. Although only nine miles from the famous haven, Ocilla remained an obscurity. We had our pride, though, and nobody could intimidate us.

> *"Ocilla does not take a backseat to any town in this part of the state. Remember that,"* crowed Ocilla's first newspaper, the *Dispatch*, in 1900.

Nine years later, in 1909, when the Yankee haven was on the way to being called one of the greatest colonies in America since Plymouth Rock and the Pilgrims, the owner and editor of the *Ocilla Star* sounded the alarm.

A village always or a hustling little city? J. J. Flanders cried in 1909.

It was a real good question. In one of his pep-talk writings, publisher Flanders told of a new game going around called the "hustle" and he said we'd better get on the ball, learn how to play the game if we ever wanted to have anything or be anybody to matter. Nobody got chewed out for letting Fitzgerald whip us. It wasn't like that. A former Ocilla school superintendent who was now the proprietor of Ocilla's little weekly, Mr. Flanders and his cohorts of the Ocilla business district were just saying that the age of "everlasting hustle" for industry was here, and if we didn't score, others in the game would wash us.

"*Let's go*," Flanders howled in the *Star*.

Spectacled, clean-shaven, humble but enthusiastic, James Julian Flanders did not have the means or the pull to make Ocilla into a modern little city he thought we could be. Compared to the powers who controlled the money and the politics, and the elite landholders, who generally frowned on industry, fearing that factory jobs would leave no one to pick cotton, Flanders was nearer to a pauper. But in civic spirit and when it came to the floating of progressive ideas on how to grow Ocilla, he was among the richest citizens, and he had a dream.

In the dream, which he shared through his commentaries, Ocilla awoke and began to dance for the capitalists that she favored, and it was a beautiful union. The right industries came, the jobs came, the right kind of people moved in, the school grew and Ocilla began to hum with new life and vigor while staying true to her farming roots. In the real world, Mr.

Flanders' editorials, although they were always very interesting, did not seem to have much of an effect. There was no revolution in Ocilla.

Maybe we were blackballed. You could never be sure.

Whatever the case was, Ocilla would never rise to the level of our friends in places like Albany, Valdosta or Moultrie and we could not ever beat Fitzgerald at their game. No.

But all hope was not lost.

At the pace of all-sufficient God, our Redeemer, keeper of "Uncle Warren," our father, Mr. Henderson, Provider, Divider of Sheep from Goat, Ocilla kept her feet moving and made her own fire, like with football, which often was spelled with two words.

Through "foot ball," Ocilla left a mark.

The average Ocilla resident had a blissful spirit. They were hearty, agrarian people, a little wary, somewhat lazy, predominantly of Southern cloth. There were some drunks among us, of course, and naysayers and the kickers fought progress at every turn but if you could put up with the politics and liked a small place away from the traps of big city life, Ocilla was a nice spot to put down roots, do business and bring up children to teach them how to live.

Besides loving Jesus—and it was Jesus who said, "Blessed are ye, when men shall revile you, and persecute you, and shall say all manner of evil against you falsely"—Ocilla folks came on strong for properly educating the local boys and girls. While you had to commend the Yankee haven for their schools, which boasted of kids from 38 states and two territories, and being the first system in Georgia to offer free textbooks to its pupils,

Ocilla was just as proud of her own institution. Two stories of red brick at Fourth and Alder streets, the Ocilla School was charming and the kids were civilized.

Basically, everyone was as happy in Ocilla as they wanted to be. The bulldog, Flanders, was never satisfied, though. Determined, he kept beating and beating the drum of progress. When anything occurred in Ocilla that resembled prosperity, initiative or forward thought, the town crier dashed from his office, pen in hand, eager to salute it.

A few years washed under the bridge.

By now it was getting late in the first quarter of the twentieth century, during the autumn time, in fact, when Mr. Flanders must've jumped out of his chair one day, rushing to investigate a grouping of Ocilla boys in the school yard. He discovered they were playing *foot ball.*

"Foot ball?"

It wasn't exactly the type of industry Flanders and his pals of the business league had long hoped would come in and push Ocilla ahead. But it looked like fun and we could all use the distraction.

"*Fascinating,*" Flanders said of the new game.

Certainly, he recognized the boys in leather hats were our sons, each a Son of Ocilla, Irwin County, at a time when this community south of Fitzgerald needed some heroes. You will find out soon enough, but our very first boys got killed. Oh, it was ugly, and even in their best years, they did not win a mighty lot of games, losing to the big frogs on foreign soil, but the boys expected to win every time they took the field. At hundred miles an hour, they came at you in the spirit of the Lord even though they very often were the underdog. You had to respect Ocilla.

Clearly, Flanders liked to see the boys win, especially if we were playing the bigger dogs, and for the sake of morale and pride we all needed to win at something besides farming and turpentine. But even in defeat our boys were not beaten for good character and that counted for a lot in the eyes of Flanders and the town clergy, who valued a good name over riches.

Underprivileged, not the most talented and playing with a short hand, these *colorful* pioneers of football in Ocilla attained a degree of celebrity for their clean, plucky play. No team was bragged on in the daily press more than Ocilla's little brigade. Between 1923 and 1928, savvy fans in towns that Ocilla couldn't compete with in the industrial arena grew fond of the gallant teams she presented on the ball field for their hustle and never-say-die attitude. Spectators used to four yards and a cloud of dust were thoroughly entertained as if by a circus when the out-manned Ocilla squad, under the leadership of a man we called "professor," hit town with its unique aerial show and clever play-calling. The Ocilla boys appear to have been among the league's first teams to unleash the forward pass as a primary weapon, on occasion tossing the ball two or three times on the same play.

Maybe it would've been cool to have lived in those days.

Back then, for lack of a bus, Ocilla boys traveled by car and went by many names. Game for anyone who wanted to play them, our gritty bunch of cotton pickers crisscrossed this old Indian country, tooling merrily on the roadways and on some dusty roads with their meager gear stuffed in amongst them like gypsies. At first, Flanders simply referred them as "our boys" or "the boys" while the daily press called them the "Ocilla Eleven" or "Whelchel's boys." A lot of times, our ambassadors dubbed themselves the Aces or the Orphans, which was freaky; most teams went by mean creatures like Bulldogs and Pirates and a great storm was just up the road at the colony. But generally, our earliest lads, the first to bear the Ocilla banner of Pride and Prosperity, would be uniquely remembered in the record as the Terrapins.

Their pants hung on them dumpily. There were no names on the jerseys and no numbers on the front or back of the jerseys—at least not for Ocilla. Some boys wore long johns under their gear on the colder days. The shoulder pads were not much more than a stack of flapjacks. The leather helmets, buckled under the chin with a single strap, had holes in the side and holes in the top for hearing and sweating through with no mask to protect the boys' snarling faces from flying feet, elbows and knees. A few poor boys for Ocilla did not have decent shoes for cleats; some played in tennis shoes or without helmets, but nothing could deter our fightin' few from the task of trying to beat other boys to pieces.

You could not estimate the value of football to Ocilla in dollars. Economically it never did a lick for us. But it was good for fan morale when the boys won, especially over Fitzgerald, and the games were a fine venue for fun and fellowship and a wholesome source of relief from the mundane realities of that period. Football was something to look forward to, to cheer over, to talk about in the drab days of autumn—even in church. For the players, football was a good outlet for their energies to keep them out of mischief, and it taught them about teamwork and life. For some of the better ones, it was a ticket out of Ocilla, like to college.

So, everyone associated with the little program made a profit.

Flanders was troubled by bad attendance at the games in Ocilla. He felt that our hustling band of ballers, popular on the road, deserved a better showing when they came Home, and while the boys did have some crazy local fans, our needy little aggregate had to scratch for every dime to pay for such as gear and road trips, and they spent a lot of time on the road where they were very unlucky.

The home record tells a different story.

The school lot where the boys fought their hearts out was a hard place, unfit for goats, full of little red rocks and stones that scarred many a boy forever. Ocilla's was probably the worst field in the league, which might help to explain the soft turnouts and why our boys sometimes were the "Orphans"—a team without a field. There was no running water or place to pee. The goal posts were two-by-four boards nailed together to form the letter H and a few banks of pine lumber was the best you ever got in Ocilla for seating. But those were the times. It was what it was. The game was football, not girls' tennis, and there on that old, rocky plain along Fourth Street, before their own whooping fans, who longed to see them beat the snot out of somebody, the boys of the 1920s won many victories in the name of their school, their families and the little town of Ocilla.

2

Rivals

Valdosta High School took a hard fought game from Ocilla last Friday by the score of 20-3. The Valdosta team had no trouble gaining thru the Ocilla line and Ocilla could not gain consistently thru the Valdosta line. Ocilla had several chances to score a touchdown but each time the Valdosta team tightened up and held them back...For Ocilla the entire system of forward passing seemed to give Valdosta trouble. This was the best gaining play Ocilla had. Vardeman and Whelchel at ends played nicely and both received several passes for nice gains. Fletcher played a good game at full back for the time he was in. McCall scored for Ocilla with a pretty field goal from the 25-yard line.

—Ocilla Star, October 9, 1924

The South lost when Lee surrendered. You knew that. You also knew that you were supposed to get over the war, move on. Fitzgerald was a shining model of peace and harmony, where Billy Yank and Johnny Reb lived and worked side by side for the greater good of mankind, so forget the past, dear friends, and let's all work together in this garden spot of the world once occupied by Indians. And yet, for many causes, it was all kinds of fun to stick it to ole Fitz on the chalked field. Seemed like Ocilla was always in the shadow of Fitzgerald, like a little brother or a redheaded stepchild, and battling their boys in football must've been like refighting the Civil War. It was a real kick to whip 'em, which Ocilla did five times out of eight in the 1920s, according to the old records. How they must've hated that—losing to us peasants.

There were a lot of reasons why football in Ocilla was hot if the game was with our nearest neighbor. Certainly, the Ocilla-Fitzgerald divide was greater than the nine miles separating the two towns. Fitzgerald was bigger than us, one thing, and our histories were different. So were our politics and our ways of looking at the world were not the same. Also, hats off to Fitzgerald. They had their act together; Ocilla, not so much, it seemed. Flanders cried and cried for someone to step up and be our leader, to take the cat by the tail and get us some industry that'd help make Ocilla a relevant little city but nobody ever wanted the ball. It was a case of every man out for himself to prosper and there was not very much leadership.

Fitzgerald knew how to grow a town, which sort of made Ocilla look bad. They had leadership and a clear goal, which made us look like squatters or something. The colony began with the dream of a former drummer boy for the Union army.

Philander H. Fitzgerald, who grew up poor, imagined a place where Union veterans could live out their days in a warm, peaceful climate. But all respectable people, not just old Yankees, would be welcome. They wound up flocking to Irwin County just up the road from slow-poke Ocilla.

In an old, grainy photograph, the mastermind of the buildup appears now to have been slightly framed with a mustache like Wyatt Earp. A visionary, Fitzgerald published a newspaper out of Indiana. Brilliant, he also was a lawyer and his dream colony, a symbol of reconciliation over the Civil War, was progressive for its time. Ocilla was not very progressive. Among their achievements that Ocilla could not match, the colonists built a grand Yankee-style hotel called the Grant Lee, one of the first public work relief programs in America. At the end of 1896, our neighbor had two railroads, a bank, three newspapers, 250 businesses and eleven churches and they put up a bandstand with music ranging from "Yankee Doodle" to "Dixie." They even had a big parade.

That was all well and good, and everybody'd heard of Fitzgerald, where the streets were cleverly laid out with names from both sides of the Civil War, not just the North.

In his 1932 book, *History of Irwin County*, J. B. Clements of Irwinville wrote that the natives were awed.

> *This new town and colony springing up almost overnight was quite a curiosity to them, a place to visit, consequently on Sunday afternoons many would drive over to investigate. It was a popular drive for courting couples or for a young man to take his best girl site-seeing. The natives were a curiosity to the newcomers, as one of the early colonists told me that when he came down here he thought no people were in this country except probably a very few scattered squatters.*

Although a number of settlers who were looked upon by other colonists as "undesirable" tired of their southern home and got out, initially some nine thousand seekers came. This, now, was at a time when hatred of Yanks ran deep in the heart of many Georgians. But give Fitzgerald credit. He and his partners hung in through some tough sledding when their venture was called "Shacktown" or "Slabtown"; and after the storm, Fitzgerald was a model—one of America's first truly planned cities, and if it made them feel any better, they weren't the only ones who had their hands full with little Ocilla between the hashes.

Our boys did not discriminate; they got after everybody and did Ocilla's bidding in a way that made us proud. They hailed from the town of Ocilla and from the woods and the fields in the outskirts where all the cotton grew, and relished a shot to lock horns with big frogs from the bigger schools in the bigger, faster towns who probably had thought of Ocilla as a little backward.

These battles were waged in the daytime. There were no lights in those days, just what God gave—His sun. Kickoff was about two or four o'clock, depending. Unlike schools that seemed to have a stable of coaches and players, Ocilla High only had one coach at a time, and to put out a team worthy to war with the league's big dogs, our coach had to be quite a schemer. Boys living in the reaches of Irwin County who'd have made good ball players did not attend Ocilla High and were not eligible for our football team. And because some Ocilla boys were in the cotton field when school took in, a turnout of 15 to 18 ballers for practice was the most you could expect to see in Ocilla.

Sometimes the Ocilla squad hit the road without any

substitutes, making do with the traveling eleven, while the conference heavyweights had 35-40 boys apiece and they kept shuffling in fresh men, which was how they got us a lot; they wore Ocilla down.

The league's hardest nut for Ocilla boys to crack was Valdosta. The boys 65 miles south of Ocilla always treated us with the respect and civility that you would expect from a class outfit like Valdosta High School. They never put Ocilla boys down or acted in such a way as to make Ocilla feel like second-class citizens. Although Ocilla could not seem to ever get over on Valdosta, we thought of them as a big rival, and until about 1929, when the walls began to crumble, games between Ocilla and the Wildcats were good quality.

But let's get back to Fitzgerald. You know, it's possible that town never liked us much down here in Ocilla even though we were so close and were supposed to be friends. From the looks of things, the rivalry between us and them that later trickled into football originated in the turpentine days, back when Ocilla and the village that we'd come to know as Fitzgerald were siblings or whatever you call it when hamlets are in the same county, in this case Irwin County, and compared to Fitzgerald, Ocilla's history was as dull as a plate of lima beans. And yet one had to admit a name like "Ocilla" was unique.

While it may be obvious to many that Fitzgerald was named after a human being, the jury is still out on "Ocilla." One school of speculation says the name spawned from a river, either the Satilla or the Ausilla, or a combination of the two. The theory with the best legs says "Ocilla" was a take on Osceola, which is pronounced ah-see-OH-la, which in part means "black drink." Osceola was a legendary warrior. You probably read about him in school. He led the fight in the Second Seminole War against the government. The government pushed the tribe to Indian Territory west of the Mississippi River. So, we pick Osceola as sort of our namesake.After the Indians were put out and white settlers arrived, the land that is today southern Georgia was divided into three districts they called "Mother" counties: Appling, Early and Irwin. After 1819, the state began to cut into these lower Georgia giants like a jigsaw puzzle to make new counties, such as Lowndes, which had been part of Irwin. The seat of Lowndes along the Florida border would be Valdosta.

Mother Irwin birthed many a county in these parts.

Ocilla appears to have originated in the 1880s as a turpentine still. Later, we were just an ordinary little rural community trying to make a go in Dixie when J. A. J. Henderson, dubbed the father of Ocilla, and who served as our mayor, postmaster and, for a time, a state senator, inspired the construction of a large sawmilling plant that rivaled Fitzgerald's big mill.

It was game on.

In 1897, a railroad was built that connected Ocilla —specifically, Henderson's mill—to Fitzgerald and the world beyond. That same year, Ocilla was legitimized when the city charter arrived from the state of Georgia.

By 1900, our population had doubled to a whopping 805.

In his book, Clements noted that after the mill went up,

This place began to grow and flourish and was soon recognized as the rival of the neighboring city of Fitzgerald. It was the rival not only in a business way but also its rival in desiring (the) courthouse.

The courthouse at that time was based in Irwinville, the county seat and which you might remember from your history book was the capture site of Jefferson Davis, president of the Confederacy.

Fitzgerald went for it first. There was a county-wide referendum on moving courthouse operations from Irwinville to their place. They lost. It wasn't game over, however, and in 1906, Fitzgerald divorced Mother Irwin when the state carved out another piece of Irwin and a piece of Wilcox County to make a new county, Ben Hill, of which Fitzgerald would be the seat.

A year later, Ocilla took her shot. And won. It was a bitter, friendship-busting referendum but Ocilla prevailed, winning the right to be the seat of Irwin County.

Then in 1909 came J. J. Flanders on his horse with some big ideas for growing Ocilla into a sparkling hub by way of manufacturing.

Town lots have been laid off on all sides of us, enough, if populated, to make Ocilla half as large as Atlanta.

Naturally, that would never happen. But the 1910 Census did show an upswing. That year the population of Ocilla was 2,017. The increase was due largely to the railroad, new businesses going up and moving the courthouse operations to Ocilla from Irwinville, which was nicknamed the "Graveyard of the Confederacy."

About this same time, interest in high school football was growing across south Georgia.

Fitzgerald didn't hesitate; they jumped right in.

Albany's Indians, Moultrie's Packers and Valdosta's Wildcats also were among the trailblazers. The trio got started with football in 1913 and then Thomasville got up a team and warred with them, forming a mighty foursome.

Old sports records indicate that Fitzgerald High had a football team as early as 1908. Fittingly, their stormy troops were the Purple Hurricane, or simply the Hurricane, sometimes

"Canes" for short, and in Ocilla, for a lot of reasons, we always looked forward to beating them as bad as we could.

3

Husky Bunch

Show Your Public Spirit. Elsewhere in this issue appears a call for a meeting tonight to organize a business league.

Most people with whom we have talked seem agreed that we ought to have such an organization. The question is, what are we going to do about it? When an Ocilla man gets away from home and tells people that he is from Ocilla, the question almost invariably asked is, "Where is Ocilla?" Our invariable reply has to be "Nine miles from Fitzgerald." Everybody knows where Fitzgerald is because that town is advertised. A few of the people of Ocilla have determined that henceforth we are going to be on the map. We know that we have the goods, and we are going to let the rest of the world share the secret.

A business league, promptly managed, will put new life and vigor into our little city and it must be confessed that we need it. There may have been a time when one could sit down and let prosperity come to him but that time has passed. This is the day of everlasting hustle and the fellow who does not know how to hustle invariably gets left. What is true to individuals is equally true of towns. Other towns—our neighbors—are hustling, are getting before the country at large, and are acquiring industries, and we must get busy, or be hopelessly left. Sit down and wait for the other fellow to bring prosperity, and it will not get here. What kind of spirit have you?

—*Ocilla Star*, July 30, 1909

With boys in the school yard tossing to one another a brown, leathery oblong object that might have reminded someone of a blown-up hog bladder, football began in Ocilla in the year of 1922. The exact day cannot be determined. The spirited youngsters were discovered by Mr. Flanders in the month of October.

Why football? Certainly, our upstart band of grid-iron enthusiasts realized that a lot of boys across the district were already doing it, and besides the fact that football was another way for us to get something over on Fitzgerald and our other neighbors in this part of Georgia, the Ocilla High lads were inspired by what they saw in magazines about the adventures of the Georgia Bulldogs and Georgia Tech Yellow Jackets.

It was tough, though, and they would need the Lord's strength to bring them through the trials.

Ragged, with barely any shoes for traction, this start-up crew from Ocilla, late arriving to the party, did not look much like the All-American outfit. They only numbered a dozen or so, all awkward, untrained young men who knew as much about football as they knew about climbing the Alps. Yet, they displayed an eager spirit and huskiness that gave curious fans a reason to be optimistic about their chances.

The key to their success would be coaching. We felt very strongly about coaching. No doubt good boys raised right to respect authority, all they needed was a leader, a man of high moral character who knew the game to show them the ropes and they'd beat the socks off anybody.

When it was decided that no one at the school knew enough about the game to be the coach, the boys went to see the local veterinarian or horse doctor. This man, T.B. "Doc" Gissendanner, had played football while at Auburn University. Although he probably had never actually coached, "Doc" was a good player when in college and he took the boys under wing and we all looked forward to winning many titles.

While the upstanding citizens of the Ocilla community did not know much about football, they knew the devil when they saw it, and sports here was a glorified form of recreation to ward off the evil among the youth. The devil, in 1922, was guzzling booze, gambling, swimming in pools—also known as dipping vats—gazing at girly calendars on door-backs in public places, night riding in cars, promiscuous dress and other forms of loose morality. If her young people—her future—went down the wide road to bad character, loafing, mental illness, premature aging and untimely death caused by sin and letting yourself go, Ocilla was a dead duck. Boys in their teens who could drive a motor vehicle were especially at risk of going to the dogs as many were sought by bootleggers to haul moonshine.

Basically, our young people were bored silly, which led to idleness and mischief in a small country town. The devil lurked around every corner. It was believed that one way to shield our boys and girls from sin was to involve them in clean, organized, physical activities in their spare time, which was any time they were not in school, at church, studying, working or asleep. Mr. Flanders realized that even the jumping jack, also known as the side-straddle hop, promoted good physical health, relieved stress and increased blood flow to the brain, which improved one's thinking.

Golf was a popular pursuit for Ocilla men in the old days. No fewer than two dozen Ocilla establishments, including the *Star*, closed after lunch on Thursdays so young men employees could get some relief in the form of clean, physical activity. A fair number of these penned-up workers went out on their half-day off to play golf at the Ocilla course. While golf was accepted in Ocilla as an outlet for men and some boys, the most popular game at school was basketball, which in the 1920s was an outdoor sport in Ocilla. A number of townspeople liked to watch it, and baseball, too. When it came to sports, Ocilla, in 1922, was pretty much a round-ball town.

Then the *Star* reported on page one October 12:

> *The boys of the High School have organized a foot ball team and are now busy practicing the game. T.B. Gissendanner, an old foot ball player, has agreed to coach the team and is already putting the boys through their paces.*
>
> *A public subscription was taken this week among*

> *citizens of the town and enough money was raised to purchase the equipment needed.*
>
> *The school has never before had a foot ball team and not only the boys but all the people of the town are taking an interest in this most fascinating school and college sport.*
>
> *Our boys are a pretty husky bunch and ought to give neighboring schools something to do to beat them. We will see more about that later.*

One member of Ocilla High's first football team was Myron Harper, if you take it from the man himself. In a letter to the *Star* in 1976, Harper recalled that 1922 was his first and only season. He said he played on the line and graduated in the spring of 1923 in a senior class of six girls and four boys.

> In his letter to *Star* publisher Bill Bradford, Harper in 1976 recalled that he and the other boys who formed the very first team *contacted all of the Ocilla merchants who generously contributed enough money for us to order one dozen padded football pants from Spalding's in Atlanta. The late Claude McNeil was very instrumental in us raising these funds.*

Harper did not remember the early boys having any shoulder pads, helmets or formal cleats. *Accordingly, each of us gathered up a pair of our old shoes and had the shoe cobbler build cleats at 35 cents per pair.*

On Oct. 20, 1922, the first recorded football game involving Ocilla boys was conducted against, who else, but Fitzgerald? Fitzgerald, on their turf, proved to be our daddy. Thankful, in a way, for the whipping at the Yankee haven, our boys spat on the ground and took their pride back to Ocilla. This was a Friday.

On the following Monday, Ocilla hosted its first football game of all time. The result was a narrow victory over someone's dummy squad. Everybody at the game was jubilant. Reported the *Star*:

> *Ocilla High School boys had their first game last Friday afternoon and went down to a crushing defeat at the hands of the Fitz Hi team. The score was against them to the tune of 64-0. This was the first game they had ever played and for some of the team the first game they ever saw. So they did not feel so much discouraged over the result, but came back home realizing they had learned something about the game and were ready for the next battle. The Fitzgerald boys showed good form and put up a pretty game. Monday afternoon our team met and defeated the Tifton Aggies (scrub team, of course) and in as pretty a game as one would want to see defeated them on the local grid by the score of 6-0.*
>
> *This was the first game ever played in Ocilla and a large number of people attended the game and many converts were made among the older fellows. Even J.L. Paulk and Major Harris came back talking about organizing a team of fifty year olds. Now our boys are daily practicing under the coaching of Dr. Gissen-danner and are thirsting for more gore, having once tasted blood.*

From that point in the season of 1922, the record grows hazy; data is incomplete, sources are conflicting. But it is no exaggeration; the inaugural mark was dismal. One game in 1922 was especially bad form, the drubbing on Ocilla High far worse than the devil beating his dog. Our boys were crushed in an especially gruesome and heinous way and one supposes there was no mercy rule. Afterwards, as they lay dead, as dead as one could be beaten without suffering a literal death, Ocilla was probably the laughingstock of the sport.

4

'Credible Team'

Licked to a Frazzle

It's a sad tale, mates. A tale of plenty of grit and nerve but of choosing the wrong bunch to pick upon.

When our aggregation of feet ball artists, who have just begun to play, and who had tasted blood for the first time when they played the Tifton Aggie scrub team last week, being a bit chesty over having drubbed one Aggie team, decided that they could do the same thing to another Aggie team, and this time the regular Aggie varsity, and decided that they Eleventh District Aggies were the particular Aggie team they wanted to drub Monday afternoon, they made a bad selection.

Let us get the sad tale told without more misery. We got beat a 144-0 score.

Lack of experience going up against a team that has had a good deal of experience is the whole story. But our boys are game. They are not afraid to tackle strong teams, knowing that hard games are needed to develop them in the gentle art of busting them all to pieces.

Our team will play Nashville Friday afternoon in Ocilla.

—*Ocilla Star*, November 2, 1922

After the trials of 1922, had our boys packed it in, let the program pass out, you'd have understood, and maybe a lesser bunch might've surrendered. But that's not what happened. We had our pride. Cast down but not destroyed, the boys wanted to play on and the Lord said, fine, go ahead, and while no divine promises were made, there came to Ocilla a man of the Methodist faith to help these ambitious boys of ours compete.

Straight-laced, leader of men and boys, who knew how to train up kids in the way they should go in the world, E.V. Whelchel was everything the school board had hoped for as Ocilla High's top man. Wise to the ways of football also, and having served stateside during World War I in the Army, Emmett Whelchel came to us from over in Douglas, Georgia, to be the principal of the upper grades, which was the high school, and to teach a science class. We called him "professor," a courtesy title given to our principal, and in the old days the principal was athletics director by default and coach of all the teams.

Taking over for Gissendanner, whose house burned in late September of that year, 1923, Prof. Whelchel added football to his long list of duties. It helped that eight who'd played in 1922 formed a nucleus for a good coach to build around and that year things came together the way the Lord intended. We did not win the conference. Maybe we weren't supposed to. But we won every time in the column for good character and sportsmanship while bagging six games out of nine on the fall slate, one of the highest marks in the league. We stunned a member of the "Big Four" and knocked Fitzgerald down a peg.

God was good. Yes, very good.

Dubbed the "association," this league was formally the Southwest Georgia Athletic Conference. It was the only group of its nature in southern Georgia and probably the first of its kind in the whole state. Based in Albany, the conference started up in 1919 and lasted for about 14 years and during that time claimed as many as 32 members.

This league was the best venue for organized play in the 1920s, and membership had its benefits. A conference champion was named and boys were honored at season's end for stellar work. Regardless of school size or athletic ability, members played other members, although the *elite* ones—the power clubs from schools in the bigger towns—rarely picked on the littler squads, called the *minors*, unless it was as a warm-up for the season. Eight to ten games made a normal season. The team with the most wins or fewest losses took home the mythical title of conference champ and there were no playoffs, although in 1931 there was a "special playoff" between Valdosta and Bainbridge.

Topping the *elite* list of clubs were Albany, Moultrie, Thomasville and Valdosta. These so-called "Big Four" were the older, established, superior teams with more boys and greater talent who hogged the awards and took turns winning the championship, except in 1930 when Fitzgerald claimed the title and 1931 when Bainbridge ended with the most checks in the win column.

The smaller, poorer programs, the *minors,* received little, if any, mention in the daily papers, had no shot of beating a conference power, taking the title or having a boy named to the post-season all-conference team.

Then along came Ocilla, one of the most interesting teams in the league.

With his goal in life to be a top administrator, Whelchel didn't see coaching as a long-term deal but he seemed to enjoy it while in Ocilla, where he was like a father to the boys, wanting them to succeed not only in sports but also in the classroom and in life. Under his hand the boys learned how to line up properly, get in a stance, block, tackle, punt, pass, kick and other aspects of the game they'd need to know to have a chance to succeed.

Most of all, they learned how to be men.

"That was Daddy," says Carolyn Mills, the coach's daughter who was born in Ocilla. "He didn't always win, but he stood his ground. That's how he raised his children."

In June 1923, the boys got up a game with Tifton High, and lost 32-12. It's not clear if Gissendanner was still coaching the team. Whelchel had the boys in hand when school took in. The first game was played on September 21 when we lost 9-0 at Ashburn. A week later Ocilla hammered Douglas, 30-0, on the school lot and later escaped Nashville with a 6–0 win.

The *Star* said on October 11:

The foot ball team of the Ocilla High School is playing ball. Their first game with Ashburn hardly counts, as they were merely beginners and the big score run up by Ashburn in the first quarter was before they found themselves. Since that first quarter in their first game, they have not been scored against. ...Prof. Whelchel is making a credible team out of this bunch of youngsters, and Ocilla is proud of the showing they are making. They play a good team, Eastman, here Friday and a hard game is in prospect...The boys have a good chance to win, but you can make it much easier for them by giving your support and backing. So show a little civic pride in your school, and come out to encourage the boys next Friday afternoon at 4 o'clock.

There was no game that afternoon with Eastman. The Bulldogs forfeited, giving Ocilla the victory. That was not extraordinary. A lack of transport, lack of men, washed-out roads, disease and other factors common in the 1920s often forced forfeits. Likewise, a number of games were set on the fly, depending on who was ready and able to play.

After the no-game with Eastman, our boys finally got their shot at Fitzgerald when the 'Canes agreed to a game. They came to Ocilla on October 19, 1923, and our boys did not seem the least bit intimidated. Proving worthy of our neighbor, Whelchel's corps let the cannon balls fly and drove Fitz down on the rocks.

Ocilla had been successfully defended.

The takeaway was that Ocilla boys, for all the rap they might've gotten, could play a good, clean game—and beat a quality club. Although no trace of it could be found later in the Fitzgerald papers, as if the occurrence at Ocilla was of no importance or had not really happened, you can bet the drubbing of ole Fitz was page one news in Ocilla. Two weeks later in

Fitzgerald, we hurt their feelings again, 7–6, in Fitzgerald, according to the records.

Then Eastman was ready to play and they tripped the Ocilla boys, 14–12, in Eastman.

But the season of 1923 did not end there.

Prof. Whelchel contacted Harold Saxon, the head coach in Moultrie, about a game, and they set it up for Thanksgiving Day. After a 6–1 season in 1922, Moultrie High was 2–5. Still, the Pack expected to take out little Ocilla with hardly a grunt, for they were Moultrie and our boys were just Ocilla and Moultrie ought never lose to Podunk.

Wrote the *Moultrie Observer:*
Ocilla High appeared here yesterday with a fast, well-coached, stocky team and defeated Moultrie High to the tune of 13-6...Ocilla got the ball on the kickoff and by a series of line plays and a delayed run off Moultrie's left tackle and end, scored a touchdown without losing the ball....For Ocilla, Hall was the outstanding star. Henderson at left tackle was good as was Colson at right end. The whole Ocilla team was on edge and took the unsuspecting Moultrie players off their feet time after time on delayed runs and flukes through center. Moultrie boys expected an easy go, and the game put up by the visitors came as a distinct surprise.

If the minors needed an inspiration, they now had one in Ocilla.

5

'Strongest Eleven'

Ocilla people will see their first foot ball game of the season Friday afternoon when the Tifton High School team comes here for a game. The Ocilla team has played two games this season, losing both, and they are about ready for a turn in the tide. This means that they are going to put up the fight of their lives to wrest a victory from the Tifton stalwarts ... and the fact that they have never lost a game on the local field is an added incentive to the local boys. Revenge for a past defeat is part of the program. It is a foregone conclusion that a good crowd will be on hand to cheer the local boys on to victory.

—*Ocilla Star*, October 9, 1924

Then in 1924, we got the short end of the stick six times out of nine, if you take it from the old data. We just didn't have the guns, if you want an excuse. It was frustrating. While the bigger clubs seemed to reload year after year, little Ocilla usually followed up a good season with a rebuilding effort, and after 1923 we lost eight first-stringers to graduation, leaving our coach with young, light players who'd not seen much battle. However, if you were looking for an easy bunch to kick around, stay away from Ocilla. Our boys that year, although inexperienced and short-handed, fought to the last man. Ocilla was a team to watch. And speaking of the coach, 1924 was a big year for Prof. Whelchel. He was promoted from principal to superintendent, giving him control of the Ocilla School's daily operations in all grades, first through the eleventh. Had we kept with tradition, the new principal—Roy Vinson, who did not have a coaching background—would have taken over the ball teams. But Whelchel opted to stay on as coach and athletics director, and he not only held the football program together at a shaky time, he forged it ahead by adding two more of the league's Big Four—Albany and Valdosta—to the fall slate, both on the road.

Superintendent Whelchel's philosophy on scheduling teams for Ocilla to play went with him to his grave. Besides not having a good field to play on and no way to collect admission, perhaps it was Whelchel's belief that to make a relevant team, like we all wanted, our boys needed to play the top squads, and playing them at their place had financial benefits under the gate-sharing rule. Also, the Ocilla boys received more exposure on the big stages, which raised their level of notoriety and that was useful

FIRST STRING, 1924-25— The photo above shows the "first string" of the 1924-25 Ocilla High School football team which won a state championship. B. L. (Ham) Henderson, who was omitted in the identification of a picture of the entire team published on Nov. 30, provides the following information on the above photo. On the line from left to right, Hugh Colson, end, who went on to attend Southern College in Lakeland, Fla.; Martin Whitley, tackle; Clark Nobles, guard; Tom Hollingsworth, center, who also played center at Dahlonega; McKinley Hudson, guard, who continued his football at Mercer University, Macon; G. W. Dismuke, tackle; Marion Dickens, end, who made all Southern and All American at the University of Georgia. In the backfield from left, Carlyle Vardeman, quarterback; John W. Fletcher, r.h.b., who also played halfback at Tifton A.and M.; B. L. (Ham) Henderson, l.h.b., who attended Tifton A. and M. and played halfback there and Herman Hall, fullback, who went to Dahlonega where he played quarterback. Mr. Henderson, whose address is Rt. 1, Enigma, said that of the team members, G. W. Dismuke, Tom Hollingsworth, Hugh Colson, J. W. Fletcher and Herman Hall are deceased. E. V. Whelchel, who coached the team, retired as Moultrie School Superintendent, and now lives in Moultrie.

The 1924-25 Ocilla Hi football team. *Courtesy of the Sandy McClurd collection* when the awards were voted on and other considerations were made.

Whatever logic was driving, Whelchel and his band of young ballers piled into waiting cars on September 26 at the school and lit out in the rain for south Georgia's largest city, 62 miles away, to open the '24 season.

Around mid-afternoon, the fleet from Ocilla snaked into Albany to play the powerhouse Indians and got whopped on the scoresheet. Although we showed good form, and conducted ourselves gentlemanly, our lively attack with the forward pass was snuffed due largely to the rain and mud and there went the goodies. Albany High had 42 lads out for football that season, and they substituted freely while Ocilla did not have the extra boys to match them. Ocilla, however, got some good out of the deal, if you liked press. Folks back home beamed over the team's showing of grit and sportsmanship in Albany. Although the boys returned home with the butt end of a 26–0 score, The *Albany Herald*, the region's largest daily, patted them on the back, saying Ocilla boys were *well-trained...the strongest eleven Albany ever faced in an opening game.*

Then a week later Valdosta beat us but the score was only 20–3 and the 'Cats knew they had been in a fight, and the Friday afterwards, fans who hadn't traveled with the team got their first sight of the boys in action when Tifton came to the school lot. One of the league's top teams that year, the Blue Devil club gave us our first loss ever on the home field.

Otherwise, if you overlook the Tifton game, home in 1924 was good to the little Ocilla team. On the rocks, the boys skinned Nashville, Sylvester and Cordele. Out of town, in addition to bowing to Albany and Valdosta, we bit the dust at Cordele, Waycross and Moultrie, although not in a big way, and there isn't any record of Fitzgerald playing Ocilla in 1924 and you'd have thought the 'Cane would've wanted revenge for the lickings we put on them in 1923. Web data shows that Fitz played eleven times in 1924, winning five, losing three and tying three. They did not play big guns Albany or Valdosta, like Ocilla did, and their game at home with Moultrie was one of their ties, which was no easy affair.

Moultrie was back in power in 1924. Prior to the contest, the *Moultrie Observer* assured Packer fans that the "scrap promises to be lively" between Moultrie and Ocilla.

> The daily paper reminded readers of Ocilla's upset win in 1923 on Thanksgiving, adding, *Another victory for the visiting lads would not be objectionable to them.*
>
> According to the *Observer*, *In a wire received from Coach Whelchel, he reports that he will be here and ready to play at 4 o'clock and that Moultrie will know that she has at least played a game when the final whistle blows.*

For a lot of minutes our boys gave the Pack the business. It was one of Ocilla's better games although we had to chalk it up in the loss column.

And that was the season of 1924.

Or was it?

At the Irwin County Library, there is a local history book in the archive section that contains old pictures and one of the pictures shows the 1924-25 Ocilla football team. In the grainy black-and-white depiction, the dressed-out players are lined up on the ball with their helmets on. Boys identified as Herman Hall, John Fletcher, and B. L. "Ham" Henderson are standing with quarterback Carlyle Vardeman in the backfield looking serious; growly-faced Tom Hollingsworth is over the ball; Clark Nobles and McKinley Hudson are the guards on either side of Tom; the tackles are Martin Whitley and G. W.

Dismuke; Hugh Colson and Marion Dickens are lined up at the ends next to the tackles. The wonderfully nostalgic photo did not appear in the *Star* until many years later, and it's strange because when the picture was published, the caption credited the 1924-25 Ocilla High boys, who did not win the conference, with winning a state championship although this claim was downgraded later to an "unofficial title." The write-up did not say who we played for "state" or where or when, and neither the *Star* nor any of the area dailies ever mentioned a state championship, and Mr. Flanders surely would've said something had it happened but you could never be sure about a lot of things in the old days because in a 1976 obituary for Marion Dickens in the *Star*, Dickens *attended Ocilla High School where he starred on the school's unofficial state football championship team in the mid-1920s.*

David Waller, chief historian for the Valdosta Wildcats, isn't convinced. He says any state championship in the 1920s would have been in the eye of the beholder, since official state titles weren't awarded until 1947. Prior to that time, although teams were free to play anybody anywhere at any time and call the game as they saw fit, to Waller's knowledge there were no playoffs that would have resulted in a state crown official or otherwise.

"I just don't believe they had it. They weren't capable of putting it together at that time."

On a somber note, 1924 was tough for Ocilla's number one cheerleader, Flanders, when Ens. Merritt Flanders of Ocilla died in a Navy sea plane accident in October while stationed in San Diego. The town grieved, putting football on the back burner. Letters and cards of sympathy poured into the *Star*. J. J. Flanders and his wife, Harriett, struggled mightily with the loss of their only child. And for many years after, they marked the anniversary of their son's death with a tribute to him in the paper.

6

Marion

In the third quarter Dickens ran through Tifton's entire team while they played tag at attempts to stop him, scoring the first and only points of the game. Dickens was the greatest ground gainer of the afternoon, his long runs at end and through the line netting great counts in yards. Dickens played an unusual and extraordinary game through the four quarters, carrying the ball 80 percent of the times it was carried by the Ocilla team.

—*Tifton Gazette*, October 29, 1925

On July 21, 1907, Callie Dickens gave birth to the middle of her three boys. She named him Marion, which was significant. The boy thought "Marion" was for a girl and it pushed him. His mother had wanted a girl child and she made him help with cleaning the house. Driven to prove he was a man, the raven-haired Dickens, who grew up in Ocilla, excelled in the most strenuous of affairs, like football. In fact, although not the fastest man alive, Dickens left a legacy as one of the best players to ever cross a chalk line in south Georgia.

Known later in life as "Dick," Marion Bailey Dickens, when he played for Ocilla Hi in the 1920s, was called in the press t*he great Dickens* and t*he great Marion,* although, growing up, he preferred to be called "Mayrun" or "Mairn." An unusual lad and wise beyond his years, Dickens was a straight shooter. He possessed an air of confidence and quickly caught the eye of Coach Whelchel. If it was sports, Dickens was game. He was Ocilla's earliest version of Jim Thorpe. "He said he had to be tough because his mama gave him a girl's name," says his son, Johnny Dickens, of Huntsville, Alabama.

In June of 1923, Marion Dickens represented Ocilla in the pole vault at the state track and field meet in Athens. The *Star* reported: *Marion won third place for Ocilla High School by vaulting 10 feet, 6 inches. Only lost first place by four inches. Marion claimed that he would have won first place but was not in practice as the vaulting pole at the school house is broken and he was afraid to practice with it.*

Ocilla was fortunate to have a string of gifted ball-handlers in the 1920s. The first in the line was Dickens who won a boatload of all-conference honors for agility and toughness while playing football for Ocilla Hi from 1923 through 1926. "He used to say he wasn't the fastest guy in the world, but he ought to be able to reach out and touch the fastest guy on the butt," says Johnny Dickens, whose father also was a stellar point guard in basketball and a crafty baseball pitcher. He broke the state record in the broad jump in the spring of 1927 with a leap of 21 feet, 6¾ inches to win first place and grabbed first in the discus. His younger brother, Johnny, also played some ball for Ocilla. But he wasn't Marion. Few kids outshined Marion Dickens.

Dickens was no saint; he had his human failures. But he had a good nature and on the field, when he made a tackle, Dickens was the kind of young man who'd reach down and help a fallen opponent to his feet. Offensively, a big part of Whelchel's scheme was getting the ball to Dickens so he could—depending on the play—run it, catch it, or throw it. Ocilla's wide open offense fit Dickens' multitude of abilities nicely, and Whelchel was a master at utilizing the skills of his gifted performers.

At the University of Georgia, Dickens was a three-year letterman and one of the best players for the Bulldogs. In 1931, assistant Bulldog coach Rex Enright told the *Atlanta Georgian*,

> *Dickens has the best temperament of any player I have ever encountered. He was about three minutes late for practice the other day. He came up to me and said, 'Coach, I'm sorry but I took a nap and overslept.' Most players would have tried to slip on the field without being noticed.*

The coach's comment came as no surprise to anyone in Ocilla who remembered the Dickens boy playing sports.

> *All of us know about Marion Dickens,"* Flanders wrote in the *Star*, commenting on the *Georgian* article. *"When he was a player Ocilla lost only a few games. Ocilla is proud of Marion and the record he is making as a football player.*

In college, Dickens thought about being a lawyer but decided it wasn't something that an honest man such as himself could make a living at and became interested in philosophy. While attending UGA he met his first wife, Ethel Moody, and they had a daughter, Marion, whose nickname was Dynamite. The higher learning at UGA was so extensive, Dickens would later say, that it took him almost ten years to get back to feeling normal.

One thing led to another with Dickens. During his lifetime, he did some teaching, coaching, played a little pro ball for the now-defunct Providence Steamrollers, and boxed—though not necessarily in that order. And he hated "damn Yankees," as he called them.

For a while, Dickens lived in Florida, where he became an avid fisherman with a green thumb. He was a fence-post philosopher, witty, swore some, loved kids, and during Prohibition brewed his own beer. He taught math at a junior high school in Florida where all the kids called him "Daddy" or "Uncle Dick." His friends and neighbors called him "Dick."

Dickens retired back to Ocilla in 1970 and a short time later was placed into the Osceola Nursing Home. While at the center, he lost his left ear to cancer. But he never accepted being convalesced; one time he escaped from the facility for the thrill of it.

In musings about her dad, his daughter once wrote, "His face became reminiscent of an old Indian, weather-beaten and wrinkled, while his body remained supple. His vanity showed only in that he never let his hair turn white. He faithfully used milk tonic to prevent graying." Suffering from emphysema and pneumonia, the first player to put Ocilla on the map in football died in 1976.

His daughter also wrote, "It took me many years to understand why my father had to work so hard at being masculine. He fought his emotions, for instance, and I never saw him cry, even when he was very sad ... Aunt Mae (my grandmother's sister) indignantly told me, 'That was the sweetest little boy that ever lived, Honey, and your grannie tried to make a girl out of him. She wanted a girl so bad and when she had three boys she just picked on the middle one to help her in the house.' So he was fighting his sissy name and his mother to be a man."

7

'Outstandingly Clean'

Valdosta will have a real test this coming Friday. The Whelchel-coached team from Ocilla, one of the best in the conference, is coming over and it looks good...Their forward passing attack is as strong as ever, according to report, and they have developed something in the way of a line plunging effort, with Hollingsworth doing most of the work. They will certainly be a hard outfit for the Cats to stop. Valdosta fans who are looking for a team that possesses a colorful attack will do well to see the game.
—*Valdosta Times*, October 12, 1925

That year, 1925, if you can believe the data, Dickens and his accomplices played eight games, the first six on the road.

How'd we do? Well, there again, it depends on what you want to believe.

Many years after 1925, the Star gave that bunch credit with winning the "mythical title" of state champions.

Yep. Here we go again about titles.

Just like in the old picture from the 1924 season, the 1925 team is shown in the *Star* with a caption that states, in part:

> *... It could be the team shown in the photograph above was the last from Irwin County to win a state football championship. The photo is of the Ocilla High School team of 1925 (it may have been 1926). The team was unbeaten that year and played in a league comprised of such schools as Valdosta, Waycross (Ocilla won this one 70-0), Albany, Tifton, Moultrie, etc. ... Many of the team members shown above are new deceased but those still living can recall some interesting experiences on the gridiron in those high school years that led to the championship year.*

Well, that did not happen, not if Mr. Flanders could be believed, and if the high school historians web site is true. That year, armed with just four able subs, the boys fought to 4-3-1 finish, according to available data. Sadly, we fell at Fitzgerald. Also, we got beat by two really heavy hitters, though just barely, to complete a 2-3-1 road swing. But, hey. At least we had a winning mark, which was a pretty good day's work if you were Ocilla, and the record says our boys were unbeaten on the rocks, hammering their two Home foes by a combined 128-0.

According to the *Star* and other media, we opened the 1925 season again with mighty Albany.

Flanders noted: *Of course, it would have suited Ocilla better to have licked the stuffing out of Albany last Friday, but a nothing-to-nothing score looks like a mighty fine team for Ocilla.*

Next the boys were in Moultrie where the final was 13-3 for the mighty Pack.

The *Moultrie Observer* said:
Dickens, Ocilla's right end, was the star performer for the visitors. This lad made some pretty runs and with 15 seconds to go kicked a field goal from the 19-yard line. This was the first score made against the local team this season. Moultrie was clearly outplayed during the whole game with the exception of a few minutes of the fourth period. Ocilla showed much more signs of being a well-trained team, running better interference and producing a dazzling attack with the forward pass.

A week later, Dickens and company hit the *wonderful machine* that was Valdosta and almost wrecked it. In the pre-game hype, the *Daily Times* lauded the work of Ocilla High's Elder Hollingsworth and Carlyle Vardeman. But Dickens stole the show even in a loss. The only scoring that day in Valdosta was a touchdown and a point after kick.

The *Times* attributed the Cats victory to *"the grace of God and the assistance of Lady Luck."*

The 1925 Ocilla Hi team: Bottom row, l-r: G.W. Dismuke, Louis Crouch, Tom Little, Martin Whitley and Hodson; first name not available. Second row, l-r: Hugh Colson, Charley Taylor, McKinley Hudson, Carlisle Vardeman and Marion Dickens. Top row, l-r: Herman Hall, Wilbur Edwards, J.W. Fletcher, Herman Dismuke, Charles Dickens, Tom Hollingsworth, Elton McCall, Clark Noble and coach E.V. Whelchel. *Courtesy of the Sandy McClurd collection*

> *Dickens, alternating between defensive end and offensive half back, was the big star for Ocilla. He was easily the most brilliant end to ever play against the 'Cats. In range, speed and power, he outdistances every high school flankman ever seen here. In the backfield, his mad rushing at the line accounted for over half the Ocilla gains. The simple fact is that Ocilla has one of the best teams in the conference. It was about as heavy as the Cats. It had range, speed and perfect condition on its side...The Ocilla team was one the most outstandingly clean teams to play here this season. They had none of the usual mean little tricks that most football teams have. They did not pile on or commit any of those minor beaches of good sportsmanship that are not provided against in the rules. Both teams were occasionally over anxious, and Ocilla drew two offside penalties and the Cats three. These were all the penalties imposed.*

Later, the boys gnawed the horns off Tifton and got by Ashburn before closing out the long road part of the schedule in Fitzgerald. The rivalry, interrupted in 1924, was revived on November 6, 1925, and the 'Canes had a good squad and one boy, Hayes, enjoyed probably the best game of his life that afternoon against Ocilla.

Ocilla got the ball to start and drove a short distance before a pass was picked off. Fitz got six when Hayes scooted around an end. Late in the contest, the score was still 6–0. We had the ball at midfield and appeared bogged down when suddenly Dickens broke loose. With hardly any time left, our wheel horse gave us some hope as he took a toss from Vardeman and raced madly toward the goal. But here came the Hayes boy, dragging down a gassed Dickens from behind to save what would have been the tying score. On the next play, Dickens threw to

Vardeman, who was tackled at the five-yard line as time expired.

Angry, the boys came home and whipped Waycross, 59-0, and Sylvester, 69–0, in a game in which Dickens put a period on the 1925 season by scoring seven touchdowns on the Pirates.

Ocilla presented one of the best defenses in the conference, allowing only 32 points all season. As usual, our boys were the smallest team represented in the awards. Dickens made first team all-conference at end and received some votes for halfback. One of our freshmen, Joe Crouch, made second team end; Charlie Taylor of Ocilla made second team at tackle.

Thomasville took the conference title with a record of nine wins and a tie.

Then in late December 1925, we lost J. A. J. Henderson. The father of Ocilla died from what the *Star* reported was "acute indigestion." In his Christmas Eve edition, Flanders paid homage to Henderson in an article titled "A Builder Gone." The article appeared alongside a tribute of sorts to coach Whelchel. Of course, Whelchel was not deceased, but a movement had come afoot in Ocilla to name the playing field for him. Flanders wrote of his friend:

> *Those who know of his work among the boys are loudest in his praise. They realize there is something of value that boys can learn in school not found in the books of the regular curriculum. They have found out that... a boy learns that the really important thing in life is not so much the winning of victory as in the manner in which he plays the game. Whelchel has done this and more for the boys of the Ocilla High School. A fitting honor that the field should be named for him.*

8

Whelchel Field

The present football season for the Ocilla High School...closed with the game with Moultrie last Friday the 19th.

I am a great lover of clean athletics and our football team under the direction of Professor Whelchel has demonstrated what is meant by the term clean athletics. I have visited three towns in which our team has played and have discussed the football games with leading people before I was known to the men. And in every place the party or parties have highly complimented our team for their clean and honest playing. One very prominent man said it was a pleasure to have such fine fellows to play against. He said our boys held up the standard of true sportsmanship and he had no fears for a boy's future who showed honesty and loyalty as our boys did in their games.

A good name is rather to be chosen than riches. I surely appreciate our boys and the kind of character they have shown in their athletics and am proud of the fact they have made so enviable a record of winning games, but proudest of the good name they have gotten for themselves in that they are CLEAN ball players. We are indeed proud of our boys and their coach.

—W. Harvey Wages, Pastor Ocilla Baptist Church,
—*Ocilla Star*, November 25, 1926

In the spring of 1926, perhaps after a morning stroll, publisher Flanders penned an observation:

Ocilla needs only that a few marble games be kept going by those who are not playing checkers to complete the picture of a dead town.

Though at risk of echoing the "calamity howlers" who warned of Ocilla's demise, saying that soon enough the town would be broke and peas would grow in our streets, Flanders, by his "dead town" remark, was just saying Ocilla wasn't the hustling little city of his old dreams.

Football, meanwhile, was going great guns, and Flanders was delighted over construction of Whelchel Field. The work was the result of much public spirit. Certainly, Flanders wished that those so aggressively involved in the project to honor the coach would've taken the same initiative in constructing a factory or two.

In his June 10, 1926 edition, the publisher bawled:

We can't build big industries right now like cotton

mills, but we can put in small ones like mattress factories, overall factories, and the like. Enough of these will make Ocilla hum with industries. With plenty of electricity, there is not a reason in the world why we should not have them.

As Ocilla shuffled on in her quest for industry, the football fence went up. Materials were paid for by donations. The Irwin County Fair Association contributed a share of the proceeds from the annual carnival it hosted in Ocilla. The labor was donated. The sheet iron fence that was too high to see over and too low to peep under lapped around the ball field like a bowl or half drum.

Flanders said the enclosure would be *comfortable* and *add greatly to the attendance at the games.* He was hazy on how the fence would boost attendance. Then again, the fence did help Ocilla High to raise money for its program. In the fence, there was a gate. Spectators had to pay to enter. Admission was 50 cents for adults and 25 cents for youths. The revenue could be shared by visiting teams, maybe enabling Ocilla to get more home games if the guest teams didn't mind the rocks.

Previously, fans could see events at the field from the street or gather up around the field for a better view at no charge. The fence put a stop to free ball in Ocilla while helping the gatekeepers weed out the drunks on days when the boys were at war inside.

"That was the purpose of it," an old Terrapin, Waldo Paramoure, remembers being told about the fence.

In the fall of 1926, a record 20 boys reported for football practice inside the confines of Whelchel Field.

In the opener, Dickens touched the ball only four times and made four easy touchdowns as the Terrapins took the contest from the upstart Bulldogs of Lanier County, 66–0.

The second game found the boys back in Albany for the third season in a row, and it was a classic.

> The *Albany Herald* reported:
> *Albany's Braves defeated Ocilla High School yesterday afternoon on the local grid, 18–14, but they knew they had been in a whale of a fight when the fun was over. They knew, too, that the goddess of luck had smiled her sweetest on them, for they had beaten one of the pluckiest, scrappiest, cleanest and most sportsmanlike eleven that ever trod the turf of the local gridiron, and had done it mainly through getting two major breaks.*

The biggest "break" the *Herald* mentioned occurred with only a few seconds to play. Ocilla, down by four, was first and goal at the Indians' ten. Dickens stepped back to make a pass and was looking for a receiver when an Albany player swatted the ball from his hand. The pigskin went flopping on the ground and rolled past the goal marker with everybody diving for it. Play was stopped with 20 seconds left. Referee Red Joiner, a former Albany quarterback, ruled the ball should be brought out to the 20-yard line where it would be first and ten for Albany. Ocilla boys howled in protest, except for Dickens.

> The *Herald* reported, *"Then Dickens who had immortalized himself in the eyes of the Albany fans already, did the whitest thing a man could do. Quieting the argument, he said, a bit regretfully, 'The ball belongs to Albany. It was a touchback.' Maybe those weren't his exact words but that in effect was what he said. It meant the loss of the game, for with 20 seconds to play, it was*

inconceivable that the ball could be taken from Albany and pushed over the line."

Flanders wrote a two-line salute to the boys: *The Ocilla High School football team is making a name for clean sportsmanship, and that is far better than winning games. But they are going to win their share of games as well.*

After heartbreak in Albany, the boys took two on the rocks, including a big upset over Tifton, 35–0.

The *Star* said, *Ocilla's line was like a stone wall, besides breaking through on the defense to throw the Tifton backs for losses.*

Then it was on down to Valdosta again. The 'Cats of coach Herndon were coming off victories over Pelham, Quitman and Nashville and a loss to Albany. Ocilla and Valdosta both needed a win to stay in the hunt for the title, and Ocilla stymied the Cats before Valdosta broke our heart,14–7.

Wrote the *Valdosta Times*:

The great Dickens was submerged from scrimmage but he proved that he is the premier back of the conference... Dickens was everything that has been said of him. He is a fine player, a gallant foeman and one of the whitest men that ever made cleated shoes fly between the line marks of the gridiron.

The game drew an afternoon crowd of 1,300, the most for any home game in Wildcat history to that point.

Back at home for game five, Dickens and his thorny

sidekicks showed Fitzgerald no mercy. The Canes blew into Whelchel Field at only 1–4–1 but they were supposed to be a top team that year and our boys rolled them to our satisfaction, 46-0.

Wrote the *Star:*

Fitz High was no match for the Ocilla boys here Friday in a hard fought, though clean game. They were outplayed all through the game. ...Every man on Ocilla's team played well, their line was like a stone wall and it was never broken and never bent. Hollingsworth played the greatest game he has ever played. He never failed to gain, he made three touchdowns and kicked three extra points. Dickens played his same old brand of football, never failing to gain and adding four touchdowns to his total to bring it up to seventeen for the season.

The next two games were dogfights. Ocilla got Waycross, 9–0, on a Thursday in Waycross, and eight days later gutted out a draw, 16–16, in Moultrie to finish fourth place in the conference.

Albany won the championship with a 9–1 mark.

Dickens scored 116 points that year and made all-conference at halfback, first team. Elder Hollingsworth, a junior from Ocilla who scored 82 points, was recognized by the conference for his work as utility back. Ocilla was again the smallest team represented in the all-star balloting.

After the season, the boys were treated to a feast at the Eureka Café in Ocilla. Passersby just looking in the window might've thought the boys had won a championship of some sort. Flanders never mentioned a title.

In his "Ball Boys Entertained" article about the first-ever recorded dinner honoring Ocilla football players, he wrote:

The dinner was given by the fans of the town who

wanted to show their appreciation of the good work of the boys. Besides the team there were a number of friends who were hosts. Prof. E.V. Whelchel was toastmaster and called upon every member of the team to make talks, and every member responded with an appropriate talk.

To succeed the retiring, Mr. Marion Dickens, captain, who will graduate this year, Mr. Elder Hollingsworth was elected to head the team next year.

The team has made an especially good record this year. They have met the strongest teams in the conference and in every game have given a good account of themselves. Of the eight games played this year, they won five, lost two and tied one. They scored 242 points against their opponents and their opponents scored only 48 points against them.

The team next year will be as strong as any that they school has put out ... Fans are already counting on some real thrills.

9

Creep On, Terrapins!

As usual Coach Whelchel is going to give us a good football team this year. It makes little difference how it looks at the start. He always winds up with a team better than we have much right to expect. The foot ball team of the Ocilla High School has done a whole lot to bring Ocilla into the limelight and get the kind of publicity that helps us.

We pay out good money in the effort to get this publicity other ways. The Chamber of Commerce spends quite a good deal in trying to get Ocilla and Irwin County before the world. It is doubtful that this effort has done as much as Coach Whelchel and his teams have done.

Now Ocilla does not support its teams as well as it should. True, a small high school has a big school team, and we don't have as many people to pay admissions as Albany, or Moultrie or Valdosta but we do have fully twice as many people who ought to see the games as we do have. This is to suggest that our people make it a point to see every game played at home this year.
—*Ocilla Star*, September 22, 1927

Home, even though it was a hard place to play on, and nobody really liked to play in Ocilla, was very good to our boys. In fact, between 1925 and 1926, they won all six games played on the Ocilla school lot by a combined 321-0.

Then in September 1927, a new team member arrived tightly stitched, headless, leathery, with no arms or legs but who could take a pounding. The boys were in high spirits as they tried to tear Ocilla's first tackling dummy to shreds.

Also, Flanders livened up coverage of the ball team, giving the *Star* a sports section that looked more like the dailies with larger headlines, and for the first time he called our boys the "Terrapins."

The *Star*'s preseason edition was chocked with updates on the team and sprinkled with football news on various teams from around the league that appeared to be compiled from area dailies. There were no pictures but Flanders inserted a sketch of a football player in the center of the page. The helmetless, well-groomed young man in the rendering appeared to be punting. Below his kicking foot was the 1927 football schedule for Ocilla High School, and just in time for football, the *Star* introduced a sports editor called Kid Onus, which could have been Flanders himself or a student from the high school. Either way, it was all a fresh touch to football news as Flanders tried to rally fans around the team.

Onus said 18 boys, many with experience, showed up for fall practice and appeared to be heavier than usual. Flanders, through Kid Onus, did a nice job presenting the new crop of boys to the reading public. Many were called by name, which was also a different touch.

Said Onus:

Coach has made a few changes for the last few days and one of them is sure to help the team. He has decided to let John Dickens, a brother of the great Marion, run in the backfield on offense and play end on defense. This boy sure can run the ball and before the season is over ought to be nearly as good as his brother was.

Leading up to the Albany game, Onus wrote: *Everybody that can ought to go over and help the boys to win.*

After losing to Albany, 26-0, the boys hosted Valdosta. For the first time, the 'Cats had come to Ocilla. A throng accompanied Valdosta to the Terrapin pit. Fans on both sides got their money's worth.

The *Star* reported:

By the score of 7-0, Valdosta won from the Ocilla High foot ball team last Friday in as pretty a game as has ever been seen in Ocilla.

Neither team could score till the third quarter when Valdosta covered a fumbled ball and pushed it over for a touchdown. In the fourth quarter Ocilla came very close to scoring, lacking about six inches, when they lost the ball on downs. Valdosta kicked the ball back into safe territory and Ocilla's chance was lost. Ocilla clearly outplayed Valdosta in the first half, though this

> *advantage could not be turned into touchdowns. Valdosta kept putting in fresh men while Ocilla did not have the substitutes to put in and showed the effect. It was a clean game and both teams played hard consistent ball.*

It was Ocilla's first loss on the home field since 1924.

After taking a week off, the Terps traveled to face our old rivals, Fitzgerald, and for a second season in a row, Ocilla tore their hide off, 45–6, then crushed Waycross and Moultrie to end the season.

The *Waycross Journal-Herald* came close to accusing Ocilla of a dirty game against the Bulldogs. When he saw this in the *Journal-Herald*, Flanders fired off a biting editorial:

> *It remained for the young man who writes of sports for the Waycross Journal-Herald to accuse the Ocilla foot ball team of unsportsmanlike tactics. This will indeed be news to the other South Georgia towns that a Whelchel-coached team played dirty ball, and that crooked officials were selected by Whelchel in order to be sure to defeat as poor a team as Waycross sent to Ocilla last week.*

The game that year with Moultrie in Ocilla was a lot of fun for the locals who could afford the admission. Hollingsworth had a big day in the 25–0 victory. He had this one punt return that provided more electricity than Ocilla had seen all week. On this one punt, according to the *Star*'s write-up, when the Packers kicked the ball to Hollingsworth, he fumbled. The ball rolled backwards to the four-yard line. Hollingsworth picked it up and again he fumbled it. Finally, he secured the ball and raced 96 yards for a touchdown, leaving all Packer boys in his wake. It was the longest punt return in Ocilla history and was the first runback of a kick for Ocilla since Dickens popped one for 90 yards against Waycross in 1925.

Albany, Thomasville and Valdosta tied for the 1927 conference title, each with one loss. Bill Henderson of Ocilla and a Jones kid from Albany tied in the voting for first-team all-conference center. Hall of Ocilla got votes for utility line and Hollingsworth received votes for quarterback. As usual, Ocilla was the smallest school represented in the all-conference first team. The only others with boys on the first-string lineup were Albany, Valdosta, Thomasville and Moultrie.

10

'Wonder Man'

E.V Whelchel, who has been turning out great teams with extremely small material for several years, has this year two outstanding backs and a splendid line. No team in the conference has a more deadly scoring threat than Crouch and no fullback has done greater damage than Hudson. The boys on the line are typical Whelchel linemen, strong and hefty and hard to move.

—*Valdosta Times*, October 22, 1928

On October 14, 1947, the San Diego Marines were playing the Santa Barbara Athletic Club out in California. Maybe you've heard about this. The Marine fullback heaved a pass that traveled 79 yards in the air before it was caught. All the papers carried the story.

The man who threw the legendary pass was Joe Crouch. Joe was an Ocilla boy. Nobody had ever heard of Ocilla.

"It was in the San Diego stadium that Joe Crouch made football history and brought fame to his south Georgia hometown," Autry Ross wrote for the *Star* in a 1980 story about Mr. Crouch.

Acclaim for Crouch's throw was immense among California sportswriters. The newspaper in Greenville, South Carolina, where Joe's sister was teaching school, picked up on the story and claimed that Joe was a Greenville boy when in fact he was born in Ocilla on Jan 14, 1911.

In its write-up of the historic heave, *The Associated Press* got it right: "Joe Crouch is from Ocilla, Georgia."

Built like an ox and fast as a deer, he was ambidextrous. You wouldn't want to face Joe in an alley scrap. To hear Coach Whelchel speak of the kid, he was *Wonder Man*—agile, hostile and mobile. In 1928, in his senior season, Joe made all-conference as a ball-handler.

In a preview of the annual Ocilla-Valdosta clash in 1928, the *Valdosta Times* wrote:

Crouch did not reach his own last year. He was sick frequently and did not materialize into the 'Wonder Man' that Whelchel promised. This year he has more than made good. He stepped off one eighty-yard run against Albany and a score of smaller gains throughout the game. He passes with either hand, showing a slight preference for the left one, and tosses his balls like air thrusts as far as he likes.

Marion Dickens and Joe Crouch were both superstars in the

eyes of football fans across the South Georgia league. But they became different men, and although Marion enjoyed a more celebrated high school sports career for Ocilla, Joe found more fame after high school in sports than Marion did. At the University of Georgia, Joe was a bruising runner and a bear of a tackler. Known in college as "Jumpin' Joe," he played on the Bulldog varsity in 1932 and 1933 and was credited with shutting down Yale's aerial attack in 1932. After college, he joined the Marines.

Once, at a naval track meet, Joe blew away the field with a record throw in the discus of 144 feet, 8½ inches, breaking the old mark by 13 feet. Joe badly wanted to be an Olympic thrower but never got the chance, reportedly because he didn't have the money. In 1954, he moved back home, where for the better part of 20 years he served as city clerk and treasurer, essentially running the town of Ocilla. Joe died on October 17, 1982, at Irwin County Hospital. This community and the sports world had lost a legend.

A Marine graveside service was conducted at the Ocilla Cemetery.

Publisher Bill Bradford wrote:

Joe Crouch was a special man that God created to teach us something: perseverance and discipline. This editor loved him and learned from him. We'll miss Joe.

11

'Crazy With Joy'

Coach Whelchel and his eighteen candidates for Ocilla High's football team are working until dark every afternoon, trying to get into shape for the opening game which will be played here on October 5th. Nashville High will be the opponent. The team this year seems to be slower than usual about getting down the plays and learning how to exercise them as they should. Coach has been spending a lot of time this week trying to get these faults corrected. Prospects for a winning season are only fair.

—*Ocilla Star*, September 27, 1928

Finally, after four seasons, here was Albany. The Indians

had agreed to play our boys in Ocilla. Averaging 165 pounds per man, Ocilla had developed well in the first two games, both at home, despite having to replace two ends, a tackle, a guard and two backs lost to graduation.

Whelchel had the boys in top form to meet the reigning champ. To reach this game, Ocilla had hammered Nashville and Sparks-Adel by a combined 74–0. Albany had played two of three games on the road, defeating Pelham, Hawkinsville and Dawson by a combined 45–12.

The tribe came to Ocilla minus two good players, each of whom was declared ineligible for the game after flunking a test that week in school.

But, hey, that was life. You had to strap up; let's play some football.

With Joe Crouch leading the attack, the Terp offense gnawed and clawed its way down the dusty Ocilla plain on the game's first series. At the 8-yard line Albany stopped us and got the ball but we wouldn't let them move and so they punted.

The ball switched hands numerous times in the early going.

The Indians did not attempt to run the ball in the first half, throwing on every down. Three passes were intercepted, each by Joe Crouch.

At halftime, there was no score.

Upon receiving the second-half kick, the Indians unleashed their horse, a boy named Ferguson. Running on every play, they crossed midfield and were steamrolling at our 45 when the big boy, Ferguson, coughed it up and there was Franklin Davis of Ocilla on the spot. Davis scooped the loose ball and took off like his hair was on fire. The Ocilla side roared as there went Franklin, 55 yards for a Terp touchdown.

The point after was no good.

Albany rallied. Passing over and again, they moved to the Ocilla one where twice they bucked at center but Ocilla's interior line held. On third down, however, Ferguson made six on a scamper around our right end. The point after was good but their right tackle was called for off-sides. The point was waved off and since there was no do-over in those days, the score remained knotted.

Two possessions later, the tiring Terrapins crawled out to their own 45 and bogged down. The ball went over to Albany and they hit pay-dirt on a toss. The point after was no good.

Then very late in the game with Albany leading by 6 and with the ball, things looked bleak for the home boys as the Indians were driving on the ground, trying to wrap up the game, but then they made a throw, perhaps errantly, and there he was again - Joe Crouch. Joe jumped in front of the pass, snatched the ball out of the air and went to chugging.

Ocilla fans and our sidelines were jumping up and down, *crazy with joy,* according to the *Star*, as Crouch dashed untouched, 65 yards and an Ocilla touchdown.

> *It was a beautiful run,* the *Star* said, *not a man getting close enough to make a tackle, and after passing the 30-yard line, not one followed. B. Harper passed to Hall, who was standing over the goal line for the extra point. Hall made a wonderful catch.*

The Indians, back to passing on every down, made a final push to win it but there was that boy again, Joe Crouch, with his fifth interception on the day and that was how we stole their ponies.

Holy Mosey! Little Ocilla had rocked the conference.

Cried the *Star:*

> *People swarmed out on the field to congratulate the team. This being the first time that the Terrapins have*

> *ever won from the Indians. Albany brought one of the cleanest, hardest-fighting bunch of boys that ever played here and they won the praise of Ocilla people for their good sportsmanship and playing.*

It was a great victory. Great to be a Terrapin. Great to be Ocilla.

Part II

12

Terrapins Wilt

The Terrapins are expecting the hardest game of their career with Valdosta. They realize that the odds are against them but now that they have tasted victory over one of their big opponents they are determined to satisfy their craving with a win over the Wildcats. Information from Valdosta is that the game will begin at four o'clock and that the Valdosta people are expecting a crowd from Ocilla for the game.

—*Ocilla Star*, October 25, 1928

Unbeaten and tied with Moultrie, Thomasville and Valdosta for tops in the league, little Ocilla was in good shape at long last to claim the coveted title of conference champ. The high-flying Terrapins took Monday off as a reward for beating Albany. The day of rest helped assorted Terp wounds to heal in preparation for the game Friday with mighty Valdosta.

But as the *Star* noted, when practice resumed Tuesday for the annual Ocilla-Valdosta clash, our boys, the toast of the league, seemed stove up. Whelchel, the toast among coaches, put in some new plays to try on the 'Cats. In a ragged, two-hour scrimmage, ball-handling and timing were a problem. Defensively, the first string was kicked around by a few scrubs. Two of our key starters missed the whole week's practice with injuries.

Meanwhile, as the Terrapins struggled to return to form and shoulder their fame, sports writers in Valdosta sang the Ocilla praises:

> *The Valdosta Wildcats have a hard road to travel this week. Whelchel is coming and his Terrapins have a team that last week toppled a Big Four eleven in the dust. It is true that the Terrapins beat the Braves by but one point, but that was enough to put the game into the records.*
>
> *Crouch will be a thorn in the Wildcat side, and Hudson, stocky and fleet of foot, will aid and abet him in his evil doing.*
>
> *The Terrapins have never licked the Cats but they have never been subdued. Once, scheduled by mistake as an "easy" opener, they frightened the Cats so badly that the next year's team had chills and fever. Last year they routed the Cats into the sand, chased them about the field, and mistreated them in many ways. The Cats won, but they won by a single touchdown.*
>
> *Whelchel always presents the most colorful team in the association. He uses the same plays every year, experts aver. But they look new to the teams opposing him. He always digs up a star ball carrier and a stellar linesman, and goes through the hardest schedule on the conference sheet with only one or two defeats. And most of the games are on foreign soil, too.*

Always among the cleanest and most sportsmanlike eleven of the circuit, Ocilla is a great crowd getter and a very popular team. The Cats expect their visit this year to be marked by a large attendance at the game.

It was an interesting game, like you'd expect with Valdosta. But they nailed us, 13–0. That did not end our chances of being conference champ, however. The Terrapins were still in the hunt going into the next game, which was at home against heavy Fitzgerald. Well, the boys managed to get over on the 'Canes, though not as handsomely as we'd liked, and then, for some reason, the Terrapins began to unravel.

It was one of the mysteries of the period.

After crawling Fitz, the boys fell at home to Tifton, 14–12, and got smoked at little Quitman, 31–13. Moultrie crushed our shells 37–6 at Moultrie and Douglas rolled us 33–6 on Thanksgiving Day as the season of 1928 that began so nicely fizzled into a disappointing 4–5 record.

Then came the year of stock market collapse. Hard times. And speaking of crash, the Terrapins opened the season of 1929 with four road games and got run over by a combined score of 154–0.

Where had our good boys gone? Whelchel could not stop the bleeding. Perhaps it was injury or the bad economy and maybe boys quit school to find work or just lost interest in the game. The turtle program was being strangled. We did not have any horses and Flanders, maybe in a sign of the times, scaled back the *Star*'s coverage of football. The take-down of the once-lively sports section was obvious when Kid Onus was given the boot.

The *Albany Herald* reported:

By playing somewhere near their normal form in the second half, the Albany Indians were able to muster enough strength to down a light but fighting Ocilla eleven, 28-0, here yesterday afternoon. Almost from the outset it was seen that the visitors didn't have much chance of defeating the Braves, but they have a good account of themselves...With an eleven of sophomores and juniors built around only two veterans, Captain McCall and Roberts, of last season, Coach Whelchel did well in rounding out a capable eleven that is sure to improve as the season progresses.

There was no improvement. Valdosta blew Ocilla away 70–0, in Valdosta. Waycross, Moultrie and Fitzgerald all raked the light and merry Terrapins over the coals.

The boys were 1-1 at home that year, losing to Douglas and beating little Quitman.

Some in the student body grumbled that Coach Whelchel had become too predictable with his play calling.

The boys wound up the season of 1929 with a pitiful 1–6 mark to put a lid on the Roaring Twenties and it was a sad state for everybody in Ocilla who'd been rooting for the Terrapins.

Publisher Flanders had ceased to comment on the team anymore.

Whelchel was ready for his check.

Carolyn Mills, the late coach's daughter, who was born in Ocilla, says the parting was amicable. "I know when he left he was given a silver football. It has his name on it."

Whelchel had loved Ocilla. Living here, coaching ball and

befriending the good people of the community, "was the highlight of my daddy's life," says Tom Whelchel, citing the "high morals and good character" of Ocilla people. He says his father took the job as principal at Adel-Sparks simply as a step up to a bigger school in keeping with his career goals. The elder Whelchel used to chuckle when he talked about game days with the Terrapins. "He said you had to leave town early in case the car broke down."

13

Mister Waldo

Believe it or not, Ocilla has won a game of foot ball and it was right pretty game, if any should ask you.

The loser in the 28 to 20 contest was Pelham. These high school boys journeyed here Wednesday afternoon and played the game with our boys who had gone the whole season without winning a single victory.…For the local boys the three players whose work deserves special mention are Whitley Berry, Clifton Harper and Waldo Paramoure. Berry, by his shear plunging, battered through the opposition time and again for many substantial gains till he was hurt so badly that he had to retire.

Clifton Harper, though the smallest boy on the team, is one of the best. His passing to Waldo Paramoure, who was much above the average in receiving, was the real feature of the game.

—*Ocilla Star*, November 26, 1931

One lovely Ocilla day in 2006, a sunny day in the spring, warm and soft as a puppy dog, "Mister Waldo," with his sweetheart by his side, opened the back door.

"Come in," the old Terrapin said to the visitor who'd just then knocked at the cozy brick home of the Paramoures on Beech Street.

"I don't remember ever winning a game."

His head full of hair, Waldo Paramoure looks sharp, sporting a Polo shirt, creased slacks, shined shoes. The "Mister" before his first name is a lighthearted title of respect still afforded a number of our older gentlemen.

"Ninety-one," he said, when asked his age in years.

Waldo was not born in Ocilla. Yet, he has lived here so long it's like he's a native. His parents, John and Cora, moved their family to Ocilla when Waldo was 14 from Effingham County, Georgia, so the elder Paramoure could work in turpentine. There wasn't any glory in turpentine for a boy in 1929 so Waldo went out for football instead. A friendly, good-natured lad, "I weighed every bit of 120 pounds."

In his roomy den, the old Terrapin folded his frame onto a small sofa while the love of his life, known fondly around town as "Miss Iris," sat on the edge of another seat close by.

"No, no," Waldo said, when asked if he had some old shoes, a helmet, pants, yearbook, anything to mark his playing days as a Terrapin. "I've got so many scars on my knees from the rocks," he said with a chuckle, referring to Whelchel Field. Now the oldest vintage Terrapin alive, Waldo's nickname on the grid was *Unconscious,* although he was also known as *Dizzy*, and while his brother, Charles, never played football, the two boys were often confused as teammates.

When asked why he played the game, Waldo replied, "Back in those days, there wasn't a whole lot to do."

That's his way of saying that life in Ocilla was a struggle for good boys with red blood in their veins. There were no bowling alleys, YMCA, or skateboarding. Beyond church, school, and agriculture was a black hole. What was a boy to do? Play Wii?

For a kid wanting to show off his moves or just trying to prove something to someone or to himself, there was no better outlet than football and football was already a big deal in southern Georgia when Waldo got to Ocilla.

Nobody put a gun to his head to make him play. He had options. When Waldo realized what those were, he came to an easy decision. So one afternoon in the early fall of 1929, he crawled into an old, faded uniform, laced on a pair of new brogan shoes, squeezed his head into an old leather helmet worn by boys before him, and jogged merrily around the rocky confines of Whelchel Field for practice.

Although he didn't make the team that first year, 1929, "I did get to travel with the team."

Waldo can remember riding to games in cars that had rumble seats, and he said "great coach" when asked about Mr. Whelchel, his first football mentor.

How did the team look? "We had some trashy uniforms," says Waldo, who devoted a good deal of his adult life in Ocilla

Waldo Paramoure with his wife and high school sweetheart, Iris, in 2006. *Courtesy David Pierce*

to the dry-cleaning business. He adds, “There was no money to buy shoes.” He remembers boys had to buy their own shoes for “two dollars a pair” and took them to an Ocilla shoe store where the cobbler would hammer metal tips into the soles to make cleats.

How, one wonders, did Waldo ever survive? Well, he just got in there and kept battling. Ambitious, he hustled and didn’t let anybody just walk all over him. He played all four years of high school. While he never reminded anyone of our great warriors of the past like Dickens and Crouch, Waldo dazzled in his own right as a player on some teams that were pretty bad. A whip of a boy, a lesser lad would’ve been ripped to pieces and probably walked away from the game. Waldo stuck it out and never broke a bone or lost a tooth or an eye while playing for Ocilla during some hard times for the club.

His first year in Ocilla, as an eighth grader, Waldo was kicked around a lot by the older boys, but he came to the fight. He showed some skill with his hands, and you had to respect his speed. Although he would never play college ball or realize the pleasure of playing on a team that beat Fitzgerald, Waldo was a stick of dynamite. From his end position, he developed into a fine receiver and a ferocious tackler for Ocilla.

He and Iris, whose maiden name in school was Purvis, were students at the Ocilla High when they fell in love. After graduating, and after the wedding, they moved to Savannah where Waldo worked in the shipyards. After the war, they moved back to Ocilla and Waldo enrolled at South Georgia College in Douglas. For many years, the couple owned and operated Paramoure dry cleaning that fronted Fourth Street. Waldo retired from the Ocilla Housing Authority in 1982.

When he adds it all up, he has no regrets. His mind is at peace, his heart light as a dove. When he thinks of the past, he wouldn't trade a thing. God has been good. Very good. Looking back, even though "we didn't have much of a team," Waldo felt a lot of love in the Ocilla community. He was a lucky boy. He couldn't have asked for a better life.

"Fun times … It was a good time growing up here."

14

Hard times

The Terrapins crept down to Albany Friday to engage the Albany Indians in the football classic of the season, with the score standing with 72-0 at the end of the 4th quarter....In the second quarter the Ocilla team played as hard as they could but were so out-numbered by the Indians that long before a Redskin got tired a good substitute was sent in for him while the Terrapins did not have an extra 'shell' apiece....Albany called time for their squad to pick sandspurs off their backs. In the first quarter two Albany men were knocked out and taken off the field. Many other substitutions were made on the Albany side. Flanders and Harper were both knocked out at the same time for Ocilla. Although our boys lost, we

are confident they played a clean, square game.
—*Ocilla Star*, October 24, 1930

You knew it was going badly for the Ocilla team when a 42–0 loss to Sparks-Adel was considered a "100 percent improvement."

That year, 1930, the losses were heavy. Boy, things had really gone downhill since that big victory over Albany just two years earlier. J. D. Salter came from South Carolina to be the high school principal and athletics director, replacing Whelchel, in the fall of that year. Maybe he did not know about football or his heart was more into basketball, but all Salter did for football in his first year was schedule just three games: Eastman, Sparks-Adel and Albany—all on the road. The hard-time Terrapins were wiped out by a combined score of 182 to zip.

Mr. Whelchel, who was now heading up the Sparks-Adel program, took Ocilla to the woodshed with mostly second stringers.

*They outweighed us ten pounds to the man,*groaned a report in the "Ocilla High Recorder" section of the *Star*. *Although we lost the game the team showed 100 percent improvement over last Friday.*

The *last Friday* contest referred to in the article was the "sand spur game" with Albany. *The Indians took out their fury on the Ocilla Terrapins,* wrote the *Albany Herald*. *Ocilla's passing attack was woefully weak.*

So went 1930.

The Lord was about ready to call it.

To start the 1931 season, the *Star* reported seeing a ray of hope.

On August 31, Coach Salter issued the call for foot ball practice and about eighteen young and ambitious boys answered the call. The chances are that the Terrapins will have a much better team this year than last. Only a few stars were lost through graduation. All but four of the players have had a little experience...All in all the boys down at Whelchel Field are expecting big things this year.

The boys let Nashville beat us up.

The Ocilla boys were too light and seemed to realize it, said the *Star. They did not put up as stiff a fight as they could have done.*

Later, ole Fitz washed us. According to the write-up in the paper:

The score does not indicate how hard the small Ocilla players fought. When a large man hit one he would not lay there groaning but would get up running. The tackling of Paramoure and the fine punting of Paulk were the highlights of the play of the Ocillians. The Ocilla team now shows some spirit in what they do and with Berry, the plunging fullback, who had his nose broken in the Nashville game, and Harper the big tackle the team should show a marked improvement.

The boys of 1931 gave up 163 points while scoring 41. Students were writing funny poems in the paper about the ball team.

Football fans in Ocilla were getting a headache and reaffirming their love of basketball was made easier in the spring of 1932 with the construction of a gymnasium which Ocilla folks had begged for since 1921.

Promised to seat 1,000 spectators, the gym was built by volunteer carpenters and laborers. Profits from barbecues, baseball games and boxing matches helped pay for the materials. Ocilla's jewel, located down the hill from the high school, was dedicated at a public gathering March 11, 1932. The gym would accommodate boys' and girls' basketball, the Irwin County Fair and other public events.

In the fall of '32, after the gym went up, the *Star* crawled out on a limb in trying to keep people from losing all interest in football.

> *The prospect for Ocilla High to have a winning football team this year is very bright, in fact the squad is the largest and most promising that has ever been assembled here. Coach Salter has about thirty or more candidates out every afternoon and has been drilling them for the past few days getting them hardened...."*

Although they did not tangle anymore with the likes of Albany, Valdosta and Moultrie, our boys put up a decent effort that year, finishing 4-2-1. The game with our neighbors in Mystic was the opener. The anticipated beating of lowly Mystic was celebrated in Ocilla by the junior and senior girls throwing a post-game party at the home of cheerleader Dorothy Pittman to honor the football team.

> *The party was a reward of victory,* a student wrote in the *Ocilla High News* section of the *Star* dated October 6, 1932. *Centuries ago the reward of victory was a branch of olive leaves but we modern maidens have*

modern ideas...We called it Depression prom to let everyone know about the depression before refreshments came abound.

On October 28, 1932, there was a morning pep rally for homecoming. Girls led the cheers, boosters made talks and some Terrapin boys came forward to say a few words. The rally was called to jack school spirit for football while a parade that afternoon encouraged townspeople to come root the home boys on to victory.

Admission to Whelchel Field was reduced to 25 cents for adults and 10 cents for students.

The peppy parade snaked through the streets of Ocilla—a caravan of 50 horn-honking cars decorated in Terrapin purple and gold and packed with whooping faithful—and ended at Whelchel Field for the homecoming game with Blackshear.

Musicians played their instruments during the game from a makeshift bandstand at the field.

In the second quarter, Waldo Paramoure scored on a long pass from Fat Harper. At halftime, paying customers performed a snake dance around the field. Ocilla ended up winning the game 38-0.

Salter scheduled the last game of the 1932 season to be against Fitzgerald. The record says we had to forfeit, leaving the reason to the imagination.

15

The Last Stand

This is a story about the strongest supporter of the Ocilla High athletic teams. He is an old negro, Warren Johnson—Uncle Warren, as he is called by his white friends.... When the district basketball tournament was held here last winter, Uncle Warren attended every game. Before the tournament started he predicted that Ocilla would win it. On that hectic Saturday night that the finals were played, Uncle Warren was the first one there. That afternoon he went into the woods and prayed that Ocilla would win.... Uncle Warren says he never played football, but it was just because he never had the chance. When asked about football recently, he said, "Boss, I love it. I think it is de biggest thing in de world." Uncle Warren is on the evening side of life. The sun will soon sink on a long and useful life for him....A football game in Ocilla without Uncle Warren would not seem like a football game. There would be something missing, something that could not be replaced.

—Guy Berry, *Ocilla Star*, October 12, 1933

It was a terrific, storybook ending. Ocilla couldn't have scripted one better. In a stunner, Ocilla High pulled off a thrilling victory over McCrea-Helena by the score of 33–32.

Of course, that was in basketball!

Basketball? Oh, yes, who could forget basketball? Ending what the *Waycross Journal-Herald* described as *the most exciting final game imaginable*, the Ocilla hoopsters of football softie J. D. Salter captured the eighth district tournament in March 1933 on a basket with just a few seconds left, giving Ocilla the district title. An overflow crowd of some 1,200 of which 400 were from McCrae jammed into our new gymnasium for the Saturday night thriller.

Ocilla residents had gone all in for the tournament, opening homes to out-of-town players needing a place to stay overnight. Ocilla was in a showcase in a way football had never enabled it to be. Players from 17 schools journeyed to Ocilla to participate in the games, and many were shown around town by hosting adults. Nothing like it had ever happened in Ocilla, and fans struck up a jubilee.

Ocilla was a basketball town again.

Meanwhile, the bleachers and the old tattered uniforms and grimy helmets told the sad story of football in Ocilla. The wooden bleachers at Whelchel Field were in disrepair. Those who came in for the games mostly stood on the sidelines, and that year J. D. Salter abandoned Ocilla football, delegating those duties to high school teacher Paul Lewis. Only 25 men reported for practice.

Guy Berry wrote for the *Star* in a depressing article:
This year the entire squad will be green. Only a few boys have ever played the game.

In a later piece, Berry wrote:
After three weeks of grooming his charges in the manly art of football, Coach Lewis has about whipped his boys into shape for their initial game of the season...They are going to be weak at kicking. Coach Lewis would like very much to have someone that could kick. In fact, he wants one so bad that he has offered to swap his entire kingdom for a punter...These boys have worked hard in an effort to have a winning team. It remains for the people of Ocilla to show their appreciation by coming down and yelling for them. The admission is only 15 cents and 25 cents. And it will be well worth your money.

Though hard to watch, because the boys were not very interesting anymore, we weren't the worst team in the league that year. We beat Hawkinsville twice and Patterson once. But the boys of Ocilla Hi were no competition for the other clubs.
Barry reported:

This week the boys are hard at work for their hardest test of the season. They are going to play Fitzgerald and everyone knows that Fitzgerald boasts of one of the best teams in South Georgia. Those who go to Fitzgerald to see this game may rest assured that the Terrapins are going to be in the fight from the opening kick-off until the final whistle blows. The boys will need all the rooting they can get, so come on Ocilla. Let's go!

Fitzgerald shredded the Terrapins, 78–0, the worst licking our neighbors had ever put on us; and a week later the boys got drilled in Douglas, 50–0.

A top team, Tifton, was next on the slate.

The game should attract a lot of fans from Ocilla. The Tifton team is coached by an Ocilla boy who made good, Elder Hollingsworth, Berry wrote.

Tifton pummeled the Terrapins, 32–6.

The Lord had seen enough of the abuse. The boys played their last game on Friday, November 17, 1933. The Sparks-Adel coach, E. V. Whelchel, stood on the visitor's sideline of the rocky field that still bore his name. To welcome him back, many of the Ocilla boys on the team showed up blonde. Guy Berry reported in the *Star:*

This is going to be the Terrapins' last stand for the season. It will be the 'Blonde Terrapins' when they line up for the opening kickoff Friday. Most of the boys have dyed their hair. Everyone knows what a record Coach Whelchel had when he was the coach at Ocilla. And fans in Ocilla will know what to expect from his team Friday: a clean, hard fight. This is homecoming game for Ocilla. And every person who ever graduated from Ocilla has a special invitation to come to the game.…It will be a gala day in the sports history of Ocilla.

In a sense, it was historical, and by the way the game ended deadlocked at 13. Somehow that was a fitting conclusion, with

Whelchel back in Ocilla, and only a few people bothered to come out to see it.

And so, the dog died. God called His band of Terrapins to come home and the walls tumbled down. Flanders never said who threw in the towel. Or why. Too much losing and no titles certainly had to be strong factors. Maybe a lack of support caused boys to pick up their interests in basketball or something else. Surely, the new gymnasium gave football a hard kick in the head; basketball in Ocilla prospered with the gym. Whatever the causes were, and while Fitzgerald and the other teams played on like nothing had happened, our little football program, which had brought a measure of prestige to Ocilla in the 1920s for clean, scrappy play, died after the 1933 season and stayed dead until after World War II.

16

Up From The Ashes

Football, the game of games, is back in Ocilla High School...None of the boys have ever played football so they are just as green as grass. However, the entire squad is working hard as Coach Edge drills on fundamentals and tries to get the squad into good physical condition. In a few minutes' scrimmage thus far the play has necessarily been ragged but most of the boys are responding to coaching and improving daily. Other than shoes, the biggest need of the team is two cars to transport players home after practice in the afternoon.

—*Ocilla Star*, September 19, 1946

After the war, Ocilla went football crazy. The fall of the year had become just a little too lonely.

The boys of old had never met with such backing.

It was 1946 and the boys got new digs; maybe that would help them to win. Many traditions were made, like game-day motorcades with whooping fans that formed on Irwin Avenue leading out to the new field by the golf course where spectators stood, sat on the grass or perched on car hoods watching the boys take on boys from other towns. Students sold purple and gold "feathers" with *Ocilla* down the side to wear on your shirt to show your support for the team. Notices of upcoming games at the golf course field were scrawled onto the street blackboard and merchants ran advertisements in the *Star* urging the boys to victory.

It was all quite a rush for a half-dead town still struggling for jobs and development.

High above Mr. Flanders must've been beaming.

Back the team...We want a touchdown! We want a touchdown!, barked Davis Pharmacy in a quarter-page ad.

Out of ten chances that year, the boys got the good end four times. They lacked for gear, such as cleats, and were very inexperienced. The optimists among us could see that the boys played much better ball than the record suggested, and there was always next year to look forward to. The Terrapins of '46 were game as a bantam rooster at a buzzard brawl, and nobody beat the pure snot out of us like they used to when the Terrapins were a bad outfit. The Fitzgerald paper took notice, saying Ocilla boys of '46 were *entertaining* to watch, although we did not play Fitzgerald in a regular game.

The key to reviving the program was a group of Ocilla men

led by Ocilla High alum Raymond "Knot" Tucker, who starred on Ocilla High's 1937 state title team in basketball, and school bosses hired E. P. Edge, a former Mercer University standout, out of Wrightsville to be the head football coach.

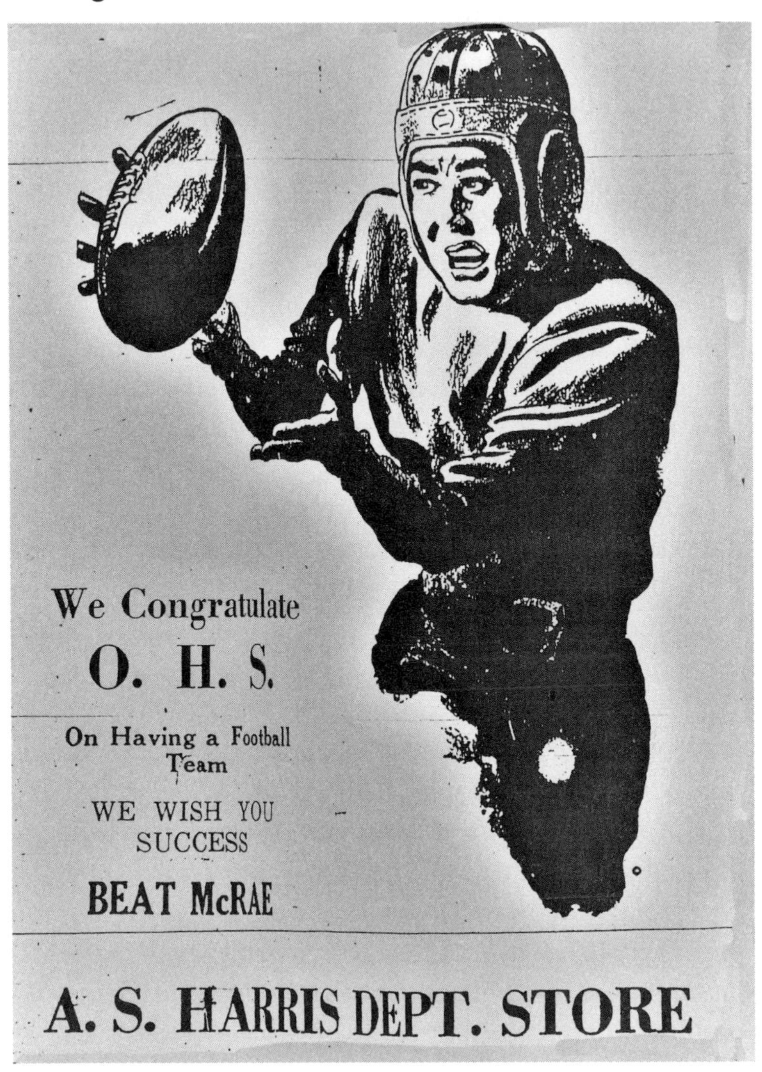

Ocilla merchants showed support for the Terrapins with advertisements like this one from Sept. 19, 1946. *Courtesy Ocilla Star / copied by David Pierce*

Having the merchants behind the boys certainly was a call to rally around the new Terrapins and the Star said, *for the purpose of pledging our full-hearted support*, 25 Ocilla stores closed between two and five o'clock for the season opener with McCrae-Helena in Ocilla. Later on that month, because the closings were such a success, a longer list of merchants agreed to do it for all home games the rest of the season.

> *Your cooperation in this will greatly aid the school in meeting its indebtedness for football equipment and expenses incurred in its first year of football. Without attendance and gate receipts, athletics in the school cannot function. And we feel sure that each and every one of you, and us, are interested in seeing competitive athletics reach a new high in our school.*

Unfortunately, Ocilla's number one cheerleader was not on hand for the hearty resurrection of the Terrapins. Harriett Flanders wrote a tribute to her husband that appeared on the front page a week after his death in 1942.

> *He took great pride in his paper. During the last thirty-three years he put forth his best effort to build up his town and county. Even in his declining health his interest was alert to make his county and town one of the best in the state. With strong convictions and the stamina necessary to carry out these convictions, even in the face of opposition, yet never offensive, he based his principles on upright methods.*

Byron Maxwell acquired the *Star* from Mrs. Flanders.

We will try to maintain the high standards and straight forward policy of the Star with which you are familiar, he wrote in the April 27, 1944 edition.

By 1946 Ocilla Public School was bulging under a countywide effort to consolidate pupils, except for Irwinville. The enrollment was a whopping 700 with 300 in the upper four grades. Thirty-one boys were taken into football. Some of the young men like Newt Hudson were pressed into service by boosters, since volunteers with much athletic ability were scarce. Five boys were lost to farm work during the season, which might've hurt our chances of very much winning. But Newt Hudson, fresh back home from Navy duty, and centerpiece of the revival, stuck it out even though he farmed and was just a little guy.

Ocilla was lucky to have Newt, a future state representative. The young Hudson showed some good moves at fullback and was our top producer, scoring 39 points followed by 32 points put up by Jack Wilkes. Though only 155 pounds, Newt was wiry from farm work and military service. Doggedly tough, he was good on his feet; and although slippery, he'd pound you if he had to. Newt grew up a hardworking boy on his daddy's dirt farm in the outskirts of Ocilla. After chores before sunup, he walked the train tracks to school in Ocilla and hoped to be an agronomist. He dropped out of Ocilla High after his junior year to enlist in the Navy. After his tour, he returned to Ocilla to finish school as a senior, and that's when he was backed into a corner by Knot Tucker.

"I didn't want to play football," Newt says now. Besides, he wondered, being a former school dropout and Navy veteran, "I didn't think I was eligible. But they got me eligible."

The next he knew, he was toting the pigskin for the new-era Terrapins, sharing backfield duty with old friends he'd left behind for the Navy.

As the season wore on, Newt Hudson recalls, "We all had some missing teeth."

The *Star* published a team photo of the boys dressed in their gear. Coach Edge is also pictured along with the water boy, whose name was listed only as "Strange."

While Knot Tucker and his pals were on the front line in the effort to bring football back to Ocilla, Claude McNeil had a big hand in locating a new field for the boys to play on. McNeil's idea for a "sports park" north of town by the railroad track and golf course began to brew in 1939 when the Ocilla mayor envisioned a lighted complex of some 32 acres for *"and all sorts of athletic events,"* including horse racing, according to the *Star*.

Metal from the old Whelchel Field next to the school would be used in the construction of the racetrack "grandstand." In 1946, the newly formed Ocilla Athletic Association acquired the property by the railroad track for development as a sports facility. Newt Hudson and the other boys cleared out a place to play ball. The field in the pines, rimmed by the golf course, would host football games in Ocilla for the next 60 years. The old Whelchel Field lot became a practice field for the reborn Terrapins.

The horse track McNeil dreamed of was never built.

On game days in '46 the boys dressed in the gym and rode a bus to the new playing field at the golf course. That year, after a tough loss to McCrae-Helena in the opener, the *Star* reported:

The progress shown by the Ocilla team is remarkably good and the Ocilla-Sylvester game to be played Friday afternoon at 2 p.m. in Sylvester is expected to see some fine plays. Anyone with a car available to help transport the team to Sylvester is requested to be at the school house at 12 noon Friday to pick up a load, as a school bus will not be free at that hour to take them. Others wishing to see the game are urged to meet at this time and form a motorcade to help take as many football fans over as possible.

A later game with Douglas was one of two the boys played that year under the lights in Fitzgerald. Vic Smith covered the Douglas game for the *Fitzgerald Leader*. His story was reprinted in the *Star*.

Ocilla's underdog Terrapins played a highly-favored Douglas Pirate eleven a good, solid, scrappy ball game here last Friday night before bowing to a last-half rally, 24-6. Outweighed and badly out-experienced, the Terrapins hung in there doggedly and battled the Douglas outfit to a scoreless deadlock at halftime and actually outplayed the Pirates for most of the first half. .... The team hasn't set any worlds on fire but it has played hard and tried hard and it boasts an offense that is not only entertaining to watch, but likely to score on anybody. Ask Douglas.

In Wrightsville that year, the boys found the hospitality refreshing, even in a loss. Reported the *Star*:

Long before game time the rain started and continued through the first three quarters of the game. As a result, the field was muddy and the ball slick. Long end runs and passes being practically impossible, the two teams hammered through each other's line up and down the field. The Terrapins fought hard on both offense and defense, but when the final whistle blew, Ocilla was trailing 20-0. After the game Wrightsville proved themselves real hosts by serving both teams hot coffee.

17
First Lights

Although defeated 40-0 by Fitzgerald's Purple Hurricanes, Ocilla's Terrapins scored a moral victory Thursday, November 13, on Fitzgerald's field. Local reports from Fitzgerald had it that the Hurricane would defeat the Terrapins by 60 points with their B team and that the mighty Hargrove would make 30 points. At the end of the first quarter the score was 6-0. At the end of the second quarter the score was 12-0. In the second quarter the Terrapins once held the Hurricane on the one-foot line for four downs. In the third quarter Fitzgerald again made only one touchdown, to give them 20 points. But a battling Terrapin eleven tired in the fourth, and the final score was 40-0 for the Hurricane.

Sixty points? Only 40. B team? The Hurricane first string played the entire game. Hargrove's 30 points? He made 12.

—*Ocilla Star*, November 20, 1947

In 1947, with nine first stringers back in the lineup, we expected the boys of E. P. Edge to show us something. That was the first year state titles were awarded and Ocilla wanted to punch her ticket to the dance. That would have to wait, however. Although there were many thrills in winning a half dozen games, the most in a season since 1923, we lost like old times to Fitzgerald and did not make the playoffs; Edge was let go.

The wonder of '47 was the lights. It was the first year for lighted poles in Ocilla. How cool was that? The power company, at the urging of Mayor McNeil and the football boosters, put up lights on wooden poles at the Ocilla field by the golf course so our boys could see to play at night like most everyone else. Kids must've really flipped out to see a lighted field. Ocilla was one of the last teams in the district to get lights. Kickoff was normally at eight o'clock. Under the lights of home, the boys of 1947 were 3-1.

Forty lads turned out for fall drills that year, the most ever for an Ocilla team, and the boys seemed to be in high spirits. Jack Wilkes and two other boys wrote a preseason piece that appeared in the *Star*:

The men are having a free-for-all for the vacant spaces left on the first team this season by the graduation of

Griffin and Hudson, although you already know who will take their places: the ones with the biggest feet.

The trio quoted Coach Edge:

After having these boys out for a few hard practices, I can easily say our team this season will far exceed that of last. We are sincerely hoping to have some of the most exciting games this season that have ever been witnessed by Ocilla or any other high school team.

In a *Star* writeup a week later, Edge indicated he had never made those statements.

Prospects at this time are dim for a winning football team from Ocilla High ... Peanut digging and cotton picking mean many boys have to go home on the early busses every afternoon, and cannot get in the hours of practice they badly need.

The first game played under the lights in Ocilla was on October 3, 1947, in the season opener against Sylvester, a Class B team. By then, Georgia high school football programs were divided into classes. The Terrapins were in Class C, which was teams from the smaller schools.

After being pummeled by Sylvester, we found the win column, downing Blackshear. In that game, 145-pound Robert Fain became the first Terrapin to score points under the Ocilla lights. Robert's touchdown came on a reverse around left end for 30 yards.

Besides Blackshear, the victories in '47 came over Nashville, Sparks-Adel, Hawkinsville, Eastman and then in the dramatic season finale, played on Thanksgiving Day in Baxley, the Terrapins held off a late rally to win, 21–13, but we had not won enough games to make the postseason. The *Star*'s article about the Baxley game included the first action photo from a football contest. In the picture, a boy identified as Jack Wilkes of Ocilla was rushing toward the goal line with the football.

Asked now about his playing days in Ocilla, Wilkes says. "It was good. I was all right." His biggest complaint was the "dad-gum" hard field the boys practiced on in the school lot, and as to our rival, "We didn't do too good against those big ole boys from Fitzgerald."

> When the season of 1947 was over, M. S. McDonald wrote in the *Star:*
>
> *The Terrapins wish to express their appreciation to the people of Irwin County who have supported the team so liberally by attending their games and contributing their financial support. In return for the support the boys pledge their efforts to make future Ocilla teams noted for their ability to fight from the first to the last whistle and, win or lose, play a good game.*

Then in 1948, N.S. Deaver took over as coach, replacing Edge, and we were expecting a good hand but the boys were a little sorry and did not have quite enough spirit, even though '48 was the first season we had a team of cheerleaders.

The boys opened with a loss to Terrell County and never really got any traction. The game was technically a home game even though we played it at Tifton; road work was blocking the entrance to the golf course street in Ocilla, and Tifton High made their field available to us. The next Friday night, the Terrapins were shredded by Cordele, 38–13, which cast light on just how far we were from being a contender. Because of ongoing construction at the Ocilla our field, the Cordele game was played at Fitzgerald.

The *Star* stated:

> *The home boys were out-classed in weight, experience, and reserves, and they still need long and hard drills in the fundamentals with special emphasis on blocking and tackling...Their spirit needs improving along with individual desire.*

Later we thought maybe a 40–7 victory over Douglas was a turning point in the season. After Douglas, we jumped on Adel. The *Star* announced that a motorcade would leave the Ocilla City Hall that Friday night and head to the Adel field.

> *All those planning to...join the group and are asked to decorate their cars with the home team colors.*

Adel blew us out, 39–0, and a week later we got ripped at Tifton.

The boys were not winning like everybody had hoped. The finale of the '48 season was at Fitzgerald and it went about like you would expect. Fitz, dubbed the "Goliath" of Georgia high school football, broke our backs in forty places and went on to win a state championship. Their stud, Lauren Hargrove, had missed an earlier game with blood poisoning but he was back in the lineup when they played the out-manned Terrapins. In the game, with only a few ticks left on the clock, a Fitzgerald player intercepted a James Coley pass. Ocilla was passing the ball on every down, trying to score, even though all hope for victory was lost. After the interception, the Fitz High coach reinserted the Hargrove boy, nicknamed the *Fitzgerald Phantom*, apparently to run the score up on Ocilla as much as possible. On the first play after the pickoff, Hargrove rambled 77 yards down the right side for a touchdown. Then he broke through the line for the extra point and stayed in the game to kick off to Ocilla's Coley who was tackled down at our thirty as time ran out.

Fitzgerald was just too much for Ocilla. The final score was 59–6.

They never liked us anyway.

18
Country Boys

The Ocilla boys are showing a high degree of competitive spirit and several of the boys who played the first game of their life last week are expected to profit from the mistakes charged to inexperience.

Coach Steve Summerhill had the boys well-occupied during early-week practice. Players waiting their turn to substitute in scrimmage were kept busy clearing off the newly-mowed field. The turf will be in good shape for the home opener on Ocilla's well-lighted field. The stands are in readiness for the crowd. And the athletic association is in need of a financial boost.

Let's turn out and give encouragement to these young

-sters Friday night, and enjoy a good ball game while doing it.

—*Ocilla Star*, September 29, 1949

Troy Roberts of Ocilla remembers he played football "to keep from picking cotton." Between the football field and the cotton patch, "we didn't have nothing else to do."

Troy, whose daddy, Rafe, never missed a home game, first played for Ocilla High in '49. "Me and Harry Portier decided to go out. Harry didn't stay long. He changed his mind but I liked it."

Many believed farm boys made the best athletes; able to give and take a pounding.

Football filled a lot of holes with fun for boys who went for those kinds of shenanigans.

"We were playing Dawson," Troy says, "I broke through the line, and me and John Langdale stood the runner up, and he lost the ball. It landed right in my hands and John says, 'Run, Troy!' and so I ran, and I scored a touchdown."

Pete Martin says he got a tooth knocked out tackling a boy from Tifton named Johnny Lipsey, and laughed it off. "That joker broke through the line. I dove and caught his heel in my mouth." Pete recalls the cut took six stitches but it never fazed him.

Pete was never able to rest on Saturday mornings after a Friday night football game because there was work to do on the farm. "I got up and went to the field. I picked cotton. I stacked peanuts, shook 'em by hand."

At 220 pounds, Carroll Green loved to hit people. One of Ocilla's bigger boys of the day, Carroll remembers a game with Hawkinsville where one of their players was running wild on the Terrapins. "Coach told me to go out there and get that guy. I caught him blindsided…broke his leg. It was a clean hit."

Going to away games was a lot of fun, especially the food. Troy says, “We always ate at a nice restaurant. I remember the Green Frog in Waycross.”

“We got to eat away from home,” bawls Pete Martin, citing restaurant food as a perk of playing football, and coming back from road games, “we’d sing some, talk about the game, try to take a nap” on the bus.

Those days yield a lot of good memories for old farmer Robert Fain. Although just 145 pounds in high school, he was toughened by farm work. Robert grew up about a block and a half from the school. Despite exhaustion, bruises, scrapes, the hardness, and dangers of the game, “I really liked it,” he says. “I played all four years…I tried to come back to school to play a fifth year but they wouldn’t let me.”

Not all boys for Ocilla High were from farm families. Carl Hodnett, for example, was a city boy, but he was country in nature. He weighed 200 pounds and worked for his father’s Ocilla plumbing business. “Threading pipe kept me in shape.”

No boys for Ocilla in those days were more country, or tougher, than the Barrineau brothers. Emory and Raymond never came off the field during the games, those rough and tumble Barrineaus.

“I just loved it,” Emory says of football. “I weighed 170 pounds. That was a pretty good-sized boy. We didn’t have stuff to eat like they do now to gain weight.”

To get home after practice, Emory walked from the field to Highway 129, where he hitched a ride to Whitley near Lake Beatrice. From there, he hiked three more miles on a dirt road to the family farm.

When Raymond was six years old, he broke his ankle in a bizarre accident while horsing around on the farm. He had

Coach Steve Summerhill with Indian Captains C.B. Jeffries, l, and Emory Barrineau, about 1950.
Courtesy Ocilla Star / copied by David Pierce

heard that cats always land on their feet so he was testing the theory by tossing a few kittens out of a hay loft in the barn. As he ran toward the loft door to throw the next kitten far as he could, Raymond slipped on loose hay and flew out the door himself, breaking his ankle in the fall. His ankle wasn't reset correctly, so it didn't heal properly. He said having a bad foot didn't bother him much in the games, although "when I'd get home and take my shoes off it'd hurt." But he really enjoyed football because he loved to hit other boys.

Emory, now a resident of Tallahassee, Florida, says he was the first Ocilla High boy to ever wear a face mask but not because he was sissy. His nose bled easily. "They put that bar across to stop them from hitting me in the face with their fingers," he explained.

An older brother, Cecil, was the ramrod of the family farm when Raymond and Emory were in high school. Although the boys had many chores to perform, in the fall when football started, Cecil let them play football.

"He loved to watch the games," Raymond said of his older brother. "He never did try to stop us from playing…We never won no state championship…but we held our own."

Except with Fitzgerald, that is. Beating Fitzgerald was not anything the Barrineau boys or anybody from Irwin County ever imagined could be possible.

"They had a heck of a good team," Raymond remembered. "They had a little more to pick from than we did."

"One time," Emory recalled, "we got beat like, 75–0. That was way back in the day…We were just a little ole school. Only had a few boys. Fitzgerald had a bunch of boys, big ole boys…two, three coaches. We were just outclassed."

Emory used to think that Fitzgerald trained boys at an early age just for football. Ocilla wasn't that well organized in the sport. The vast majority of boys coming into Ocilla High had never played football, and Ocilla only had the one coach.

Emory, who was drafted into the Army for service in Korea, played last in 1950; Raymond, in 1948. Despite its risks, football in Ocilla in the old days meant a lot to those who played the game. "I just loved it," Raymond says. "Back then, the rougher it was, the better I liked it."

Says brother Emory, "We were just a bunch of ole country boys, that's all."

19

Indians!

Ocilla's light, inexperienced high school football team, operating from the T-formation under the direction if a new coach will make its debut at Fitzgerald Friday night, September 23, against one of the Goliaths of Georgia high school football—the Purple Hurricane, 1948 class A champion.

Steve Summerhill, who is used to trouble as chief umpire of the Georgia State baseball league, is not worrying particularly about the result of his first game as Ocilla coach.

"A touchdown against Fitzgerald is the most we can hope to accomplish in the game," he said this week, as the Terrapins rounded out their second week of practice.

"We realize we are badly out-classed, so we hope all our boys come through the fracas without physical hurt and can thereby meet our Class C opponents on close to even terms."

—*Ocilla Star*, September 15, 1949

In the fall of 1949, without a ceremony, they put the *Terrapin* down. The creature was deemed too slow and ineffective. How could anybody win or be feared if they were named for a turtle? There was a new breed of student at Ocilla High School who wanted a mascot with more pizzazz and more swag that they could sink their pride into and maybe we'd win more games. So, prior to the season opener with Fitzgerald, the seniors were asked to pick a new name for the team.

"It was our class that voted," remembers former cheerleader Myra Griffin, whose maiden name in school was Sandifer.

When the votes were tallied, Bulldogs and other creatures were beaten out by *Indians*.

Feelings were conflicted. Pete Martin, a half-back that year on the first team of Indians, was glad to see the Terrapin gone. "I wanted it changed. They moved too slow." Others were disappointed.

But considering that Ocilla was probably named for Chief Osceola, and with so many arrowheads around Ocilla in the dirt, the Indian was the logical choice by most who voted.

"We had so much 'Indian'," recalls Myra, a part-time worker at the Irwin County Library. "Our class ring had an Indian on the side."

Big dog, little dog, floppy-eared pup! C'mon, Indians, eat 'em up! became a cheerleader favorite at the games.

That year, 1949, Steve Summerhill was brought in to be the coach, replacing Deaver, who'd lasted one season, but changing coaches, like changing names, didn't help us any. These boys, the first to be called Indians, and averaging 150 pounds, struggled to three wins against seven losses. In three years since the Terrapin resurrection, we hadn't done much but the game that year with mighty Fitz was not as ugly as was predicted; the boys put up a fight, losing by only 39–0. Luckily, no Indian boy was hurt.

"We were scrappy, but it seems like the other schools had a better team," recalls Mary Jane Espinoza, whose last name in school was McMillan. She says she and her fellow cheerleaders "thought we were doing wonders. It was mostly moving together. We practiced for hours, trying to get everybody to do the same thing."

At the start of the 1950 season, the Star reported:

Friday evening is slated to be a festive occasion for local football fans and townspeople alike. Coach Summerhill and his teaching associates, the pupils and a few interested local people have been hard at work all week working up some added attractions which will give the fans more than just a football game. To start festivities off with a bang, a motorcade will form at the high school around 4 p.m. ...and tour the city to let local residents know that Ocilla High school is playing a football game that evening and that they plan to open their 1950 season with a win over a tough Mitchell County team from Camilla.

The article wrapped a team photo of some 37 Indians. Another picture in the spread showed Summerhill in pleated trousers and white shirt standing between co-captains C. B. Jeffries and Emory Barrineau in full gear.

We lost to Mitchell County 6-0 before reeling off six victories out of the next seven games but, again, the boys did not make the playoffs and due to classification rules, there was not a game with Fitzgerald.

The game with Cordele that year was scheduled to be in Ocilla but Cordele boosters decided they wanted it at their place and offered the Ocilla Athletic Association a $300 guarantee in gate receipts to play the game at Cordele. Ocilla took the terms with the understanding that our home season tickets would be honored at the gate. Cordele agreed. They beat us 19–0.

Then in 1951, Summerhill's boys, hard-hit by graduation and some other circumstances, defeated Toombs Central, 13–6, for their only victory.

Again, we did not play Fitzgerald and a game scheduled with Patterson never took place.

We just couldn't get any footing in '51. Nobody wanted to hear excuses, but besides losing seven starters who had graduated, three other Indians counted on to play quit the team to join the military, one boy moved away, one was too old to play and three others were ruled ineligible due to academic difficulty.

The lone win in 1951, over upstart Toombs Central, was homecoming for the Indians. *The day's events included a colorful parade of elaborate floats in the afternoon,* according to a cutline below a photograph of the queen and her court in the *Star*.

The loss that year to Cordele was by forfeit.

The *Star* explained what happened:

> *The Cordele field was flooded last Friday with continued rain adding to the poor condition of the gridiron five inches under water at some points. Coach Steve Summerhill said the decision to forfeit the game*

> *was based upon the probability of injury and illness to the players, the certainty of ruining uniforms, especially the expensive football shoes and the fact that Ocilla's low standing in the region made the game pointless. It would have cost more than $100 to make the trip. With the added rest, the Indians hoped to have a better chance in the remaining games.*

Ocilla in 1951 was not very much of a football town.

20

The Promoter

From the start of the game, it was apparent that the Indians were out-classed. Camilla had just too much speed and experience for Coach Strickland's young team. The Indians were game and willing but totally unable to cope with the long range thrusts of the more experienced and heavy Panthers coached by Chilly Penn. An estimated crowd of 2500 saw Camilla strike in the first period on a pass from Bateman to Watson for 38 yards and a touchdown ... One of the bright spots of the game was the performance of 150-pound Hollis Register. Register was called the finest player on the field by many spectators. Danny Paulk, Roger Dill, Carl Hodnett and the entire team battled valiantly but it was just not their

night. In practice this week the Indians are stressing tackling, the main weakness of the team as a whole."
—*Ocilla Star*, September 25, 1952

So, in the summer of 1952 Steve Summerhill was let go. He probably hated how badly things had gone. In fact, there were hurt feelings all over the place that year, even if you were the pig.

That was the year the big merger took effect, giving the world Irwin County High School. The boys of '52 were the first to be called the Irwin County Indians and at one game fans were entertained by a pig chase.

That year the boys lost six games out of ten and failed to make the playoffs but unlike in years past they showed some promise toward the end with a strong group coming back.

Our new coach in '52, H.L. Strickland, who went by the name "Herb," was a whip-cracker who knew not only how to train a team but how to rally the community for football, a skill that was sorely lacking among previous coaches. For one, you had to beat the bushes, stir everything up. Football was a product. You had to sell it, not only to athletes in school but to the community at large, and that's where Strickland was a master. Luckily for Strickland, he had some boys who'd put on a good show.

Nobody ever said Summerhill was a sorry coach.

"Good coach, no doubt about it," says Ocilla restaurant owner Max Alford, who played for Summerhill and Strickland in Ocilla, "but he was not a charismatic guy that could go out in the community and stir the community up the way Strickland could do."

Under Strickland, people began to feel a connection to the football team in a way they never had.

"He was a promoter," says Alford. "He went into the

community and got people to do things for the program, give them money, get a bus for them to go do things. There wasn't another coach who'd done that."

Coach H.L. "Herb" Strickland in 1953. *Courtesy ICHS Library / copied from 1953-54 yearbook by Lucy Pierce*

Irwin school bosses, no doubt feeling we'd hit rock bottom and knowing of a string of talented boys coming up in the ranks, hired Strickland away from Sylvester to invigorate the sagging program in Ocilla. A former Auburn player, Strickland did not have a stellar record at Sylvester High, posting a four-year mark of 23–16–1 with no playoffs. But he did really good in Ocilla, at least for one year, and old boys who played for Strickland give him credit for lighting the fire of pride over football that still burns in the hearts of Indian fans.

Danny Paulk, a junior on the '52 team, remembers Strickland as "a blood 'n guts coach. Summerhill was a softie."

Mr. Alford, who coached football for two years in nearby Douglas, won't argue Summerhill's ability to coach, "… but he did not have the community behind him like Strickland did when he was the coach."

The merger was a bitter pill for some, although it enhanced the football program by bringing in new talent. Emotions were tender when Ocilla High went out of business. The consolidation into a centralized high school, based in Ocilla at Sixth and Almond streets, was especially a blow to the Irwinville vicinity for it also killed old Irwinville High, a powerhouse in boys' basketball, and in many towns, losing their school was a death knell. Football in Ocilla gained hugely, however. There were many prospects among the wave of boys coming from Irwinville High. Strickland recognized talent when he saw it and probably was the best coach in Ocilla since E.V. Whelchel of the 1920s at digging up, or recruiting, ball players.

One boy the Indians gained from the Irwinville exodus was a little fellow named Hollis Register, who could run backward faster than most men forward. Hollis and another Irwinville transfer, Jimmy Clements, put on the pads for the first time in 1952. The two had never seen the game played, but Hollis especially picked it up and made good. At only 5-feet, 8 inches tall and 150 pounds, he was cat-quick and could outjump the new boy, Charlie Barnes.

Hollis was picking cotton when Strickland visited him in the field about playing football in Ocilla. The coach shook hands with Hollis's dad, who resisted letting Hollis play. A lot of farmers who relied on their sons to help pick cotton and do other chores were that way. To give up a son to football was to lose farm labor.

"I was going to play," Hollis says, adding that he'd already made up his mind to go out for football when Strickland met him that afternoon in the cotton patch. However, due to their resentment over the school merger, "my own family wouldn't come watch me play ball" for Irwin County High.

To Hollis, the merger "was the best thing that ever happened to me. It got me knowing people like Danny Paulk, Roger Dill, boys like that" and with them came a lifelong camaraderie.

Of course, anytime there was a coaching change, feelings were subject to get hurt and morale to suffer. It was no different when Strickland, for one thing, suggested to the *Star* that the 33-man team he inherited from Summerhill in '52 was a poor excuse for a squad. "We had a really good team (but) we had a lot of problems," recalls Carl Hodnett, one of only three senior starters on the 1952 outfit.

Hodnett recollects "a lot of controversy" surrounded Strickland's first season here that interfered with the team's focus.

One issue that bothered boys like Hodnett was with the new kid, Charlie Barnes, described by the *Star* as *the fastest and most experienced man on the team, good runner, blocker and tackler.*

When the school chiefs hired Strickland, Charlie came over

with him from Sylvester, perhaps making it appear the two were a package deal. Mr. Hodnett says the coach named Charlie a starter right out of the gate and appointed him to a captain's role before the boy had ever played a down for the Indians, who had already chosen a captain. Some Indian veterans felt it was unfair for Charlie Barnes to be treated like a prince.

Hodnett, who played end, remembers the Barnes affair generated a lot of talk and speculation. People were told that Charlie had lived in Sylvester with his grandmother while playing there for Strickland and while his parents, Bud and Louis, operated a store in Ashburn. Later his mom and dad moved to Ocilla where they established an electronics store, leading some people to suspect the couple got put into business here just so Charlie could play in Ocilla for Strickland.

Max Alford said there shouldn't have been any confusion over how it went with Charlie and Strickland.

"His parents were in business with Charlie's uncle in Ashburn, but they had already established a business here before Charlie came here," explained Max, who later became Charlie's brother-in-law. "They established it like six or eight months while he was still in Sylvester … They knew he was going to move to Ocilla when he finished out that year in Sylvester. So he came here his junior year and so did Herb Strickland … but there was no conspiracy. Charlie went where his family was."

Regardless of the circumstances surrounding his becoming an Indian, nobody argued that Charlie Barnes was a good boy and talented back who wanted to be a Georgia Bulldog. One of many juniors on the 1952 squad, Charlie sat out the season opener against Mitchell County while his eligibility to play for Irwin was in the hands of the state's athletic hardship committee. The committee ruled he was good to go. Charlie also missed most of the Blackshear game when he came out with an injury.

The '52 team did not win until October 24, when they upset single A Bacon County, 31–0, at home. They defeated three of their last five foes by a combined 99-6 and the outlook for 1953 looked bright to fans long starved for a contender.

Inspired by Strickland, football also had begun to appeal to the peewees, which was vital to the program's long-term success. According to the *Star*, sixty-five midgets from the elementary school played games at 6:15 p.m. prior to the Cochran game, and some also played at halftime. In promoting the tikes, the *Star* wrote, "All these boys have full equipment and have shown plenty of fight and determination."

The varsity tied Cochran that night, 13–13.

There was no game that year with Fitzgerald.

Among the losses in 1952 was a 13–2 setback to Terrell County High out of Dawson in the third game. For Irwin, the highlight of the evening, besides the safety and a 35-yard scamper by Hollis Register, was a greasy pig chase at halftime. A purebred Duroc Jersey pig was lathered and let loose onto the Ocilla field for boys of the local Future Farmers of America club to pursue for the entertainment of the crowd. The boy who sacked the pig got to keep it. The *Star* did not identify who, if anyone, ever caught the animal.

Said the *Star:*

> *This was the final game of the season for the Indians. and although their won-lost record was not too good, they provided the fans with some very interesting football. ... This was the last game for Carl Hodnett, Ronald Paulk and Tuffy Hudson. Although these three boys will be hard to replace, it is believed that the Indians will have one of the strongest teams in the region next year.*

21

Desire To Win

The mighty Irwin Indians rolled for six touchdowns Monday night in scalping a valiant Sylvester team, 41-0. The game held promise of being a tight, close affair until the second half was just a few minutes old. After that the final score was simply a question of how many times the Indians gained possession of the ball. Murderous downfield blocking on the part of the Indians repeatedly paved the way for runners to rip off long gains and touchdowns. Conditioning also played a major part in the victory.

—*Ocilla Star*, September 31, 1953

The first of our boys to wear red and the first of them to attend a summer camp, the 1953 Irwin County Indians learned how to win, and when that happened, fans crawled out of the woodwork as the team and the community began to tie together. We'd never look at football the same way again. You could talk about peanuts. You could talk about cotton and that was fine. You could sit and talk politics all day. Football was something else now and as the wins mounted, "All of a sudden everybody talked football," Danny Paulk remembers.

That hadn't happened in Ocilla since the game was resurrected here jubilantly in 1946. Only now it was 1953 and the boys in red were hanging the Ws. That made a huge difference in shaping everyone's attitude for decades to come.

"Ocilla is a tremendous football town," observes Mr. Alford, who recently returned to his boyhood town after many years in Texas in the furniture business. "I attribute Ocilla's start to becoming a real football town to Herb Strickland."

No question, Strickland was a figure. In a 1998 *Ocilla Star* article about Danny Paulk and a few of his old friends in the early days of the Indians, Danny said of Strickland, "We loved the man. We would do anything for him. He gave us and the entire community pride and a desire to win."

A tough dude, Danny, who appears now in khaki trousers and an old ball cap at his business, Paulk Pecan Company, on 2nd Street. Growing up in Ocilla, Danny earned the rank of Eagle Scout and later attended Emory University in Atlanta where he earned a degree in petroleum geology. He also did two years in the Army.

In 1953, Danny was joined in the Indian backfield by two other seniors: Charlie Barnes and Hollis Register. Danny had a great arm; he put that baby on a dime. He was also a good runner. With Charlie and Hollis behind Danny, with Max Alford at end, and a solid line, Strickland in '53 had the tools he needed to finally build a winner in Ocilla.

"We felt like we could beat anybody," Danny says now,

"and most of the time we didn't have any trouble."

The Indian starters were all two-way players. And no team in Ocilla history ever entered a season in better shape physically. In his second season, Strickland drove the boys hard at Lake Blackshear in mid-August. Our boys had never been to camp, and while this affair—summer camp—sounded like it'd be fun and serene and maybe they could get in some fishing, it was a nightmare.

"Coach Strickland separated the men from the boys," recalls Warren Alexander, who played some at half back on the '53 team. At camp that year, "boys were cutting out right and left, hitting the road."

Hard workouts at the lake were the order of each morning with the bullfrogs and the crickets, and boys could never get enough to drink, so thirsty were they from drills. "They served milk in metal pitchers," Danny Paulk remembers. "That ice-cold milk. You couldn't get enough. They took care of you but they worked your butt off."

On the night of September 11, 1953, the raging Indians of Class B hosted Clinch County to open the season sporting the new outfits. The jerseys were red; the days of looking like Fitzgerald's little brother were over. Strickland had wanted the change, believing purple and gold were odd. The home outfit was a red jersey with gray pants and gray helmets with a red stripe down the middle. Actually, the coach had wanted burgundy shirts; but that scheme was unavailable by the uniform supplier in Albany, so the basic red was chosen and made to stand for something.

That night, in the first of six home games, the boys

thundered over Clinch, 38–0, and a week later, with a motorcade of fans along, the Indians hit the road to Camilla where Irwin had to pull out all the stops to win it, 14–7, scoring on a fancy play in which Barnes pretended like he was running a sweep but he stopped and threw to Max Alford who had slipped behind the Camilla secondary and was waiting all alone.

In the third game, the boys hammered Strickland's old team, Sylvester, on a Monday night in Ocilla, the game having been postponed from Friday due to weather.

> *Possibly the outstanding feature of the game in the opinion of the overflowing crowd was the sensational running of Hollis Register who rushed for a total of 224 yards on 17 attempts and scored four touchdowns,* the *Star* reported.

The community ate it up. After games, fans of the boys came out of the stands to greet them in a spirit of pride and joy. Especially after home games, "Jack Wilkes' mother and a bunch of old ladies, they came out on the field and we formed a circle and chanted, *'Two bits, four bits'*…It'd just make you so proud to wear that red jersey," recalls Warren Alexander.

That year, due again to the restraints of classification, Irwin County did not play Fitzgerald.

"They were in a higher class than we were," says Danny Paulk, explaining why the rivalry was not renewed. "We had our competition going but it wasn't on the football field." Danny says there was an old saying in Ocilla that went "Fitzgerald had the boys and we got the girls."

Game 4 of 1953 was played in Dawson, some 85 miles away, against the Terrell County Green Wave, and Irwin put a "W" in the win column but only by eight points. As soon as they got off the bus back in Ocilla, the sleepy, worn boys were punished by Strickland for lack of effort before they were allowed to go home.

"We were at the football field, running wind sprints at one, two o'clock in the morning," Danny Paulk recalls.

From that point the boys blew out Wacona, Folkston, Bacon County and Blackshear by a combined score of 157–27.

On the Tuesday following the Blackshear game, the boys and their dates were feted to an evening fish fry at Ocilla's Cumbee Park. The fish used for the occasion came from Marion Green's pond. Mr. Green had drained one of his ponds in the county and let the football team come out and catch the fish as the water went down.

The Friday after the fish fry, the Indians clinched the Eastern Division 1-B by slashing Cochran 46–0 after the kickoff was delayed a half hour due to revival services at the Ocilla Baptist Church.

For the first time in history, there was a football trophy in Ocilla and the Indians gained statewide recognition.

This was the team we'd all been waiting for.

With the east region hardware in the bag, the boys closed out the regular season by pummeling Patterson in Ocilla on a Thursday night, which was homecoming. The following week there was a bye, which enabled Strickland and boosters to take the boys to see the football game between Jesup and Valdosta. The team left town early the next morning, Saturday, as a group to see the Georgia-Auburn classic in Athens.

Football in Ocilla was flying high.

Win twice more and we'd make state.

In the Region Final, the Indians beat Quitman by four touchdowns in a game that was played at Tifton. It was the first football playoff victory for an Ocilla team as the boys claimed another trophy and pushed their mark to 11–0.

Ocilla had never seen the likes of it and it was beautiful.

In the next game, which was for the South Georgia title, the offense spat and sputtered on a wet night in Waycross before Coach Strickland got it moving, and the Irwin machine went on to crush Glennville High, 35–6, and we all celebrated as the victory vaulted the Indians into the state B title game with some school in northwest Georgia called Model where they did not know anything about picking cotton and peanuts.

Everybody tried to make it. Everybody was crazy, hungry and a little nervous; one win away from being on top of the world.

22
'Quagmire'

Irwin High and several hundred fans will make the trip to Rome Friday to see the Indians in their attempt to defeat Model and become the State Class B Champions. The Indians will meet at the high school gymnasium Friday morning at 7:30 a.m. and be ready to leave by bus at 8:00. They will spend Friday night in Rome and return home Saturday or Sunday. ... The Irwin High Band is scheduled to leave by chartered bus Friday at 12:45 p.m. There will be a chartered Greyhound bus carrying some 35 fans to Rome. The bus will leave the bus station at 12:00 noon Friday. Roundtrip fare will be $7.50.

—*Ocilla Star*, December 10, 1953

While their proud, anxious fans made their way to the game as best they could, traveling 257 miles, the boys left Ocilla aboard a yellow school bus that morning and played the game that night. The Irwin band was there and got soaked. It was unexpectedly rainy in Rome, cold, and the red-clay field at Model High was slick with mud and had very little grass.

"It was a quagmire," cries Danny Paulk.

Max Alford remembers seeing snow.

But it was the same on both sides of the ball and the Blue Devils, whose strength was the running game, who came in with record of 12-1, having lost only to Villa Rica, roared out to a 19–6 advantage in a steady drizzle on their home field.

> Said the Star: *Things got off to a bad start for the Indian team and the several hundred loyal fans that followed the team from one end of the state to the other.*

Like champions, however, the Indians battled back and tied the game by the half, at which point, *"Indian fans felt good about the situation,"* the *Star* said.

But in the second half, as the slow drizzle turned to a light rain, the Indians fumbled three times, one leading to a quick Model score, and then gave up an interception in trying to match Model's easy six.

> *The ball was too slippery to maintain possession of for any length of time,* bawled the Star.

"Our strong suit was throwing the ball" Danny explains. The cold, wet conditions threw the Irwin offense out of gear. Strickland couldn't fix it. Danny couldn't save us. Hollis and Charlie couldn't save us. And down went the tribe, 25–19.

> *There were times that they looked dead of their feet, which was all a fast team like Model needed,* the *Star* reported. *The Indians came out first in only one department. They made 11 first downs to Model's 8.*

"We should've won the game," cries Max Alford. "I think we had a better overall total team."

Meanwhile, Danny and his buddies are firm in the matter as to the field conditions, which fit Model's offense better than ours, and 60 years later, the old boys remain sensitive when "Model" is mentioned in their hearing.

Says Warren Alexander, "Had we met on a halfway decent field..."

"We all think that," says Charlie Barnes.

The *Star* saw numerous reasons we lost in Rome.

> *The difference could have been the hard charging Model line, a Model back named Shellnut, the long bus ride that Irwin took, the faulty eye of the officials or the rain that slowed Irwin's powerful backfield, or a combination of all these. Model made the most points, anyway, and won the game.*

Hollis Register recalls, "It was a mess up there" and says he'd have gone on to play at the University of Georgia except he was too short. But as to Model, "I got about a 65-yard run for a touchdown."

When the game was put into the record, the Indians left the field like gentlemen with heads high. Proud to be from Ocilla, Irwin County, south Georgia, our many fans, some in tears, came out onto the field to greet the boys, and to congratulate the peanut pickers on the best season ever, although it ended in disappointment. That night the fatigued, downcast Indians ate like kings and stayed in a warm, clean motel. On Saturday, the sun came up. Though dark with unfulfillment, the boys spent the day sightseeing like champions on a bus through Atlanta, which many of them had never seen.

Coach Strickland was named the Class B Coach of the Year by the *Atlanta-Journal Constitution*. Jerry Trantham, the Indian center who also played linebacker, was named Georgia's lineman of the year. Charlie Barnes made All-State running back, first team. Roger Dill and Hollis made All-State second team. Eight boys received All-Region honors.

The three trophies earned by the team were put on display in Ocilla at the A. S. Harris department store, and that was good but it'd been a real pretty display with that "state" trophy.

Nevertheless, "We had a great year," Hollis Register acknowledges, believing that the winning attitude that exists in Irwin County for football began with his group.

Danny Paulk agrees, and as to the camaraderie that formed between the boys, Danny carries in his pocket a crinkled piece of paper with the handwritten names and phone numbers of boys he played football with in high school. Now and then someone from the old team drops by at his business to catch up on town gossip and reminisce. Danny says the boys of '53 possessed great chemistry, and football "bonded everybody together" on the team for life.

"He's right about that," says Charlie Barnes, whose boyhood dream of being a Georgia Bulldog football player came true. Two years later Charlie shelved his cleats after tearing up his knees and his nose at Georgia. His heart remains warmed by the fond memories from his football days in Ocilla. "We had a good time, had a good coach and had some good players. We were anxious to play and wanted to play. We had a good group," says Charlie, who married Max Alford's sister and now resides in the Lake Blackshear community. "I remember all of them like my brothers."

Seven Indians won All-Region honors in 1953: L-r, Ernest Berryhill, Danny Paulk, Charlie Barnes, Hollis Register, Jerry Hancock, Jerry Trantham and Max Alford. *Courtesy ICHS Library/ copied from 1953-54 yearbook by Lucy Pierce*

23

Held In Check

Nearly 2,500 persons jammed Ocilla Athletic Field last Friday night and saw a spunky Irwin football squad hammer out a 26-12 victory over Tifton's big Blue Devils. The crowd, the largest to witness a game here in several years, saw the underdog Indians thrust two scores over in the first period and one in the second to roll up a 20-0 halftime score and hang on in the second half to win....Coach Hicks reports the Indians were shaken up pretty much in the bruising battle...but he believes he'll be able to field eleven men against the Hurricane. Team spirit was running high this week as anticipation of belting the scalps of Tifton and Fitzgerald in the same season descended upon them.

—*Ocilla Star,* September 22, 1955

From 1954 through 1959, we whooped and hollered. It wasn't that. We turned out in big numbers and built fires. Ocilla was a "football town" now and every year we wanted to believe might be the year we'd finally do it, get back to state and this time win it. The school held pep rallies and the boys really hustled. They were scrappy, never quit, and were fed well and we had a star here and there, perhaps none more special than Marion Roberts while two other Indian boys - Billy Alexander, fullback, and Kice Stone, end, - both made All-State in 1958. Unfortunately, after the joy of 1953, with all those victories, the results of 1954 through 1959 were not to up to snuff and each year ended in disappointment as the playoff train that stopped in Ocilla for the first time in 1953 blew by us like a ghost.

It was awesome to get over Fitzgerald three times, and once we nipped Tifton. But in the span of six years following the marvelous run to state, which had electrified the fans and helped to put this town on the map, the boys moved up in class a lot where they were too often outgunned, too slow or just unlucky and never made the post season cut.

Strickland had shown us what it takes to win—it was a community effort. Everybody had a part. The warriors in red, their coaches, cheer girls in pleated skirts below the knee, boosters, moms and pops and the other spectators were all in it together. Everyone who came out to the games showed their pride by their presence and getting beat was never easy.

That Irwin would not be a power every year was painfully evident in 1954 when the great Strickland had no more tricks and many holes to fill left by graduation and although we buried Fitzgerald in 1954, we got pounded in moving up to Class A and losing was hard to get used to again. Tifton, Cordele, Americus, Thomasville, Cairo and Cook all burnt our teepees in 1954 and we put only four games into the win column.

The Irwin High Indians string of regular season games without a defeat was broken last Friday night when they were defeated by the Blue Devils 37–13, the *Star* reported in 1954. *The Tifton line, which outweighed the Indians approximately 30 pounds per man, tore huge holes in the Indian forward wall for Imp backs to rumble through.*

There were many obstacles to making the playoffs if you want to hear about them. Our boys weren't always very talented and lacked the strength to compete at a high level. Sometimes it seemed nobody knew how to block and injuries were untimely. Maybe some coaching wasn't top form, and under state reclassification, Irwin was put into a region with bigger schools that we really had no business playing. There was always an excuse and fans were wondering when we'd get back to being a power again. Byron Maxwell of the *Star* did a nice job covering the teams. He published play-by-play accounts of the games and inserted pictures with the articles. Some photos were of boys in their games, others of players posing in their uniforms for the camera.

As to our coaches, "blood 'n guts" Strickland, who'd carried us to the doorstep of greatness, called it quits in 1955, handing the bonnet to his top assistant, Aubrey Hicks, and took up school administration in LaGrange, Georgia. In late August 1955, the *Star* ran a page one picture of six Indians in the old school yard departing Ocilla for summer camp under chief Hicks at Lake Blackshear. The lads are clean-cut though not very husky with duffle bags as if drafted for duty in the Army. Although we beat Tifton in 1955, Hicks was not successful. The team was the most woeful seen here in years, going 2-8, and after one season Mr. Hicks left the reservation. Later, the blond-haired, hard-nosed Hicks, known to the boys as "Snake Eyes," became a Hall of Fame coach in Alabama. Nobody can say for sure why he couldn't win in Ocilla.

In 1956, we handed the bonnet to Gene Alexander. Brought in from South Habersham to lead Irwin back to prominence, hopefully to a state title, Alexander was never able to satisfy the Indian family's thirst for the playoffs, although in his first season we almost made the tournament.

> *The team is extremely short on capable reserves...and one or two injuries would seriously hurt them,"* Alexander told the *Star* prior to the 1956 campaign. *"There are 29 boys out for the team with only about half that number with the physical capabilities of playing in a game.*

But the boys of '56 showed us something, bowing their necks, and were in the fight for the 1-AA North title down to the wire before losing by an eyelash to region winner Americus.

A year later, in 1957, with Marion Roberts, a sophomore, at quarterback, the hard-battling Indians of the 1-AA North won just four times, including a tough loss to rugged region foe Tifton.

> Said the Star:
>
> *The Tifton High Blue Devils handed Irwin High its first regional defeat here Friday night, 13-0, before a crowd estimated at about 3,000. ... Although the heavier and stronger Tifton squad kept the Indians offense in check most of the night it still required two cheap touchdowns to defeat the scrappy Irwin eleven. Irwin*

suffered a big loss when Ennis Veal was carried from the field in the third period with an injury. He suffered fractures in the lower part of his back and will be in the hospital for perhaps a month.

At one point in '57, quarterback Marion Roberts and his accomplices faced the iron-man task of battling strong AA contenders Cairo, Warner Robins and Bainbridge in a span of eight days due to a flu outbreak in Ocilla and Warner Robins that postponed games. The underdog Indians went down to defeat in all three. The Cairo game was homecoming for Irwin but the annual parade was cancelled and school was closed because so many kids were out sick.

Resuming hostilities with the old rival was a kick. There was always pride and a bit more on the line when the game was with Fitzgerald.

In '54, when Irwin jumped a spot to join Fitzgerald in Class A, the Indians drubbed the 'Canes for the first time since 1928. The score, at Fitzgerald, was 13–0, and as one might imagine, and as the *Star* pointed out, *"Fans in the county were jubilant over the victory."*

Then in 1955 the Indians were very slow and it was crying time.

Reported the *Star*:

The Fitzgerald Purple Hurricane invaded Ocilla last Friday night and nearly blew the heavy-footed Indians out of the park, rolling up a 45–6 score. The Irwin boys who appeared stale and dazed at times never gave up and fought a futile battle right to the end.

In 1956, Alexander's first year, Irwin spoiled Fitzgerald's party.

The *Star* crowed:

The Irwin County High School Indians reached their peak Friday night as they humbled the Purple Hurricane of Fitzgerald 37–19 before a large homecoming crowd at Blue and Grey Park in Fitzgerald. The Indians completely dominated the game. ... A determined Irwin crew showed they meant business. ... The Irwin second stringers played a majority of the last quarter. It was a rough and tough battle all the way with the Indians' superior conditioning and hard charging giving them a decisive advantage.

In 1957, it was Irwin's turn to moan. Groaned the *Star*, *A good team with an overwhelming desire to win was the Fitzgerald Purple Hurricane last Friday night as they defeated the Indians, 25–0... With Crumbly out with illness and Portier sidelined after the first period, the Indians had no offense to speak of, making only three first downs all evening. Losing five fumbles didn't help their cause any either. Only Billy Alexander, playing his first game at halfback, gained any yardage against the heavier Hurricane line.*

The Indians battled the Purple Hurricane again in 1958 and '59, each on Thanksgiving Day. The 1958 turkey classic before a large crowd in Fitzgerald was scoreless at halftime before Fitzgerald picked up a pair of safeties and made a field goal and a touchdown to take the game from outmanned Irwin, 13–0.

In 1959, Irwin grabbed the bird in a home game that sealed the lid on 1950s football in Ocilla, winning 20–8. Irwin's final TD of the decade was scored by senior Marion Roberts on a 16-yard run midway of the third quarter. The *Star* called it "a determined run in which he bowled over would-be tacklers."

Marion Roberts shows his form on Florida State's team picture day about 1963. *Courtesy Oscar Roberts*

Marion loved to play hard-nosed football. His last season was 1959 but he played in the Indians' 1960 spring game, despite nearing graduation. Certainly, at 6-feet, 185 pounds, Marion was one of the best players we ever had and it was too bad his teams always came up short of the playoffs. His little brother, Oscar, says Marion, for a quarterback, was a bull. "He was just tough," Oscar says. "They talked about how when he'd run the ball he'd come up on the tackler and go toward him and run over him." A raw-bone farm boy, Marion made a career out of coaching football at the high school level. But before that, when his playing days in Ocilla were over, Marion in 1960 took his skills to Florida State, where he was fullback. *This wiry Georgian ... is a fierce competitor who impressed coaches during spring training with gutty determination despite injuries, according to an FSU review in 1961. He's already one of the team's best blockers and could become a dependable runner.*

All the homefolks were happy for the Roberts boy, and there was a sense of pride in knowing that a son of ours was logging time at FSU where the name Ocilla was probably foreign.

Part III

24

'Nice Little Town'

This could be the 'big year' for the Irwin County High football team. That is the opinion one gets after looking over the size and experience of the squad and the 10–game schedule ahead of the team.

The squad lost only four lettermen off last year's squad that had a 6–3–1 record in AA competition. This year they have dropped down to Class A and the caliber of opponents is not expected to be as good.

After ending three weeks of practice tomorrow, the Indians have one more week ahead of them to get ready for their opening game of the season next Friday night when they play Coffee County on the Comets' home field.

Coaches Gene Alexander, Reynolds Allen and

Richard Smith have been busy teaching fundamentals and getting the boys into shape.

—*Ocilla Star*, August 25, 1960

Although jobs were scarce, and you had to work in Fitzgerald or Tifton if you didn't farm, Ocilla was actually a hopping little business district in the '50s and '60s. On Saturdays, you could hardly find a place to park in this town. That was the day people came from near and far to buy from merchants and to fellowship. There were stores and shops open 'til way past dark, and the picture show on Fourth Street was a place for escape.

The little, dark-haired man behind the movie projector was Lanny Roberts. An Ocilla figure, Lanny ran the reel-to-reel apparatus in a small room next to the popcorn counter. Due to sickness, he never played football; but everyone knew Lanny's heart was in it, and in 1969, his name would be put in lights at the stadium.

Those were some good days for living and growing up in Ocilla.

While not everyone here had it so wonderfully, there was a positive spirit in the community, and the children were safe to play in the yards and safe in school where teachers stressed neatness, manners and academic excellence and you could rest assured that everyone had a part in raising the children.

"Ocilla," says John Hodnett, who graduated from high school here in 1961, "was a nice little town. Didn't have to worry about a whole lot of crime."

In the fall it was pleasant as summer relaxed its hot, steamy grip and let us breathe again, and for seven falls out of ten in the '60s we had a good football team. While the world over seemed to be swirling like mad, with the Vietnam war and psychedelics, the football scene in Ocilla was a carnival of lights, dances, decorated motorcades and bonfires and that was the decade the band played our own special fight song, "The Indians," as it was written and composed by Irwin High band director Leonard Wagner.

Words scrawled in red urging the boys to victory were part of the 1960s and school books down to the elementary level were wrapped in red-and-white protective cover paper bearing an awesome Indian logo. Merchants got behind the boys in red to make football fun and unique in a community where change was never easy but where the boys felt loved and supported and the cheer girls all were pretty and gayful and everybody felt lousy when the boys lost.

On game day Fridays, football ribbons were sold at school to wear on your jacket. The boys were doted on like heroes and they wore their jerseys to class; red ones for a home game, white ones for travel. At the lighted stadium in the pine trees by the golf course, the Indians took the field to the sound of the fight song. It stirred the spirit so much that even though you were not playing, you were ready to fight. At halftime of most home games, the field lights were cut while the pretty Indian majorettes twirled fire-tipped batons on the field as the band played. When Irwin made a touchdown, the fight song was played and rose-cheeked cheerleaders flung miniature footballs into the stands for excited people to grab as souvenirs.

The cheer girls traveled to away games by car. They had to keep an 88 average in school to be on the squad and were not eligible to participate until their sophomore year.

"The crowd really got into stuff," says Sandy McClurd, whose name in high school when she was a cheerleader was Sandy Hudson. "In our crowds back then, the men wore suits and ties." Mrs. McClurd graduated from Irwin Hi in 1966 and it was along about the mid-'60s when Irwin cheerleader skirts crept above the knee for the first time. Cheerleader mom

Marjorie Coley of Ocilla designed the higher-hemmed outfit for the girls to wear on game nights as they rooted on the Indians. "It was so much fun. Mrs. Martha Ann Cook was our cheerleading coach. We didn't have buses and all to ride in so Mrs. Norma Elliott would drive one car and Mrs. Cook would drive the other. We didn't have any camps. We didn't do stunts or competitions and stuff like that but we had a lot of fun," says Mrs. McClurd.

On US Highway 129, the road to Fitzgerald, Willett's truck stop was situated near the entrance to the golf course and the football field. There was a diner in the front with stools before the counter and pies in a glass case behind the counter and in back rooms were showers for the truckers. In the fall on home game nights, you could see the lighted football field through the pine trees on the south side of the parking lot and hear the roar of the crowd.

And through most of the 60s, fans had a lot to roar about. The fight song was played many times and a truck load of balls got tossed by the cheer girls as the post-World War II baby boomers reached playing age. Three men who played on the 1964 squad went on to be drafted into the NFL. For a small-manned team from a little town in the boonies, that was a point of pride.

25

Down The Drain

The big game of the season, the one they must win, is on tap for the Irwin Indians tomorrow (Friday) night when they journey to Waycross to battle the Ware County Gators for sub-region 1–A honors. Should Irwin pull this one out they will be sub-region kings regardless....Irwin will be at full strength and are in good shape physically with no injuries. Coaches Alexander, Allen and Smith have had the boys polishing up both their offense and defense this week and also cooking up a surprise or two for their opposition. The Indians must play their best if they expect to scalp the Gators in their own back yard."

—*Ocilla Star*, October 20, 1960

Finally, after seven years, we had a contender and everyone was hog wild again. It'd been a long drought since we'd done anything. But here, now, in 1960, there was joy again in the pines and we felt like we had the horses to go all the way.

Our hopes of a "big year" were legitimized when the boys of Gene Alexander, with 14 seniors on the squad, slashed their first six foes by a combined 147–33 and in the process vaulted to No. 2 in the Class A rankings. The scalps taken included Lowndes County on a Saturday night in Valdosta, 6-0.

The hard-charging Indians, led defensively by heavyweights John Hodnett and Jerry Harper, with Jimmy Mixon at quarterback, were a reminder of that great 1953 outfit that went to state. Maybe now we'd go and get it.

Besides the upset of Lowndes, the boys in red rolled over Coffee County, Cook, Bacon, Jeff Davis and Thomas County Central before taking their tomahawks and the dreams of so many of the Indian faithful to Waycross for a big showdown with unranked Ware County.

Although the Ware school was larger than Irwin's, the Gators were in our region, so we had to play them. Ware was unbeaten in the region and 3-3 overall.

The scenario could not have been simpler: beat Ware County and Irwin was champ of the 1–A East and playoff bound for the first time since 1953. The loser was out of the race. So, everybody loaded up and went over to Waycross for the game with Ware. In fact, hundreds of boisterous Irwin fans thinking of a state title made the 70-mile trip confident about beating Ware and they all screamed on the first play when the big Hodnett boy swatted the ball from the passer. Buddy Barrentine caught it. Twelve plays later, the Indians put up six, and everybody roared.

At that point, *It looked like the Indians could name their score,* the *Star* cried in the next week's edition.

Indian co-captains, L-r: John Hodnett, John Wingate and Charles Zaruba in 1960. *Courtesy ICHS Library / copied from 1960-61 yearbook by Lucy Pierce*

This is where it would be nice to say that big John and his cohorts went on to beat the Gator brains out. Only that isn't how it was. Our boys got into some bad firewater or something and coughed up the lead on the way to being stoned.

Bawled the Star:

.... all hope for regional and state honors for the Irwin County High School Indians went down the drain.

> *...Ware got every break in the book plus some questionable calls by the officials, which tended to break the Indians' spirit. Greater desire and determination of the Gators assured them of the win.*

The final was 21-7.

It was a damning defeat for Gene Alexander and everybody went back to Ocilla sick.

The boys ripped Berrien County and Worth County in meaningless affairs and battled Fitzgerald to a 0–0 tie to end the season at 8–1–1.

The middle of a trio of footballing Hodnetts, John, who made All-State tackle that year, first team, flirted with colleges but never played after high school. In 1998, he retired as chief of police in Scotland Neck, NC., a town he says is "about like Ocilla."

John suffers from numerous physical infirmities but has no regrets much about how his life has been, except every now and then when football season cranks up he has flashbacks of the Indians not making the playoffs in 1960. He says football in Ocilla "meant a lot to a lot of fellows" in his age group on the team like Harvey Davis, a stellar lineman. Harvey became a Superior Court judge in the local circuit. The courtroom of the courthouse in Ocilla is dedicated in his memory.

"The most I regret was the loss to Ware County," big John says. "I went in on the quarterback and hit him as he was throwing, and we intercepted and went on down and scored. And then we just...fell apart, I guess."

Calls went out for Alexander's head.

26

The McNease Years

There's a new fight song for the Indians being sung at football games this year ... and it seems to be catching on quickly. The words and music were composed by Leonard Wagner, band director, and the song was introduced to fans two weeks ago. Can't give the music but the words to "The Indians" are these:

The Indians. The Indians.
They're the boys from Irwin County High.
They're rough and their ready
For the battle that is drawing nigh
So on boys to victory
We know you're gonna do or die
And every time you score, we'll
Give a mighty roar

For the boys from Irwin County High
—*Ocilla Star*, October 28, 1961

In the summer of 1961 Gene Alexander stepped down as head coach in Ocilla.

No, that isn't exactly how it was.

"They ran Alexander off," says Pat Hodnett, little brother of Carl and John, "and brought in that coach with that son of his." Hodnett is referring to Harvey K. McNease. McNease, whose son was Kayo, was hired away from Vidalia in 1961 to whip the Indians into a power but he couldn't get it to work. It was a hard, sometimes laughable two years for the Indian family.

Respect for McNease was always a little soft among the men and it wasn't until after summer camp that the newspaper got his name right. Three times in camp of 1961, where the drills were said to be "spirited," the coach was referred to in the *Star* as "Harold" McNease.

In one edition, the paper said:

Sunday night, after the roll is squared away and an informative talk of things to come by Coach Harold McNease, the gridders will attend services at the Ocilla Baptist Church.

In another issue:

Football practice began early last Monday and every morning since for 35 candidates for the 1961 Irwin County High football team. Coach Harold McNease has the boys up at 5:30 a.m. each morning for a two hour practice session before breakfast.

At the end of camp, having asked McNease about the upcoming schedule, the Star reported:

They will really have to scrap to whip us; we won't be

any pushover. So says Coach Harold McNease ...

Nobody could pin all the perils on McNease, however. His first year was a bad hand. When he took over the program it wasn't a studded outfit. We'd lost 14 seniors to graduation and the returning players were *"in terrible physical condition,"* McNease told the *Star*. Many boys also were young and some were hard to reach at the mental level. Several had been loyal to Alexander and those who were also fond of assistant coach Ralph Cook, were loath to accept McNease's style. A good number who dressed out for football that year were freshmen who did not know how to play right. The most promising of the green lads were forced into the lineup and it wasn't pretty.

One of the young, inexperienced boys who was activated for first-string duty was freshman Glenn Thompson, nicknamed "Big Daddy," a raw-boned farm kid who says now that he played football because it was "a popular thing to do" and was "something to win at" when nothing else around Ocilla held much glory.

Against our other boys, the jolly giant appeared to top 6-feet, 5 inches but he didn't know all there was to football and that was the year he was hung with the nickname.

Glenn remembers jogging onto the field for practice one afternoon in the fall of '61 when Indian booster clubber and home game public address announcer Knott Tucker spied him. In his gravel voice, Knot growled, jokingly, "Big Daddy."

Coach McNease, center, with assistants Ronald Luke, l, and Ralph Cook in 1961. *Courtesy ICHS 1961-62 yearbook / copied by Lucy Pierce*

"He stuck that name on me," Glenn says. "I've got kin people who don't even know my real name."

Getting back to McNease; good fellow and a proud papa surely. He even had a good head for football, putting up three winning seasons out of five while in Vidalia, once going 9–3 in a playoff year, so he had an idea of how to train a team. But he couldn't get anything going in Ocilla like everyone had hoped he would and people wondered why he was viewed as a step-up from Alexander. There seemed to be a disconnect between McNease and the boys. Old timers who remember playing for McNease point to his son as a source of the conflict. The boys could hardly believe that McNease pushed his son to be the wheel horse of the team; that he tried to make sure his boy touched the ball in scoring situations, and that was part of the disgust players had with the coach.

"He tried to make an all-star out of his son, Kayo, and he wasn't. He wasn't even an average player," says Ronnie Cantrell, who was a senior end on the '61 team. "He ran with his head down all the time."

Jack Gray, the senior bull of the backfield in '61 at the fullback slot, remembers a similar scenario.

"McNease came in and put his son in there ahead of some others who were probably a little better. I think that was his main problem."

The booster club, which claimed 133 members, did all it could, feeding the Indians hearty meals and patting them on the back at every occasion to keep their spirits up during a hard time. Many in the club met on Monday nights to eat, talk and be shown the game film by the coach. At one meeting, in September of 1961, someone suggested Irwin County start a football program for fifth and sixth graders, like other school systems had for years. It was a long overdue but brilliant idea. If Irwin County wanted to be a winner on a consistent basis, we needed a good feeder system. That way when they reached varsity age, the boys would be familiar with the sport and some would've already been scouted for talent. Knot Tucker, whose son, "Little Knot," played on the varsity, was assigned to investigate a possible youth team for Irwin County. The next night the boosters hosted a barbecue supper for the players in the school cafeteria where the cheerleaders had decked the halls with Indian-themed posters.

Through the first nine games of 1961, the 1-A East Indians were 3–5–1 overall, 2–2 in the region and out of the playoff picture, when they met with Fitzgerald of the 1–AA North. We didn't have a chance against them anyway but McNease, incoherently, made sure the loss to Fitzgerald would be severe.

What was supposed to be "senior night" for the Indians in recognizing our 12th graders turned into the Billy Chambless show after McNease benched all the twelfth graders before the game and this boy, Chambless, no doubt fired up over remarks McNease had made about him, ran our boys off the field.

Ronnie Cantrell recalls that a day or two prior to the game with our old rival, McNease made a stupid remark, either in the papers or on the radio, suggesting that Chambless was not such a hot player and Billy stuck it in our face. The great Fitz back scored five touchdowns and threw for a sixth score, earning player of the week accolades from *The Associated Press.*

As to benching the seniors on their big night, and it was their last game, and they were supposed to play their hearts out, McNease "decided he was going to put in the next year's group and the seniors sat out and they just ate us up," Jack Gray says, trying to explain how the Irwin boys managed to lose the contest to our oldest rival by the score of 61–19.

Indian fans hoping for a tighter affair with Fitzgerald went home in a daze.

27

Fans Jeer

During the meeting...club members expressed concern over the amount of jeering and general harassing that members of the Indian squad are being subjected to by local fans. The club members agreed that such acts are certainly uncalled for, and made it known that persons guilty of these harassments do not feel they can offer much encouragement to the boys, at least could withhold abusing remarks. One of the purposes of the Booster Club is that of moral support to athletic teams in the school, and it was pointed out Monday night that much support is needed throughout the county.

—*Ocilla Star*, October 11, 1962

The boys of Harvey McNease were hard for the natives to love. In a crushing blow to the team's morale and confidence of the fans, the 1962 season opener on August 30, the Indians got smoked in Douglas by the Coffee County Comets, 38–7. McNease had said the Indians were improved. Then in the second game, which was in Ashburn, we got snipped, 7–6. In game 3, the boys snuck past Berrien County in the pines before starting 1–A East play against Bacon County. The Red Raiders from Alma came to Ocilla and smashed the wigwam, 26–7, and the hoots and howls started. It was a tough time for being an Indian.

In game 5, which was homecoming, Irwin managed to scalp little Hahira. The next morning, the boys were treated to a trip to Tallahassee to see Florida State play. In a show of support for the boys, the booster club made it possible for the Indians and cheerleaders to see the game in which Marion Roberts was playing for the Seminoles. It would be good for their morale to get out of town to see a college game and maybe it would inspire them to win. Although the trip was a success and everyone had a good time, the tour did not motivate the boys to any more victories.

The offense that year, led by young Walter Sumner, was never much of a threat and the porous defense was stacked with underclassmen. Jeff Davis, Cook and Blackshear thumped the Indians by a combined 100–21, knocking the tribe out of playoff consideration and assuring McNease of a second lousy season.

On the afternoon of October 26, the Irwin High Beta Club staged a parade to draw attention to the final home game that night against Crisp County of the 1–A West. The best our boys could muster was a 6–6 draw and then they were idle a week before hitting Fitzgerald on November 9 for the season finale with the Hurricanes, who had dropped into Class A with Irwin.

The *Star* reported:

A large following of Indian fans is expected to be in Fitzgerald for the contest. The Indians, if they are determined to win, can count on the fans to give them all the support possible. It's just that way in a game with the Hurricanes.

The offense scored when the Sumner boy hit Larry Johnson for a TD from the eight. But the faster Hurricanes—and they always seemed to be bigger and faster than us—had the Indians shadowed all night and broke our tomahawks.

The Indians fought dutifully. It was probably their best effort. The *Star* was not impressed, however. Just five paragraphs, the write-up on the 21-6 loss was planted on the back page of the paper just above a piece about the movie *Bye, Bye, Birdie,* and looking at it now, that must've been an omen for McNease.

Spring training 1963 started in February. Spring was always a time of fresh starts and hopeful outlooks, and if you saw the roster, with boys on it like Walter Sumner and "Big Daddy" Thompson, there was a strong, salty junior class lined up for the campaign.

Shifty and good with the tosses, the Sumner boy had the makings of a star.

The roster for 1963 showed only three seniors. Twenty-three boys were lettermen who'd played a lot, and several of the linemen had some meat to them. It was a good squad, a possible contender for the playoffs.

But spring drills went poorly and what faith McNease had in his ability to build the Indians into a contender was sucked out of him like Coca-Cola through a straw. The team was stricken with the flu. A dozen boys missed a week's conditioning with the symptoms. At least that many more McNease was counting on to carry a big load in the fall missed a lot of football work due to farm chores and McNease did not know how to deal with it. Sickness, coupled with the boys' farm pursuits, almost brought spring training to a halt.

McNease grew more discouraged. On February 25, he reached the end of his rope.

28

Cook Turns It Around

Harvey K. McNease, athletic director at Irwin County High School, made public Monday his resignation from the post effective at the end of the present school year. The resignation was given to Principal C.A. Estes on February 25 and...McNease met with the County board of Education to present his resignation orally. "I felt that it's to the best interest of my family and the school to seek a position elsewhere," McNease said of his resignation. There was no pressure from any source which prompted the resignation, he said. "I thought it over very carefully and for a long time before coming to a decision...I felt the resignation was best." McNease, who has been athletic director here for past two years, said that whether his decision was right or wrong, he felt that a coach is paid both financially and with moral support by the games he wins. He cited the 3–6–1 record of 1961 and the 2–7–1 record last year and said that knowing what was scheduled for next season, he could see no chance for improvement of those records.

—*Ocilla Star*, March 4, 1963

No hard feelings were expressed publicly when McNease resigned from Irwin County High. School officials, while wishing McNease all sorts of good luck, were quick to fill the post, however. They had their man in the wings. On April 2, 1963, at a meeting to elect teachers, the board named assistant Ralph Cook the new head coach and athletics director.

McNease wound up in Cochran, where he led the Royals to a four-year mark of just a little better than .500.

"I don't know," coach Cook says now when asked why his old boss was not successful in Ocilla. "I guess every coach has his own way of doing things."

With Cook at the helm, the fog over the football program in Ocilla dissipated. A country boy, Ralph was well-liked, humorous and he didn't have a son on the team. The boys were his sons, and Ralph loved them and got them to play hard.

"I loved it. We really enjoyed him. He was a good coach," says Walter Tyler, a farmer who played a tough, hard-nosed role at fullback for the Indians in 1963.

Though his coaching background was a little soft, Ralph starred in football at Middle Georgia College in Cochran, where he was like a coach on the field, and then went into the Army. After the Army, he farmed with his father for two years until a drought hit and they lost the crop. His father told him to leave the farm and get a useful degree.

Ralph went to Georgia Southern and groomed his interest in coaching, which he felt was his best defense against farming, and in 1961, he got Emory Walters on the line. An old pal from their college days, Mr. Walters, a famous Ocilla attorney, was the right one to dial. Hearing from Ralph, Emory phoned up his brother, Lorie Walters, a powerful member of the Irwin County Board of Education, and told him of Ralph's desire to coach. And one thing led to the next, the way it did in politics in the old days, when who you knew was as important as what you knew.

"Emory Walters came in a farm truck ... and I wound up in Ocilla," Ralph recalls, explaining how he and his belongings were transported.

He was put to work under McNease in the summer of 1961.

Two years later, in August at the start of summer camp, with Ralph now leading the charges, the *Ocilla Star* reported seeing a ray of sunshine over the football program that did not have a history of very much winning. *The team has 16 lettermen returning, and these, plus some good new boys, make prospects for a successful season look promising. The line will be extra heavy and the backfield will be light. The line ranges in weight from 180 to 260 pounds.*

Where McNease was dark, seeing no chance to succeed, Ralph Cook saw opportunity and made it work. His presence, along with a new staff, injected the emerging team with a fresh spirit, lightening the mood of the men. Basically, Ralph created an environment in which our boys could thrive.

Notorious for his tough and gruff persona, a cigar crammed into the corner of his mouth, Ralph roamed the sidelines with gusto, often in a suit coat, and made the boys believe they could win.

The winning attitude Ralph instilled into the football program would last a long generation.

In 1963, with so many returning lettermen, the key for Ralph was how to make the pieces fit. It wouldn't be a snap; to bring Ocilla the championship fans had long ached for, he would need a good staff and a little luck.

A big piece of the building puzzle fell into his lap when he got a call from an old college buddy and Vidalia native, Kermit Elliott, then an assistant coach under Joe Compton in Fitzgerald. Kermit asked Ralph on the telephone if he'd locked down his staff yet.

"I told him 'no,' but I knew who I was going to get and he said, "Who?' and I said, 'You.' So we got together."

Ralph put Elliott in charge of the backfield. He gave Melvin Dowis the ends and Earl Burch the line; neither had worked under McNease. In addition to a strong, loyal staff and renewed optimism, Ralph also had Charlie back, and you can't mention old-day football in Ocilla without saying something about Charlie Spicer.

Thc toughcst of all boys, Charlie never played a down nor wore the Indian uniform, but with Charlie, you got more than just a kid who did the wash, packed bags and tightened cleats for our other boys. He was a raging bull.

In high school, Charlie—who later became a successful banker in Atlanta—embodied the fighting spirit of the Indian family and when the boys took the sidelines to start the games, he was with them in the charge. Although his legs were braced due to polio, and he used crutches, that didn't stop Charlie, who chomped at the bit to go to war alongside his buddies in red.

Stocky and thick through the neck, Charlie, powerful as an ox, easily whipped other boys in wrestling on the cotton mat on the gym floor. He'd have made a great linebacker. He had a warrior's heart, and if the officials made a bad call against his

Indians, Charlie gave them the business. He'd charge onto the field on his crutches in a huff, barking like mad at the refs. One time, when the Indians had the ball, Charlie charged down the sidelines toward the cheerleaders, who were chanting, "Get that ball. Get that ball," according to Gwen DeBerry, one of the cheerleaders at the time. When Charlie reached them, he hoisted his crutches into the air and screamed angrily, "We got the ball, dammit."

If every boy had had Charlie's heart, grit and desire, Irwin might've never lost.

"Charlie was almost like an assistant coach," Ralph Cook says. "He was a special person."

Besides a heavy line, anchored by Big Daddy and Vernon Pettis, Zim Royal was fast and Walter Tyler ran low and hard but nobody was slippery as Walt Sumner, a junior who gained a reputation in 1963 as one of the state's top playmakers.

"We just felt like you were supposed to give all you got," Ralph says, divulging his basic philosophy on coaching.

"I don't like to lose," he adds. "I always hated to lose."

In other words, if you were playing for Ralph Cook, "Don't go out there and jack around on the field. Just give me all you've got and if that didn't win, I'd understand."

Sponsored by the booster club, the camp of 1963 was conducted at the practice field in Ocilla. "Cook said he is going to find out who really wants to play football," the *Star* reported.

Badly out of shape, 31 boys reported to camp. In the daytime, they were worked like dogs. At night, they slept in the gymnasium like refugees—if they could drag their bones to the cots.

"I could not have gone through another one, I don't believe," says Vernon Pettis. "Me and Glenn Thompson came in way overweight, and they came out with those rubber sweat suits." A senior defensive tackle, who went into construction and wed his high school sweetheart, Vernon remembers the rubber suits, also called "fat suits," were tight so that when they were loosened at the wrist after practice, "sweat would just pour out" from the sleeves like water. "That would be cruel punishment now. In two hours' practice we lost ten, twelve pounds worth of sweat. Of course, we'd put it back on."

That was Vernon's last camp. "It was tough, no doubt about it, but I think it helped build some character in some men."

With halfback Zim Royal as captain and Vernon as co-captain, 28 hard-worked Indian boys of Class A broke camp mean and ugly and roared out of the box. They tripped Coffee County's Comets, 14–6, in Ocilla to start the season, skunked Turner County, 24–0, and stomped Berrien County, 38–0, in Nashville before opening sub-region play on September 27 in Alma. Irwin got over on the Red Raiders, 19–14, and a week later crushed Hahira, 47–13. After that, Ralph's boys took out Jeff Davis, 21–0, prior to the big showdown for the sub-region lead with Cook County, led by 200-pound fullback Donald Hayes. It was quite a game down in Adel but the Hornets got the better of it, 13-6, spoiling Irwin's dream of making the playoffs.

Walter Sumner gains yardage in 1963. *Courtesy ICHS Library / copied from 1963-64 yearbook by Lucy Pierce*

In the homecoming game against region foe Blackshear, the Indians rolled, and it was a special night for the moms. Each lady with a son on the team who was at the game wore a small placard on her back with her son's jersey number on it so as to be easily recognized in the crowd.

The Indians were 8–1 when they hosted Fitzgerald in game ten. A day before the big game with old Fitz, the *Star* predicted a record attendance and a tense affair:

> *The attention of football fans in South Georgia will be focused on Ocilla Friday night when the Irwin County Indians and the Purple Hurricane of Fitzgerald tangle in their annual gridiron classic...Fitzgerald will probably be favored to win due to their scoring record and also the fact they are rated fourth in a poll of Class A schools in the state this week, while Irwin came in sixth.*

Joe Compton's Hurricane had beaten the socks off everybody except Cook High, the big dog of the region that year.

The Indians played impressively before giving out of gas. We were on top by 7-0 at the half and put up another score in the third after a Fitz TD, but the boys in those long, intimidating stockings ended up burning our teepees, 21-13.

After the game, when the Indians had showered and dressed in their street clothes, junior tackle Wayne Pierce went home and before hitting the sack told his little brother resolutely, "We'll be better next year."

With the Sumner boy back, and all the other lettermen with him, everyone in Indian land was looking forward to kicking some doors down.

29

'Couldn't Tackle Him'

Irwin Countians have long been proud of their hometown athletes. One such athlete who has made Ocilla well known is our own Walt Sumner, son of and Mrs. Herman Sumner. A product of Irwin County High, Sumner is currently a strong candidate as a defensive back with the Cleveland Browns ...According to reports published in the Cleveland papers, he is making the veteran defensive backs sweat. Cleveland has one of the best defensive backfields in pro football, which makes it hard for a rookie trying for a starting spot. "Walt has always been a hustler, so we're sure the NFL boys are going to find him tough to handle," it was stated locally...The community is proud of Walt and wish him good luck in his try for the big game.

—*Ocilla Star*, August 28, 1969

"Walter was by the far the best player we had," says one of his former Indian teammates, Big Daddy Thompson.

"Walt was the best player I was ever associated with," adds his old coach, Ralph Cook.

Some boy, that Walter, whose first love might've been baseball. He could really sock 'em.

Many stories make the legend of Walter Herman Sumner of Ocilla, who is said to have busted marks set by Ocilla Hi great Marion Dickens of the 1920s. Like Dickens, Walter wasn't so very fast. But fast enough, and another thing was, "He could stop on a dime," says his younger brother, Franklin Sumner. "He'd take one step and be at full speed."

"You couldn't tackle Walt," says Jack Paulk, a former Fitzgerald Hurricane linebacker who played against Walter in high school. "We contained him pretty well his junior year, but his senior year, we had a hard time with him. He ran all over us." Jack remembers Walter would "wiggle a little bit" and vanish, leaving would-be defenders grasping at air. "We just couldn't tackle him."

Now you search the Internet and Walter's picture pops up with all kinds of stats from his time at Florida State as a two-sport star and later with the Cleveland Browns as a punt returner and safety—he picked off a Joe Namath pass on the first Monday Night Football telecast in September 1970 and ran it back for a touchdown. There is also video of the dapper Walter recalling his days with the Browns. Walter was honorary captain for the Browns in a game against the Cincinnati Bengals in 2012.

You could write a whole book about the man.

Quietly intense and a hero to many a young Indian boy in days gone by, Walter, like teammates Wayne Pierce, Tommy Tucker, and some others on the 1964 squad, was one of those rare grit-and-wit players who competed for the top grades. On the field, Walter racked up the accolades as the Indian quarterback. He grew up on his daddy's farm and, for most of his life, has walked happily with the song of his heart. In high school, she was known as Sandra Coley, a pretty little Indian cheerleader. They married in 1968, had three children and made their home on the outskirts of Ocilla where Walter never sought public office, although he probably could've been elected senator, and shunned the limelight that a lot of pro athletes have craved. "He never has thought of himself as an icon or anybody special like that," Sandra says. "He was always very humble. In high school, he was always focused on some study. Give him a sport and he was fine."

Whether stalking pro receivers for six years as a Brown (1969–1974) or seeing his name entered into the FSU Hall of Fame in 1982, the decorated son of Ocilla, Irwin County went about his business soberly, which may in part be a testament to those who influenced his early life.

Bobby Dix, a retired Ocilla postman and farmer, remembers seeing Walter play many times in high school. "They'd get back there to try to catch him, and he would just sidestep them," says Mr. Dix. "I can almost see him. He wasn't all that fast but they couldn't catch him."

Walter and the Pierce boy, Wayne, began losing their hair while still in high school. By the time they were seniors, the two Indian boys presented scalps much older than a teen's, so much so that coaches for opposing teams challenged their ages and eligibility.

Despite playing in the pros, Walter never got rich from football. In 1970, for example, the average pro salary was $23,000. A seventh-round pick, such as Walter, could expect about half that.

Sumner on a Browns playing card from about 1972. *Courtesy NoleFan.org*

He might have made even less as an Atlanta Brave. When Atlanta drafted him out of Florida State fresh from playing in the college world series, Walter traveled to Louisiana to meet with Braves officials, who said he'd be in the farm system. So Walter elected to go with football, where he'd just been taken by the Browns. He thought he might hitch to the Braves if things did not work out with Cleveland.

But he stuck with the Browns, and "I think he played long enough to get his retirement," says Bobby Dix.

Luckily for Walter, he knew when to quit. He had planned carefully for life after football as an accountant and came home to Ocilla when his playing days were over to settle down.

Although the field in the pines where he played in Ocilla is no longer used for Indian football, the scoreboard at the old stadium by the golf course still bears his name, alongside that of another former Indian, Jack Smith, who was a year behind Walter in school.

When Walter was little, his family resided in the Osierfield community of Irwin County until Walter was a junior in high school. Then they moved into a home that sat just a Hail Mary from the Ben Hill County line marker. The small, redbrick home was actually closer to Fitzgerald than to Ocilla. Fitzgerald wished they could claim Walter. Once a sportswriter made the mistake of reporting that Walter was from Fitzgerald. This caused some hysteria in Ocilla, where folks were sensitive about their own who'd drawn fame in a way that threw a positive light on this old farming community. Charles Harris could not let the mistake pass. According to local lore, Harris snapped up his phone, rang the paper and set them straight.

Walt's son Chad, despite having Walt for a dad, grew up feeling like a normal kid.

"He's not an easy one to follow. However, I give him credit. He never put pressure on me," Chad says. He recalled his dad driving him to his first summer football camp in Ocilla. "He stopped the car and said, 'You realize you don't have to play football.' That was the best advice he could've given me."

Some might have expected Chad to be a star like his father, but he admits with a chuckle, "There wasn't much to compare to. He was a lot better than I was. He was one of a kind."

30

Big Red!

After a sloppy first quarter play in Pearson last Friday night the Irwin County High School Indian offensive eleven exploded in the final seconds of the period for 7 points and in the second stanza notched three extra TD's; added another in the third, to overpower a scrappy but determined Atkinson County Revel eleven, 34–0. The small but hard hitting Rebel squad held the Indians only to short yardage in the 1st quarter. The Rebels stopped the Indians on two successive drives but finally floundered to the hitting inflicted on them by the monstrous Indian line.

—*Ocilla Star*, October 15, 1964

We started yelling "Big Red" in 1964. We'd holler,"Let's

go, Big Red" or "Go, Big Red" and sometimes, if the boys were dragging, it was, "C'mon, Red. Let's go."

A late Ocilla clothier gets the credit for being the first to utter "Big Red" in reference to the Indians and he was pretty well spot on.

That year, 1964, although the boys slid a notch to Class B, that was incidental, just paperwork. They were something, those Indians, and with a blue-chipper handling the ball and with all that size up front, "Big Red" was hard to beat for a nickname no matter who started it. The Indians of second-year head coach Ralph Cook were believed to be as good and as big as they came in any Georgia grouping and every team the Indians played that year brought their best game against us. So it was not possible for Irwin to sneak up on people or sandbag the opposition, and to knock off Irwin, you'd done a day's work.

Valdosta of AAA was among the greatest of teams in the land. Our boys did not play Valdosta anymore like we did back in the mule days. But if we had, "I think we could've beaten Valdosta," says Jack Smith, a junior on our 1964 club, when reminded that Irwin County used to be called "Little Valdosta."

On the field, the starters all went both ways—offense and defense—and eight first-stringers in 1964 were salty seniors, having played much ball and grown a lot in skill since those awful years of '61 and '62. Our O-line was highly touted, averaging about two hundred pounds, which back then was eye-popping. In size, the line for Irwin roughly matched the University of Georgia's at the time. Certainly, a 28-man roster like Irwin County put on the field in 1964 passed through Podunk once in a blue moon, if ever, and people here felt the boys would win every game and probably take state, if they had could get by another great team, Bradwell Institute from over in Hinesville.

There were many firsts associated with the 1964 Indians. For example, in a rousing show of support for the boys, a hefty sum was plunked down to buy the Indians new uniforms. That was big-time stuff. The home jerseys were now outstandingly red, almost blood. Our boys had been in red since 1953 but a new era had begun now as the old, faded red home jerseys of the past were put away or handed down to the smaller boys coming up.

In home games starting in 1964, the boys wore the new red jerseys with white numbers and three stripes—a black stripe between two white ones—around the sleeves, and the old high-top style shoes were replaced by low-cuts. The pants our boys wore were gray with a red stripe down the side. The travel jerseys were white with beautiful red numbers. The numbers changed with the times as well. Beginning in 1964, our tackles were given 70s instead of the old-day 40s, guards got the 60s instead of 20s and 30s and the centers took the 50s. The most impressive change that year was the red helmet, which became a trademark. The old gray look in helmets was cast aside in favor of red headgear to match the home jerseys and everybody loved it.

And one afternoon, according to team legend, our boys were at practice when they heard someone yell the words that would become immortal to many a hearty Indian fan.

"Let's go, Big Red."

Big Red?

Heads turned and there went a man we all knew, Charles Harris, driving past the field on his way to the golf course club.

Nobody had ever applied "Big Red" here, at least not in association with the football team. But it sounded smart. The boys' energies picked up, and later, whenever the prominent Harris saw the boys at practice—and he stopped by almost every day, often bringing other friends and associates—and at all their games, he'd shout something about "Red."

In hindsight, that's what was missing. Somehow "Go, Indians" did not seem to go far enough anymore. What the boys lacked was a unique personality. "Big Red" captured it all. A respected business leader and an all-round fine fellow, he was a loud one, that Charles Harris, and his phrase caught on with the community in a grand way. "Go, Big Red" became the football faithful's battle cry and it joined "Scalp 'em" and other phrases on posters and signs put up at the school and in windows of Ocilla stores urging the boys to victory on fall Friday nights.

Fans like Charles Harris made football in Ocilla special. No merchant of that time more openly cared about the boys and their academics—their futures—than did Mr. Harris, a man of big character who once chaired the Georgia Board of Regents.

A graduate of Ocilla High School, the man whom lorc says was the father of "Big Red," was born and raised in Ocilla. For many years, he and his wife, Esther, operated the business his father founded, A. S. Harris Department Store, which specialized in family clothing and footwear. They had four children—three girls and a boy—and the yellow-bricked store with three large staging-box windows in front at Fourth and Cherry streets was a local landmark.

Tall, dark-haired, always sharply dressed in a white shirt and tie, active in the Fitzgerald Hebrew Congregation, Charles gave his big heart to the Indians in all sports, especially football, while doing all within reason to uplift poor families and children of the Ocilla community.

He died in 2001. But in 1964, it was Harris, who never

played football, who gave our boys an identity that has survived to present day.

31

Cornbread

The Irwin County High School Indians fresh from a decisive victory over AA Coffee County last week, prepare themselves for one of the hardest blows expected this season as the Blue Devils from Tift County High in Tifton, march into Indian Stadium Friday night. The game will officially open the Braves home campaign for the year. A capacity crowed is expected to witness the gridiron battle. Tift County will prove to be a very tough opponent as they show considerable improvement over last year, much of the improvement credited to the arrival of new head coach, Tommy Gillebeau, formerly of Ware County High at Waycross. Irwin County will remember Gillebeau from several years back, when his

Ware County Gators halted Irwin's chances of possibly capturing a state title.

—*Ocilla Star*, September 10, 1964

Cornbread made you good looking. It also made you smart and agile, able to perform amazing athletic feats. We thought everybody knew that.

Cornbread, fixed by your Mama's loving hands, was good with peas, fatback and rutabagas. The swiftest cornbread to make if you were in a hurry to get back to the crop was called "lace." All you did was add some water to the cornmeal in a bowl, sprinkle in some salt and pepper and the secret ingredient, and only your Mama knew the secret, and stir until you had batter. You poured the batter into a skillet greased with warm bacon fat and let fry until the edges bubbled up like lace, then you flipped the cake once and let the other side fry before serving. It was delicious. Many an Ocilla boy was raised on cornbread and pot licker, the good salty water of the collard green.

In Tifton, they did not believe in eating very much cornbread, however.

"They talked about us being big, cornbread-fed," says Glenn "Big Daddy" Thompson.

Glenn is recalling a joke that went around Tifton the week of the game with our boys in Ocilla that spun off from a column in the Tifton paper about their boys being small compared to Irwin County and, in a way, suggesting the Blue Devils eat more cornbread.

Whatever was said, Glenn and some other Indians took it as a cut on the heavy set. To them it sounded like jokes that were made about fat people, as though cornbread made you fat and stupid.

On Sept. 11, 1964, at about 8 o'clock at night, it came to a head, *wham*. On the game's second play, Frankie Cowan, halfback, turned on the gas, romping 72 yards for a touchdown and the Imps were cooked for the evening. They never had a shot. Jack Smith, the junior Indian fullback, ran 15 yards for a second score and Walter Sumner ran 58 yards for a third TD.

Irwin won the spoils, 20–0, on a slippery night. But it was never that close. Penalties against Irwin and the wet weather, which caused some fumbles, kept the scoring light. Tifton was held to just five yards rushing and 18 passing.

Bo Edenfield of Tifton played in the game against our biggest boy.

"Me and Big Daddy, we didn't see eye to eye," Bo recalls with a chuckle, adding that he and the big Indian battled it out.

"Actually, Big Daddy beat my butt over there."

"They put a whuppin' on us," says Mayo Tucker of Brookfield. "We had a young team."

Mayo played against Big Daddy on one side of the ball and Wayne Pierce on the other.

"Wayne would hit you a lot harder than Big Daddy," says Mayo, who went on to play for the University of Georgia as a lineman. "I'd rather hit sponge man over there than Wayne." Mayo said he ached for days after the game. "I was actually sick that next Monday."

Drubbing the Blue Devils on the scoresheet did not satisfy the lust. When the game was 90 seconds from over, the Indians called time out. Somebody gave the signal and the managers ran onto the field with the pans of cornbread covered in tin foil.

Indian boys eager to join in the shenanigans grabbed handfuls of the cornbread from the pans. In a menacing fashion, they ate some and offered the Tift boys a taste.

The Blue Devils did not seem to want any.

"I had some in my hand, but I didn't throw any," says Big Daddy.

"I'm sure I did," says Tommy Tucker, when asked if he threw any cornbread at the Devils.

Ernest Lang was the fullback that year for the Imps. "I didn't think it was as big a deal as some made it out to be."

The ref tossed a flag and marked off 15 yards against Irwin for unsportsmanlike conduct because of the stunt.

"It was a little overdone," Lang says of the shenanigans and the reasoning behind the whole affair. "It was just a little bit of a shock that they did it."

But the game was good theater for a dead night in Ocilla, and the Big Red was just warming up.

32

‘Pressure’

The Irwin County High School Indians, ranked number two, in Class B football, attempt to hold their standings and protect their unblemished 5–0 record as they travel to Blackshear Friday night to tangle with Coach Tony Adams’ Tigers. The game will be one of the top grid iron battles on tap for the weekend. Ever since Coach Adams made the statement, ‘my boys will win the State Class B Football championship’ at the beginning of the season, Coach Ralph Cook’s braves have been mentally gunning for the Tigers to find out if they are Tigers or Kittens. Friday night should tell the story. The Indians have had rough practice sessions and reports show that they strength of the Indians is tops, mental attitude beyond capacity and the Braves are ready for another scalp.

—*Ocilla Star*, October 15, 1964

The state's No. 1 team in Class B, Bradwell Institute, was crushing everybody, just like Irwin was. A big clash between us and them was being dreamed about. But Irwin had to beat Blackshear to have a shot at the postseason. The Tigers were tough—or so they said. We wanted to slash 'em. Bad. Heck, it was easy, like boiled okra sliding on a hot greasy skillet as the Big Red locomotive out of Ocilla rumbled into Blackshear on October 16, 1964 and crushed the cocky kitties, 34–6, leaving only Camden County to beat for the 1–B East crown.

That was a piece of cake, too. Our boys skinned the 'Cats, 34–7, in Ocilla, giving this community its first football trophy, and trip to the playoffs, in 11 years.

At the end of nine games, with the sub-region title in the bag, only our old rivals stood in the way of a perfect regular season for the Big Red.

"We were all under a lot of pressure prior to the Fitzgerald game to beat Fitzgerald," recalls Wayne Pierce, a senior tackle that year. Having tomahawked nine teams by a combined 291–32, "We knew we were good, and I think the Fitzgerald game would determine if we were in fact as good as we were beginning to be recognized as."

It was billed as the top game in south Georgia for the week of November 13. The two powers nine miles apart had never met unbeaten and history was certainly against the Indians. We had only gotten over on Fitzgerald three times since 1928, all in the 50s.

The intimidation factor was at work. Fitzgerald always tried to intimidate Ocilla. Yes, they did. Some called them an "arrogant" bunch. Anyway, as Mr. Pierce was saying, "We were in the shadow of the Purple Hurricane. They certainly got more publicity than we did, but you knew from a youngster until you graduated that the Fitzgerald game was the big game of the season, and you knew that you were always going to be the underdog. They wore those stockings, and they seemed to be so much bigger, faster and taller than they really were."

The *Star* noted that both teams in 1964 had high hopes for going deep into the playoffs.

> *... state honors will be forgotten Friday night in this annual grudge battle. As the number one team in State Class A ratings, Fitzgerald will be favored by state sports writers to win the game. They have a lightning fast team with plenty of experience. Also their offensive formation, the Notre Dame Box, has caused much misery to the Indian defense for several years. Irwin will go into the game with a decided weight advantage—especially in the line. However, the Hurricane expects to offset the difference in weight with their tremendous team speed.*

Fans—some with money riding on the outcome—began arriving in Fitzgerald at six o'clock for the 8:00 p.m. kickoff. By game time, every seat in the bleachers on either side was full, and the buzz of anticipation and the aroma of grill smoke filled the air. Even the standing room around the field was packed with excited fans.

People had driven from far away to see the game. One of the largest crowds ever to witness a game in South Georgia jammed the stadium in Fitzgerald to watch the two neighbors fight for bragging rights and more on Friday the 13th.

No one had more fire in the belly for Fitzgerald that night than our big boy, Glenn Thompson, because prior to the game, Irwin coaches told Big Daddy that 'Cane tackle Larry Cleghorn had called him a "big baby" and promised to drive Glenn from sideline to sideline to show the world what a baby he really was.

The captains met at midfield with their helmets off. Irwin won the flip. Coach Cook wanted us to take the ball.

Fitzgerald punched us in the teeth and we had to punt. Then we hit them in the teeth, backing them up 11 yards, and they had to punt.

It was a struggle for a while with no scoring, both sides being over-anxious.

Finally, the Big Red settled down. Walter Sumner, leading the charge, hit Frankie Cowan on an 11-yard screen pass for a TD. The Irwin side went wild. In all the jubilation, the point after by Larry Johnson was no good.

Then in the second quarter, the storm awoke and made a score on a 23-yard toss. The Fitzgerald side went bonkers. The point after was good, and our boys went in at halftime trailing 7–6.

We had not been behind in a game all season.

Then Walter, showing why he was one of the best players in Georgia, took the Big Red on his shoulders, and things began to work themselves out. On one of his superlative plays in the third period, *the elusive Sumner,* as the Fitzgerald *Herald-Leader* described, our star *brought the fans to their feet* on a 52-yard bootleg for a score. *At least five Hurricane tacklers had a shot at him, one at the line of scrimmage, but couldn't hold him as his hips seemed to be moving in tune to the latest twist record.*

Very late in the fourth, Fitzgerald was backed up in their own territory. They had to punt. The ball was snapped, and suddenly there was a gasp in the stadium as the punter, Jack

Paulk, had the ball go through his hands and it flopped on the ground with everybody diving for it. On the bottom of the pile was an Indian with the ball secured under his belly at the ten.

The Big Red side roared.

Two plays later, Frankie Cowan of Ocilla pounded the ball off right tackle for the score. Johnson added the point after to sew up the contest, 20-7, for Irwin.

When the clock ran out in Fitzgerald, hundreds of loony Indian fans stormed the field to celebrate and congratulate the team.

The boys ran around wildly. We had not beaten Fitzgerald but three times since 1928 and it was the first time in history that a football outfit from Ocilla had finished 10–0 in a season that included a win over the hated Hurricane.

Somebody call the president.

Big Red fans were heard shouting from the windows of cars leaving the stadium.

Through the years, in playing Fitzgerald, "There was a certain amount of anxiety, and you'd been led to believe they were a superior team," Wayne Pierce says. So to beat them was a sense of accomplishment and a sense of pride for the boys from Irwin County. And from the standpoint of the rivalry, Pierce adds, "I think Irwin County grew up that night."

One other thing.

The promise to make a baby out of Big Daddy Thompson was a hoax. He's long since figured out that the big baby insult was cooked up by Indian mentors so he'd play hard.

Thompson, said the *Star, lived up to his potential.*

And it was on to the playoffs.

33

On To Blakely

All Irwin Countians were singing their new national anthem Saturday morning, 'when its Hurricane time it's SUMNER in our hearts,' following the Irwin County Indians 20–7 victory over the Fitzgerald Purple Hurricane Friday night. Led by deluxe quarterback Walter Sumner, the Indians shattered a dream of the Hurricane while making their own come true. The victory gave them an undefeated season and in licking the Hurricane they captured the neighborhood championship and put the only blot on the top rated A team's record...If ever one man has been the difference in a football game, Sumner was that man Friday night. His running, passing and kicking kept the Hurricane fighting for their lives all night. His scrambling from seemingly impossible situations kept the Indians moving goal-ward on numerous occasions. The game itself was a contest of two giants, as football lingo goes. Neither team could be pushed around by the other. Every yard was earned the hard way. Time after time each thwarted the other on drives that seemed certain to produce a breakthrough.

—*Fitzgerald Herald-Leader*, November 19, 1964

Who could beat us now?

Irwin, rocking and rolling, had outscored the first ten opponents by a combined 311-39, and if they repeated the effort put forth against the No. 1 Hurricanes, the Big Red was a shoe-in to make state if they could get by Bradwell Institute.

After downing mighty Fitz in a playoff atmosphere, the Indians of Ralph Cook were the toast of Georgia as they waited to see who they'd play in the first round. The Indians were eager to get at Bradwell whose boys had also finished perfectly, beating ten foes by a combined 404–17, including 94–0 over poor little Claxton. We'd deal with Bradwell later.

For now, everybody for Irwin was high and happy, the boys drunk with pride and getting statewide notoriety, which was good for Ocilla and Irwin County. Of course, they were just boys then, lads of a small school who drank up the glory of being undefeated, saluted as one of the great Georgia teams of the era in any class. They were not so inebriated, however, as to lose sight of the immediate horizon. It would've been nice, and somehow fitting in an historical sense, to stop with Fitzgerald in the bag and be called state champs. But there was so much more to play for beginning with a regional final.

These boys of ours were not playoff seasoned. Irwin had not navigated the post season waters in 11 years, back when the boys of 1964 were in elementary school, and there was the wait factor. From the Saturday morning after the Fitzgerald game to

Walter Sumner, #12, and teammates lay hands on the 1964 sub-region trophy. *Courtesy ICHS Library / copied from 1965 yearbook by Lucy Pierce*

Tuesday night, while being celebrated for beating our old rival, they waited to find out their first round foe, who would come out of the 1–B West, where Blakely and Pelham ended the season tied, requiring a playoff. That game was played Tuesday, November 17.

The winner was Blakely. The playoff between our boys and Blakely's was set for November 25, the Wednesday before Thanksgiving, in Blakely.

Blakely, also known as Blakely-Union, had a good team. We knew that. We had their films and Ralph had sent scouts to the Blakely-Pelham game. The Bobcats, coached by Ray Knight, had won nine games in the regular season and tied one; scored 222 points and gave 18. Blakely had enjoyed a high rating during the season and certainly were no strangers to the playoffs. Blakely had reached the post season eight times in 11 years, winning four region crowns. But had they ever seen the likes of what Irwin was bringing to the game that was viewed by many as a stepping stone to reach Bradwell Institute? We thought not.

It was 115 miles from Ocilla to Blakely and rather than go over the same day, Ralph wanted to get there early to give our boys a day of rest before the game and so the Big Red went to Blakely on Tuesday in a bus and spent the night there in a motel to await the Wednesday night clash.

Confident Indian fans trailed them in a decorated motorcade.

A few motivated men among the Indian faithful, eager to pocket some easy cash, arrived ahead of anyone to hustle up bets on the game from Bobcat fans.

Hundreds more by bus and car motored over on Wednesday for the 8 o'clock kickoff.

Fans who couldn't make the trip or pick up the game on the radio sat by their phones hoping, wishing, praying.

Go, Big Red!

By 10 o'clock, the news from Blakely began to hit home.

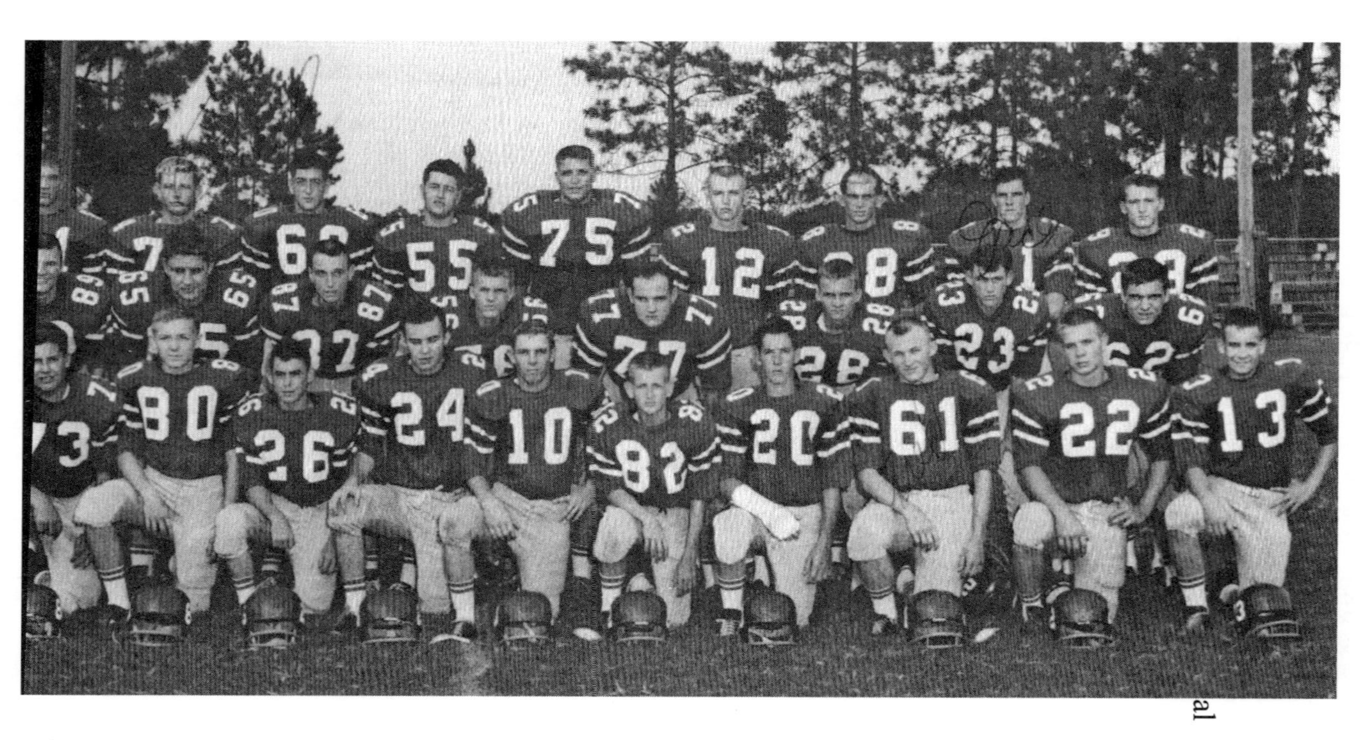

al

Glenn "Big Daddy" Thompson, #75 stands tall in this team photo of the 1964 Indians. *Courtesy ICHS Library / copied from 1964-65 yearbook by Lucy Pierce*

34
The Big Letdown

Those fighting, snarling Bobcats from Blakely upset all the gridiron prophets here in Blakely at Sandiford Field on Thanksgiving Eve, massacring the much heralded Irwin County Indians 27–14...An overflow crowd was on hand to see the 1–B shocker."

—*Early County News*, December 3, 1964

When the sun came up, and it was a lovely morning, fresh with Dixie dew, the town of Ocilla was in a pall; the disbelief was immense on Turkey Day.

One of our boys with the balding head emerged from his residence—409 Ash Street, a pink, two-bedroom, wood-frame house—and strolled through the quiet neighborhood north toward Fourth Street.

The sun that was the light of the Lord did not lift his mood.

"Couldn't believe it," Wayne Pierce says now. "Couldn't believe it."

In every quarter of Irwin County, from Lax to Waterloo, was astonishment, anger, disgust, humiliation. Every man, woman and child who pulled for the Indians hurt. The Big Red had fallen, knocked out of the playoffs.

"People were upset," says Mike Ashley, a sophomore on the team that went to Blakely. "You'd walk down the street and the people wouldn't even speak to you. It took them to about Christmas before they got over it. They said we laid down, but we didn't. We were flat."

By sunrise on Thanksgiving, word of mouth had spread some sad details. The boys got down early by four scores. They fought back when they realized they were in a football game but it was too late. Walter Sumner tried to save us but he had no more magic. Passes fell at the feet of open receivers or went sailing. The gears were busted, and with Blakely's excited boys shouting, "Don't let 'em get started," our heroes went down.

It was a crushing defeat for Ralph Cook and the Big Red family.

Said the Star:

> *... Halfback Jeff Cotton and Fullback Butch Moore proved too much for Coach Ralph Cook and his Irwin County High School Indians. The Bobcats cut the Indians to threads as they found openings in the Irwin forward wall all night and had no trouble clicking off at least four to five yards on each carry.*

In other words, "They ran it down our damn throats," says Tommy Tucker, when asked why Irwin lost to Blakely. Their fullback, says Tommy, did a lot of the damage. "We couldn't stop him."

Tommy points out that the only other teams to beat Irwin in two years—Cook High and Fitzgerald, both in '63—also presented bruising fullbacks.

Those Bobcats, by the way, knocked off Bradwell Institute, 6–0, and ended up winning the State Class B championship that most people assumed would be Irwin's.

"I didn't think anybody would beat Irwin that year," says Jack Paulk, a member of the 1964 Fitzgerald team that lost to the Indians. "That was one of the finest high school football teams I ever saw. It was just unbelievable at the talent they had."

Sick, sick, sick fans faulted the boys. They blamed the coaches. They blamed people they didn't even know. Everyone was just very sore. Some said the boys quit. Mike Ashley believes the coaching staff let the boys have too much fun before the game and "lost control of the team."

"I've questioned myself on that," says Kermit Elliott, one of our assistant coaches that season. "We weren't ready to play football, [and] I think we went to Blakely too early."

You heard it said in Ocilla that our boys, believing their own good press and frolicking in the adventure of being away from home at a motel, hit the field in a soft and lousy frame of mind against the fired-up, playoff-savvy Bobcats. Having beaten Fitzgerald and believing all they had to do was show up to down Blakely, "We got cocky," says Ashley, "and laid around the hotel all day." He gives Blakely credit, though. "We just got lazy [and] those boys hit us. They were there to play and were well coached and ran precise plays."

Bobby Dix of Ocilla, who attended the game, remembers, "We went down there looking forward to playing Bradwell Institute. We weren't even looking to Blakely, and we got canned. I just don't know what happened. We couldn't never figure it out. We were just completely out of place."

Ocilla attorney Harry Mixon says it appeared that our boys, when they fell behind, just quit and left the game for superstar Walter Sumner to win and Walt couldn't pull it off.

Also, there was dissension among the boys in the huddle when they were trying to fight back, arguing with Walter over what plays to call.

"My opinion is," says Tommy Tucker, "we went over there and stayed in that hotel and played grab-ass…Thought we were invincible" after beating Fitzgerald.

"That's a good question," Ralph Cook says when asked why Irwin lost to Blakely. "We had scouted them and we knew everything they were going to do. I think the biggest thing was, we just didn't get the job done. I don't know if it was overconfidence or what it was."

Glenn Thompson says our boys' heads were not quite in the game but he's quick to note that Blakely deserved to win because Irwin did not play very well.

The big Thompson boy made All-State that year, and Blakely was not the end of the gridiron road for him. After high school, and not wanting to farm, he signed to play ball at the University of South Carolina. Later, when there was a coaching change, Glenn transferred to Troy State. The first Troy player to be taken by the pros, Big Daddy was drafted by the Miami Dolphins in the 17th round. He soon cut ties with the fish, returned to Georgia, and began to survey land.

"I was too big for my time," he supposes. He remembers the Dolphins wanted him to play in a swaddling league for a year and lose some weight but 255 pounds was as low as he could get, so he left the team.

Regretfully, Glenn lost all his football souvenirs from his playing days. There was a fire at his home in the early 1980s sparked by an electrical short. Flames erupted while the family was away at a friend's house for dinner. Luckily, no one was injured, but two dogs died in the blaze and all his belongings burned.

The Thanksgiving morning after Blakely broke our hearts, the boy with the busted nose, Wayne Pierce, who was deaf in one ear, crossed Fourth Street and walked down the hill toward the old gymnasium, across the wide-open field where boys had shed much blood for many years.

Had he a crystal ball, Wayne would've known he'd be named Valedictorian of his class and the yearbook would identify him as the student Most Likely to Succeed. He'd have a shot at West Point, but the bad ear since childhood would prevent him from passing the physical. So, with no money for higher education, he'd end up playing football at Wofford College on a scholarship. After a season with the Terrapins, Wayne would hang up his cleats to focus on his studies, which was a major in economics. Later he would enroll at Duke University School of Law, graduate in the upper ten percent of his class, pass the bar on the first attempt and become a successful attorney in Atlanta.

But in his dictionary, under "disappointment," there would always be the word "Blakely."

While crossing the old field toward the old, wooden gym, Wayne knew that losing was a part of living; that it wasn't the adversity itself but how you handled it that most counted. The hurt, though, was gut deep and the images of errant passes dogged his mind and made him slightly queasy. He relived the fired-up Bobcats yelling, "Don't let 'em get started now!" He could not erase the images or quiet the voices. Sports and academics were his life in the little farm town of Ocilla, and now a big piece was abruptly over; and so with nowhere else to turn, he had decided to go back to a familiar place: the old gym.

There he found Ralph Cook, sorting through the boys' gear like one goes through debris in the aftermath of a tornado. Wayne was glad to see Ralph. The two sat on the edge of the wooden porch of the gym in the sunshine that came over the old schoolhouse. They talked a little about the game. But it was a tragic subject. Somehow, the old saying, *You win some, you lose some,* did not fit the moment.

When there was nothing more to say about Blakely that could be said with words, the co-captain and his coach talked about the nature of life. Coach Cook, chomping on his cigar and spitting the juice, was like, *Yeah, well, the sun comes up and the sun goes down. That is the nature of living, and there's a lot of life left for you.*

He told Wayne to keep studying and stay focused.

In a little while, words lost all value and there was no more talking and they just sat there, close, in the brightness of a crisp Thanksgiving morning on the porch of the old gymnasium.

"There were theories that we were looking ahead to Bradwell Institute, and we knew they were next, and I think there was a sense, after Fitzgerald, that we could compete with anybody," Wayne says 50 years later. "I don't know where leaving school early fits. More than anything, it was a situation where one team played over its ability and another team played under its ability."

Mr. Pierce believes the team handled the Blakely heartache well.

"A lot of us have moved on to be good citizens. I'm proud of all of us, probably more proud of what we've done since that night than prior to that night."

Still, the regret never goes away.

"Of all the people we let down that year, I feel we most let down Coach Cook. He had those fatherly-like efforts to prep us, tape us and pull for us. To this day, I wish there was some way to give him the state championship he deserved. Coach Cook always told me no matter what happened, there was a bright future ahead, that football was not all there was to life and to stay focused on academics. He will always be a state champion in my mind."

35

'Almost A Riot'

Joe Compton's Fitzgerald High School Hurricanes unleashed a tremendous offensive attack behind the running of David Garrison, Mike Eidson, Charles Melton and Jack Paulk to overpower archrival Irwin County here Friday night, 21–7. The game was a highlight of the 1965 football campaign but was not played in the type weather which was suitable for the overflow crowd who packed Indian stadium for the publicized battle between the two cities. The game was played in a constant rain all night. Obviously the Irwin County offensive unit was limited to their punch Friday night due to Jack Smith's leg injury. The workload was given to Rhett Royal who performed superbly on offense and equally as outstanding on defense by making more

than his share of tackles and assists during the contest.
—*Ocilla Star*, November 18, 1965

After the heartbreak of 1964, it was important to the good spirit of everyone in Indian country to get back to the playoffs as soon as possible, what with emotions still sore, but Walt Sumner and seven other starters lost to graduation was a hard blow and we did not do as well as was hoped.

It was good, though, that we had Jack Smith back; he was a horse and without him, we wouldn't have won the five games we did.

Jack's good friend, halfback Rhett Royal, returned to the lineup along with 230-pound strongman Ronald "Punk" Harper for the line. It was a good squad Cook put together and the boys fought to the end with great courage but did not make the playoffs.

The bright spot was defense; six times the Indians held opponents to no points. Two games ended in a tie.

Fitzgerald and Tift County, in a wild affair, both got their revenge on the Indians but it was the loss to Blackshear that kept the Big Red from the post season.

That was the first year the boys made use of a field house. The structure, built of concrete block on the east side of the stadium, was painted red and white. There'd never been such a facility in Ocilla and now the boys had a place to retire to at halftime instead of on the grass. Historically, footballers had practiced in town outside of the old gym, dressed in the gym, and on game nights were bused from the gymnasium out to the field. Having a field house put an end to that tradition, and the boys were now able to practice at the field. The facility had one side for visitors and the other for the Indians. There were showers on both ends, stalls for the boys' gear, and an office for the Indian coaches.

Probably the most interesting game that season was with Tift County, and when the contest was over, Jack Smith slugged a Blue Devil with his helmet.

"That was the cornbread bowl," Rhett Royal says with a chuckle. Jack says he reacted in self-defense. Punk Harper recalls a wild night in Tifton.

"Ralph and [Coach] Kermit [Elliott] were trying to get us off the field before it blew up," Punk says of the postgame shenanigans that were payback for what we'd done to the Devils the year before in Ocilla with the cornbread. "We went and got on the bus, and we were hollered at, thrown things at. It was almost a riot. The Tifton people treated us really, really bad."

Among the boys on the '65 squad trying to get some playing time was a skinny, wide-eyed ninth grader named Oscar Roberts. The little brother of former Indian star Marion Roberts, Oscar knew the drill in Irwin County. "You were expected to play football when you got old enough," Oscar says, remembering how it was for growing boys when he was coming along. "I didn't know anything else. I wanted to play quarterback. That's what Marion was when he was in high school."

But Oscar had to wait. Although quarterback was a gaping hole left by the great Sumner, there wouldn't be a traditional signal caller for the Indians that season. A lot of the ball handling went to Jack Smith and Rhett.

Unlike Oscar, who grew up knowing he'd be a football player, as a kid Jack never felt the call. Endowed with a load of talent, Jack grew up seeing himself farming, never leaving Irwin County, or he thought maybe he'd end up in the Army.

In high school, Jack was sharecropping. He remembers Ralph came to see him on the farm one day, asking him questions like, "Do you ever want to leave this place? And how would you like to go to college?"

Jack's eyes lit up. He really liked Ralph, an old farm boy himself, and was impressed by the prospects of leaving farm country.

Ralph took the kid under his wing.

"Ralph Cook, he was the reason I got into football. He meant so much to me at that time."

Ralph remembers the first time he saw Jack was outside the gymnasium. "I said, 'That young man is going to be a football player.' He never let me down. He was strong as a bull. He would give you whatever he had."

The coach recalls the Indians were playing some team on the Florida line, and Irwin was near the goal trying to score and needed for Jack to step it up.

Ralph signaled for Jack and barked, "Come 'ere. Do you think you can score?"

Jack nodded affirmatively with the coach in his face and returned to the action, angry. On the next play, Jack rammed it in.

"He was a tough, tough football player," Ralph says.

The Tift County game went down to the wire. That's the one the old boys remember the most about 1965.

It was a clear night and the drums of Blue Devil revenge were pounding when the Big Red rolled into Tifton. Not as brawny, heavy or as athletic as the '64 line, the Indian wall, held down by Punk, Johnny Milton and Raymond Hanley, was stubborn. The Devils put up a hard wall, too. It was a bloody tussle for points, and Jack Smith was a marked man.

During the week leading up to the big game with revenge-minded Tift, a dummy with Jack's number on it was hung in the Tift County gym where it was to be burned the day of the game at a pep rally.

It was the first season for Tift's "head hunter club," and it was Jack's head that was sought.

"They didn't like me at all over there," Jack says of the Tift boys. "I dated a girl from TyTy, but she had moved. They just meant to put me out of the ball game for some reason."

Bo Edenfield, who played that night for Tift, says it wasn't personal toward Jack, whom he described as "such a competitor." Tift knew that Jack was Irwin's best player, and it was him they felt they had to stop; but Bo denies any intent to cripple Jack.

There was no score until the Blue Devils put up six late in the game on a tricky punt return. The extra point failed, and shortly thereafter, the game ended, 6–0.

Cried the *Star*, *Over half of Coach Cook's Indians were forced to play the entire game while Tift's Guillebeau substituted freely all evening.*

Punk remembers our boys took the fight to them. "They knew they had a football game when they went home. For a little old team like Ocilla against Tifton, we played a pretty good game."

Says Rhett Royal: "We did our job but on that punt return…I don't know. I screwed up." His assignment on the return was to pursue and contain the man with the ball. "That's why I felt so bad. They fooled me. … I think about that a lot."

When the final whistle blew, because of what happened in Ocilla in '64, "we kind of figured they would come out with cornbread," Jack says, and when the cornbread did come out,

Ralph Cook yelled a two-word command to his troops: "Y'all run!"

"That ole cornbread, it had some big old cracklins in it…or rocks," Rhett remembers. "Coach Cook and Coach Elliott were trying to get everybody off the field. Jack Smith and I were walking and Coach Cook said to pick it up and Jack was taking his time. They got around him, and that's when they went to pushing it on Jack."

His nose broken and his head gashed—injuries from the game—Jack slugged one who pushing at him with the cornbread.

Mayo Tucker remembers he and teammate Bo Edenfield were "trying to feed Jack some" cornbread when all of a sudden Jack "took his helmet and starting swinging."

Mayo says he doesn't know who Jack hit.

Jack doesn't know either. "They had been trying to put me out of the game," he explains. So upon leaving the field Jack was on high alert when a boy rushed him.

"He comes up behind me yelling, and he said, 'Hey, Smith, you want some of this cornbread?' I didn't know if he was going to hit me or whatever. I had my helmet by the face mask, and when he gets about two steps behind me, I turned and swung and hit him up under the chin with my helmet, lifted him off his feet, laid him out. We walked off the field and got on the bus, and they threw bottles and everything. It got a little nerve-wracking there."

When it came time for them to think about leaving Ocilla, Jack and Punk, at the urging of Cook, went to Memphis State. Jack had thought maybe he'd join Walter Sumner at Florida State or go to Auburn, but Ralph knew a coach at MSU, and through that connection, the two Irwin County boys flew to Memphis on a plane and came back Tigers.

An injury cut Punk's career short and Jack ended up in the

pros, a sixth round draft choice by the Philadelphia Eagles. At 205 pounds, he was the largest defensive back in the NFL. Jack recalls a concussion put him out of the league; he spent a week in the hospital with amnesia. Later, he turned down a chance to return to the pros as a safety for the Washington Redskins.

For 38 years after pro ball, Jack operated a construction business, and then he owned and managed about one hundred acres of pecan trees in middle Georgia between Hawkinsville and Perry. Rhett Royal became a surveyor and Punk worked in the crop dusting and trucking business. He later wrote a book about crop dusting.

As for Ralph Cook, the season of '65 was his last.

In Ocilla, coaches were sought who could make our boys a winner. If you failed to make the playoffs, the season was not successful. You got a special feather if you beat Fitzgerald, but you never got rich. There were many reasons why coaches came and went. By the time school let out for the summer in 1966, and with a record of 23–6–2, Ralph Cook had had enough.

"I couldn't make any money," he says now with a chuckle. He led spring drills in '66 before handing in his keys. Ralph went into the fertilizer business and never coached or taught school again. He now lives in Albany, Georgia, and recently lost a good friend when his old nemesis Joe Compton of Hurricane fame died.

Ralph says he feels good and gets back now and then for class reunions.

"I am 82 years old, and I can walk and get around and function. I'm doing okay."

Fortunately for the Indian family, when Ralph took off the bonnet, the school did not have very far to look for his replacement. There was an old Vidalia boy already on the reservation, itching for a shot to be the chief.

Part IV

36

A Fighting Spirit

Ocilla restaurant owner Johnny King is spearheading a committee whose task it is to rebuild the press box at the Irwin County Indian football stadium.

The idea of rebuilding the facility was long past due until King and his committee took it on themselves to do something about it.

It was brought to the attention of the athletic booster club recently that a new press box would have to be constructed before another season starts. 'It endangers everyone who uses the old facility and especially the game photographer who is atop the structure.'

Last week, King with others including Harmon Roberts, Hugh Roberts and E.L Sprayberry purchased the lumber and began working on the facility.

The new press box will be 12 feet by 24 feet and will more than double the original size.

The committee said this week that additional finances and manpower are needed and any person having one or both of these are invited to come and participate.

The new press box should be completed within the week.

—*Ocilla Star*, August 25, 1966

Win or lose, people in the stands and around the field yelled and hollered. A "Big Mouth" award was given by the booster club to the most boisterous fan, which one year was a woman.

"I still look back on those joyous years," says Vida Dix, wife of Bobby Dix. "I can look back and see all the people" rooting the Indians on.

Not every year was swell in the win column. One of those years in the '60s when there was not much joy in the pines was when Jud Pusey was a senior.

Before he joined the Army, and was sent to Korea instead of Vietnam, Jud was the battering ram for the 1966 Indians as they fought against the tide with only three seniors on the team.

Jud says now, sitting one hot day on his porch, wearing shorts with a couple of cats close by, that the boys all hated how that season went, losing six of ten and not making the playoffs. They really hated it for their new coach.

"If players love their coach, they will give 110 percent to please him, and Kermit was that kind of man," Jud said, rolling a stubby cigar between his fingers. "He got on to you in a way you respected."

By "Kermit," he means Kermit Elliott. There was an interview process for a head coach that had to be gone through when Ralph Cook left. But everybody knew the Ocilla job was Kermit's if he wanted it. And he jumped at the opportunity.

"That'd always been one of my desires in life," Kermit says of being a head football coach. Because of his experience as

Ralph's assistant and also having coached at Fitzgerald for Joe Compton, Kermit was primed to be chief; accustomed to tough, hard-nosed football. But the cupboard was almost bare. The talent that began rolling through in 1963 had run its course.

"That was the biggest rebuilding year we ever had," recalls Mike Ashley, one of three seniors on the '66 club.

However, the Indians were in the playoff picture until late October when Camden County knocked them out by a touchdown.

Kermit felt going into the season that the scrappy boys in red would probably not win state.

> *The team is young and inexperienced,* he told the *Ocilla Star* in late August of 1966 after camp where 34 boys were trained. *But all indications are that if the boys put forth the spirit and determination as displayed during football camp, we will give our opposition a run for their money.*

Jud Pusey remembers Ocilla in those days was "a small, country town with a winning attitude." The boys tried hard to win out of Big Red pride and to feel a sense of personal accomplishment. When they lost, even to higher-classed teams, they felt lousy, having let themselves down, let the coach down and knowing they'd let the fans down, too. Losing was all round a rotten deal in the Ocilla community that was long starved for a state title.

On the bright side of 1966, as a fan you had to feel the wind would blow some future luck our way. If you picked up a game-night program and went down the roster, there were 31 boys on the list who were either juniors, sophomores or freshmen, and that was the year Irwin found a quarterback when Oscar Roberts, one of the sophomores, got his shot at the position, alternating with Phil Singletary. Oscar gave a good account and took the role pretty much full-time about midway through the season.

After losing to Coffee County in the opener, in which Mike Ashley cracked two ribs, it was time to go to Fitzgerald.

Mike Ashley says, "We were the only people who felt like we might could beat them."

Kermit had no rabbits in his hat, however. The 'Canes of Joe Compton, with a stable of backs, jumped out to a big lead and blew away the outmanned tribe, 34–12.

"Arrogant," Jud Pusey scoffs when asked what Fitzgerald was like as an opponent in his day. And the games with them were "like war. They were always a class or two ahead of us. They were dirty. They would get you down in the bottom the pile and punch you and kick you…And when we retaliated, we got flagged.

They were just a bunch of Yankees to start with."

Later on in the season, in the game with Camden, the backbreaker was a blow to Mike Ashley, who was defending a bigger, faster Wildcat receiver. On one play, "I covered him pretty well, then I slipped and he was wide open." The touchdown made Mike feel like the goat. "After the game, I went up to coach Kermit. 'Coach, I'm sorry I lost this football game.' And he said, 'No, you did not. You did not lose this game.'" That was one aspect of the 1966 season: the boys' relationship with their new head coach.

"The fact that he was such a good man, you wanted to play for him," Ashley says of his old high school mentor. "He was a person you just didn't want to disappoint. He was very sincere and very concerned about the kids. He was tough when he had to be but he had a good football mind."

"I liked him a lot better than Coach Cook," Oscar Roberts says.

Jud Pusey says, "I just love him to death."

Jud started playing ball late in school. His stepfather, a farmer, would not allow him play at first because of farm work that needed to be done. Coach Elliott talked to the man about Jud coming out for summer camp with the Indians. Ultimately, Jud told his step dad he was either going to play football or he was going to leave.

"I said, 'I'm going to play football.'"

Jud played his junior and seniors years, working on the farm when he could. "Kermit was the best friend, best man I ever knew in my life," he says. "I wish he'd been my dad."

37
An Ideal Squad

The Irwin County High School Indians will be tested to the fullest here Friday night when they host the Seminole County Indians in a football contest to decide the region 1–B championship....Attendance is expected to surpass the 3,000 mark. The Irwin Braves have been waiting three years for the opportunity to represent their side of Region 1–B in the region finals. The last time Irwin was 1–B East champs was 1964. They traveled to Blakely and were defeated....A concession stand will be open on both sides of the football field Friday night staffed by Irwin High band parents. Hotdogs, hamburgers, homemade candy, coffee and cold drinks will be available. Advance admission tickets to the Irwin-Seminole game will be on sale until 3:30 today

(Thursday) at ICHS for students and through noon Friday for adults at A.S. Harris Dept. Store, Coley's Service Station and Osceola Restaurant. Student admission is $1.00 and adults $2.00. An extra dollar will buy a reserve seat.

—*Ocilla Star*, November 16, 1967

The Indians began to kick it 1967. That year we had a fine, hustling group of those young players from 1965 toting the torch. There was much joy in the pines as Kermit Elliott's boys of '67 lit up the scoreboard and we spent most of the season as the No. 4 team in Georgia's Class B. And a sign that Irwin County would be good for years to come was seen among the boys in the junior high program raring to make the varsity and littler ones were playing tackle ball in backyards and open lots, which was typical of a football town.

We're a little lighter overall than we'd like, Elliott told the *Star* going into the 1967 campaign, *but we're a little tougher this year and will depend much on speed.*

Oscar Roberts, a junior, was leading the offense. Glenn Tucker, a 208-pound bruiser and brother of 1964 Indian standout Tommy Tucker, was converted from guard to fullback to give the Indians some punch up the middle.

The Big Red's climb to a high status began with a Friday night matchup in the rain with the Coffee County boys from Douglas. A lot of people from Fitzgerald who'd heard Irwin might be good that year came to Ocilla to watch the game between the Indians and the Comets; Fitzgerald's boys were idle that week before the annual clash with Irwin County.

Just short of sand-bagging but always one to praise the opposition, Elliott told the *Star* that he was very worried about

Coffee's reserve power and a stellar back. Kermit said Irwin would not be at full strength. *"Broken fingers may limit the service of two of his boys, (end L.H. Dill and guard Rickey Brown) and a bad knee puts a doubtful label on Larry Day who has been looking good in the backfield,"* the *Star* reported.

In the Coffee game, although the outcome was meaningless in the standings since the Comets were in a higher division, the Irwin boys with their beefed-up backfield put Class B on notice: the Big Red was back.

The Irwin High Indians proved conclusively on the local gridiron Friday night that they will probably be the team to beat for Region 1B honors, as they outclassed Coffee County's Comets, 14–0, crowed the *Star* on page one of its September 8 edition.

In the second game, Joe Compton's Hurricanes came to the reservation and blew the teepee away, 18–7. They had more men on their side and our chance at an upset was shot when the big Tucker boy went down, grabbing at his knee.

Bowing to the 'Canes was hard to take, but the loss seemed to frustrate and inspire the boys and they scalped their next eight foes by a combined 252–53 to storm into the playoffs for only the second time since 1953.

Prior to the playoffs, in an interview with the *Star,* Coach Elliott said Irwin County was 9–1 because the coaches *have had an ideal squad of boys to work with and the fact that the boys have continued to hold a close relationship with each other and maintained a togetherness. Some boys have received outstanding recognition during this period of time, but each squad member knows that by making one player a standout it's*

going to take the efforts and support of at least 10 others to make this possible.

The game that gave Irwin the sub-region was a 40–6 beatdown of Charlton County. Oscar ran 14 times for 221 yards and a pair of TDs and connected with his receivers for three more scores in being named Georgia's Back of the Week by the *Associated Press.*

He finished the ten-game slate with 1,146 yards on 183 carries and made 16 touchdowns rushing. The top tackler after ten games was Ricky Brown with 65 stops.

Winning the 1B East set Irwin up for a rematch with Seminole County, winners of the 1–B West for the 1–B title. Besides losing to Irwin on September 15, by the score of 13–6 in Donalsonville, the rival tribe had fallen to Graceville, Fla., and tied the team from Headland, Ala., but they were unbeaten in their sub-region when they invaded Ocilla for the Region final.

The game was the talk of the town all week as title fever swept through. It was the first game of playoff football ever in Ocilla.

> Said the *Star*:
>
> *Admission to the championship playoff will be $2.00 adults. Student tickets are now on sale at the respective schools at $1.00 each. No student tickets will be sold Friday night. Gates will open at the field at 6:30 Friday and local persons planning to see the game have been asked to park their autos downtown and use the convenience of a shuttle bus service to and from the field. School buses will be used for this and there will be no charge for this service.*

The Indians slashed the rival tribe, 28–7, to take the 1–B title and stretched their record to 10–1.

Next the boys battled the Bulldogs of Lyons for the South Georgia championship and it was an exhausting affair. Nobody scored until about five minutes to go when their quarterback went in from eight yards out following a long punt return. The point after was no good. The Indians could not recoup and down they went, although putting up what the *Star* called *"a winning performance."*

Later on we snickered when Lyons got whipped in the State title game, 27–0, on their own field, by Washington-Wilkes.

At the end of the '67 season, the *Star* heaped praise on the Indians.

> *All of us are very proud of our Irwin County High School football team and congratulate them for winning the region 1–B championship. Even though they were defeated Friday night in their bid for the South Georgia championship title, they can be consoled in knowing they are one of the four top Class B teams in the state.*
>
> *What makes this team so special, in addition to their excellent record, is the high moral character of every boy on the squad. Plainly stated, they are all 'good' boys. From the 'big stars' to the 'scrubbiest scrubs', they won the hearts of local fans with their spirit and character both on and off the football field.*
>
> *Of course, a great deal of the credit is due Coach Kermit Elliott and his fine group of assistants. They inspired the players to perform above their capabilities, and a total team effort was in evidence at all times.*
>
> *The squad will lose several fine players this year through graduation, but a larger than normal number will be back for the opening game next fall. With the team spirit they now possess and with the support of*

parents and fans, we can't see how our Indians can't help but 'go all the way.'

—*Ocilla Star*, November 30, 1967

38

Out-toughed At Fitzgerald

Ocilla—Coach Kermit Elliott's Irwin County Indians, the defending Region 1–B champs, gave notice that they are a team to be reckoned with as they manhandled Bacon County of Region 1–A, 34–0, here Friday night.

The Indians were paced by All-State quarterback Oscar Roberts who ran 13 times for 120 yards, scoring once, and completing 10 of 20 pass attempts for 167 yards and another score.... The Indians left the field at halftime leading 27–0. Coach Elliott let up during the third period and most of the fourth using mostly reserves. With just a few minutes remaining, the first team returned and got a final score.

—Charlie Ridgeway, *Tifton Gazette*, Nov.30, 1967

The “Eager 36,” as Coach Elliott dubbed the boys of 1968, thundered over their first six foes by a combined 198–3. In fact, they spent a good deal of the season flip-flopping with Roswell for the state’s No. 1 ranking, and in a wild affair on November 1, Oscar Roberts and his Big Red accomplices nailed down the 2–B title to punch their playoff ticket before hitting the road to Fitzgerald for game seven.

The team had dedicated the season to Lanny Roberts, who died on August 4, 1968 from complications due to diabetes, leaving a legion of friends across the state. The boys all wore black arm bands on the first night in honor of the little fellow in the black-rimmed spectacles. In addition to operating the projector at the Ocilla Theater, the slightly built, dark-haired Lanny was a radio newscaster in Ocilla on WSIZ and frequently wrote articles for the *Star*. The stadium observed a moment’s silence because everybody knew Lanny, who never played sports due to physical limitations but who supported all our teams, especially the football boys.

“He lived and died with us,” Kermit Elliott says, recalling Lanny’s devotion to football in Ocilla.

The game at Fitzgerald was rated even, with a wink to Irwin. Everybody went. The 1–A Hurricane, under first year coach Jesse Dyess, were 7–2, and they came out in intimidating new uniforms, like Notre Dame’s, that included gold helmets.

The Indians scored first after a Hurricane fumble in the opening quarter. Glenn Tucker, playing defensive tackle, fell on the ball for the Indians at their one. Oscar ran it in from that point. Fitzgerald later scored on a pass and then we hit ’em again, this time on a 52-yard romp by Bob Roland.

The contest developed into a nail-biting affair.

“Snake” Dixon of Fitz broke a long run in the third quarter to put them up 19–13.

Quarterback Oscar Roberts confers with head coach Kermit Elliott during a game in Ocilla in 1968. *Courtesy Oscar Roberts*

That's when the game really got interesting. Trailing late in the fourth, the Big Red pushed the Hurricane down to the one-half-yard line. With time about to expire, all we needed was half a yard. All the fans were on their feet. Irwin's side expected Oscar to hand off to the bull, fullback Tucker, and he'd punch it in, and we'd go home happy. Just a half yard was all.

On this one decisive play, Elliott called for a quarterback sweep.

A sweep! Oh, daddy. There went Oscar, running for his life around the right side toward the pylon, and everything just went badly. Our wingback missed a block, for one thing, and Oscar was wracked for a loss by the speedy defense and there went the ponies.

Fitzgerald's side of the field roared with elation.

The Big Red faithful threw up their hands in disgust.

"We got out-toughed is what it boiled down to," Elliott says now of failing to punch it in at the Fitz goal line. The old coach says, yes, he'd liked to have used big Tucker boy inside on that play, but the Purple Hurricane, he recalls, had the middle jammed with linemen to stop the inside run.

It was a stinging defeat for Mr. Elliott and the Big Red faithful was sorely upset.

"I never would've believed that Fitzgerald could've held us like that on the goal line," Elliott laments.

"It was sad," Oscar Roberts says. "We had 'em if we could've scored. It wasn't meant to be."

But Elliott believes that losing to Fitzgerald helped us in the long run because the boys were angry, and we drew No. 3-ranked Pelham in the first round of the tournament, which was called the quarterfinal, on November 22.

In Ocilla and in Pelham, much was made about the matchup being a battle of siblings: Oscar as Irwin quarterback against his big brother Marion, who coached the Hornets.

> *The two teams offer quite a contrast in offenses,* the *Tifton Gazette* reported.
>
> *Irwin runs out of the conventional T while Pelham operates from the seldom-seen Notre Dame box.*

The box, made famous by Notre Dame's Knute Rockne in the 1910s, was a tricky scheme. Teams who used it typically did not have a good passer. The formation resembled a square. Backs shifted a lot in order to deceive the defense. Joe Compton had used it religiously at Fitzgerald.

The Hornets, winners of the 1-B region, rode into Ocilla as hot as any team in Georgia, having won nine games in a row. Irwin was rated a seven-point favorite. A capacity crowd was on hand. Our boys were in a mean mind frame.

39

Slippin' and Slidin'

Ocilla—Judging by its surprisingly easy 33–0 playoff victory over Pelham here Friday night, it's going to take quite an opponent to derail Irwin County's quest for a Class B state football championship....

The Indians, who rebounded in mad fashion from their 19–13 loss last week to Fitzgerald, compiled 430 yards of total offense on 23 first downs, including 318 rushing. The Hornet could get just seven first downs and 75– yards total offense.

Offensively, halfback Al Dorminey was the statistical leader with three touchdowns and three extra point kicks for a 'fair' night's work. The 163–pound junior rambled for 150 yards on 14 carries, including one 70–yard scamper.

All-State quarterback Oscar Roberts completed 10 of 14 passes for 120 yards and chipped in 69 yards rushing on 15 tries....This talented 165–pound senior ran the well-oiled machine with that flair for obvious leadership.

Split end L.H. Dill was on the receiving end of eight Roberts' tosses for 72 yards. Bob Roland added 47 yards rushing and Art Davis 33.

Please don't forget the unsung heroes of any successful football team, the offensive line. The Indians opened up some holes big enough for the grandmas in the capacity audience of 3,000 to make yardage.

—*Daily Tifton Gazette*, November 23, 1968

After Oscar got by far the better of the brothers' game, the Indians had a bye week. Oscar was named Back of the Year, finishing with something like 1,000 yards and 1,000 more passing. On Friday of their week off we took interest in the Vidalia-Hawkinsville game. Irwin would face the winner a week later in the semifinal with a trip to the state title game on the line and it was Vidalia. That'd be an interesting match-up, since Kermit Elliott was from Vidalia and played football there when he was a boy. Maybe Kermit's ties mattered on both sides. Much was made in the papers about the Irwin-Vidalia clash being a homecoming of sorts for our coach.

"I've been gone a long time," Kermit told one reporter the week of the semifinal. "It fires me up a little more, I guess."

Vidalia, coached by John "Buck" Cravey, always played Irwin tough, and they brought another good team to the game in Vidalia on the night of December 6, holding a 9–3 mark that included victories over Bradwell Institute and Lyons, and while our boys ruled the stats sheet, it was a tough affair.

Irwin opened the scoring in the first quarter with a short toss from Oscar to halfback Bob Roland for six. The PAT was wide.

Vidalia hit pay dirt in the second quarter but missed the point after. The game was locked at six in the fourth when Roberts broke it up, scoring on a nine-yard keeper around left end with 10:06 remaining. Al Dorminy booted the PAT to put a lid on the scoring as Irwin advanced to the state championship game for the first time in 15 years.

The next night, No. 1 ranked Roswell defeated defending Class B champ Washington-Wilkes to get the game with No. 2 Irwin. The game at Roswell near Atlanta for the Class B marbles was played eight days later. Roswell had five boys on their team who made all-state. We had three.

With a caravan of excited fans trailing the buses, the Big Red traveled north on Thursday and stayed in Gainesville. The plan was for them to work out at North Hall Stadium but a cold front with rain moved in and forced the Indians inside a gymnasium. They had not brought any tennis shoes, so they worked out in the gym in their socks.

On Saturday afternoon, the Big Red drove to Roswell in the buses. About 500 fans in Greyhounds from Irwin County made the 200-mile trip north on December 14 to root for the underdog Indians.

Sports prophets forecasted a barn burner. Boy, you talk about cold! By kickoff, it was 15 degrees and windy like crazy. It was numbing, teeth-rattling cold. Members of the Irwin band couldn't blow their horns, so frigid was the cold. The boys from south Georgia where it never got this cold had not brought any sweat shirts. The field was suspiciously iced. Some Irwin boys suspected Roswell had wet the field so it would freeze to their advantage against the ill-prepared Indians who wore their regular steel-tipped cleats, which made their shoes like ice skates. Roswell boys wore the shorter cleats, like soccer shoes, that gave them better traction. They also wore jerseys with pockets in the front for keeping their hands warm.

When the captains met at midfield, Irwin won the coin toss. Kermit said for us to take the ball. Roswell elected to defend the side of the field where the wind was at their backs. They kicked off, and it was all downhill from there—if you were an Indian. "The first time they snapped the ball to me, all the linemen's feet went out from under them, and they fell on their knees," says Oscar Roberts.

The boys ran three plays to start the game before Art Davis was called on to punt. The ball went so high off his foot that the icy wind blew it backwards to about the Irwin seven. From there, Roswell quickly scored.

"I made a bad choice," Kermit says now, adding that he should've sent the boys on defense first.

Maybe it wouldn't have mattered. Our enemy was the field. "We were slip-sliding away," Glenn Tucker muses.

"It was so cold that night, we couldn't even think about playing football," says Ricky Brown, a senior that year who played guard on offense and linebacker. "It was so cold, and we did good to stand up. It was like a skating rink. We didn't play nothing like our game. We were not prepared for what we ran into."

Glenn Tucker remembers how on one play our center, Franklin Sumner, was over the ball when his feet slid. The ball moved just a little, and Roswell jumped on it. The referee called it a fumble and gave Roswell the ball.

"It was just a bad situation," Kermit laments.

The Big Red machine's potent offense froze up and never got started. The passing game in particular was checked. Irwin fans trying to be the coach kept begging Kermit to call more pass plays, but it wasn't much good either and down went the Big Red.

> *Irwin County fell short in its bid for the Class B state championship here Saturday night by falling to favored Roswell, 32–7, in sub-freezing temperatures and light flurries of snow.*
>
> *Roswell's touted defense bottled up the Irwin attack throughout most of the game, although All-State quarterback Oscar Roberts did complete 11 of 17 passes for 124 yards and one touchdown.*
>
> *The Indians of coach Kermit Elliott could gain only 15 yards on the ground as Roberts was held to minus 41 yards rushing. Wheelus Davis and Lamar Howell made up this deficit by rushing for 20 yards each, high for Irwin ...*
>
> *An interesting incident was the steady flow of fans escaping to their warm cars and homes. During the halftime proceedings, the lights were turned off for special effects for the Roswell program. When the field was lighted again, over half of the some 500 Ocilla fans and some of the Roswell fans had decided to depart for warmer or friendlier quarters.*
>
> *A large cloud of smoke hung over the field during the game as a result of a large fire built by the less-hearty fans at one end of the stadium. It was so cold that a hot cup of coffee left unattended during the half-time show had turned to ice by the start of the second half."*
>
> —Danny Carter, *Tifton Gazette*

Irwin finished No. 2 in the state in '68 with a 11–2 mark, and that was very good although we did not reach the goal, which was to win it all. Everybody was proud of the boys, proud, too, that Oscar went on to play at Florida State, following in the footsteps of his brother Marion and Walter Sumner.

Now when they look back, many who played for Irwin County in Roswell that night regret the ice and all.

Says Glenn Tucker, who later worked for the railroad: "I'd like to catch them on a warm night in south Georgia, then we'd see."

Under better conditions, or at least with comparable cleats, says Kermit, "I'm not saying we could've won the game, but I'm just saying on a level playing field, the score could've been a little better."

Say Ricky Brown: "We thought they watered the field intentionally. We think that they turned the sprinklers on. It was like a skating rink. We didn't have the right cleats to play on that mess."

Playing ball in Ocilla was a once-in-a-lifetime experience for the boys of '68. As men, they recall a gritty team well-supported who could've played with anybody in any class.

"For a Class B school, we had a lot," says Brown. "I can see all them old boys now when you stop and think about it."

Oscar Roberts never ventured too far away, except for playing football at Florida State, and after college he worked at a bank in Valdosta for a short time before his wife, the former Janis Luke, grew homesick so they moved back to Ocilla where they went on to raise three children, all boys, while helping manage the Luke Brothers agriculture and propane industry.

Ricky Brown took a different route to success. After high school, he signed to play football at Harding College in Arkansas. A four-year starter at guard, Ricky once made All-Conference, first team. Nothing against Ocilla, but he never came back, other than now and then to visit his Mama and them.

"Playing football in Ocilla was special. I just loved it," says Ricky, who now lives on a nice spread near Little Rock, Arkansas. "On Friday night, the whole town would shut down and go to the ball game." He remembers Johnny King and the booster club grilling steaks for the boys on Thursday nights at Robert Fain's cabin in the woods. "We used to go into Johnny's on Saturday after the game and he'd feed us a hamburger."

Ricky's made a good living in the construction business. He says he might've come back to Ocilla after college to settle down with his wife and raise a family "if I could've made a living there."

Ricky's not the only one who's ever said that about their old home town where there has never been much work for young people.

40

Lanny Roberts Memorial Stadium

Last Friday night was one of acclaim, recognition and awards-giving as Irwin County High School athletes in all fields and their coaches were honored at a banquet in the high school cafetorium.

The occasion was the All-Sports Banquet sponsored by the Athletic Booster Club in recognition of the high school athletic program and in honor of its participants. Although the awards program was a lengthy one, it successfully accomplished the goal for which it was intended...

Booster club president Johnny King welcomed the guests who numbered approximately 400. King cited some of the accomplishments during the year and called on club treasurer Joe Portier to give "a very fine financial report."

—*Ocilla Star*, January 23, 1969

It was a big night in little Ocilla. Johnny King's dedication to Indian football was recognized by the Booster Club's Knot Tucker who emceed the January 1969 sports banquet. The robust, cigar-puffing, chunkily-built King, who loved the boys like sons, was given a standing ovation when presented with the game ball used in the victory over Vidalia. Kermit Elliott was named Middle Georgia Coach of the Year by the *Macon Telegraph* and given a color television. Later, Kermit would say how much he and his wife, Norma, appreciated the TV and the work of all the boosters to make football in Ocilla a special place in the autumn time.

Coach Gary Wyatt of Florida State was the guest speaker. According to the *Star*'s account of the banquet, Wyatt *directed his talk to being a real winner. Wyatt said the real winner is he who goes about his task with a 'clear, vivid picture in mind of what he is seeking in life.' Wyatt, in his opening remarks, paid a fine compliment to a former Irwin County High athlete who has been under Wyatt's supervision at FSU, when he said, 'I would be greatly honored if my son grows up to be like Walter Sumner.'*

Then at the close of ceremonies, high school principal Adams read a statement:

Irwin County High School athletes have been playing on a field which has no name. Much consideration has been given to the naming of the football field. At most schools in Georgia, football fields do have a name. The local administration, the county administration and the Irwin County Athletic Booster Club all have approved the naming of our athletic field. Because of the dedication of this person, his dedicated contribution to his community and county, his contribution in the field of public relations and because of his dedication to the tasks of the athletic program, the athletic field will be named the Lanny Roberts Memorial Stadium, as of this date, January 17, 1969.

The crowd warmly approved with its applause and the field would be used for Indian varsity football for the next 60 years. It was the first time an Ocilla field had been named for anyone since 1926 when the old ball yard in town was named for E. V. Whelchel. It was an awesome tribute that Johnny King and his associates had made to the late Lanny Roberts. Everybody missed seeing Lanny. And then lo and behold, Johnny King was dead. Just five days after the banquet, King was in a car wreck near Ocilla and died within a week. While losing Lanny was foreseen with his failing health, Johnny King was a hearty man whose untimely death was a blow to the Big Red as well as the Ocilla business community. The football team, coaches included, served as honorary pall bearers.

John B. King—always impeccably dressed in dark trousers, black tie and white shirt—was from Fitzgerald but spent a lot of time in Ocilla where he was elected president of the Irwin County Athletic Booster Club. A former Marine, Johnny returned home to Ware County after World War II to try farming. In 1956, he moved to Fitzgerald where he started a restaurant, the Purple Duck, before leasing the Osceola restaurant in Ocilla, where he was adopted as one of our own.

Johnny's efforts to strengthen the program in Ocilla were legendary. He gave much time and energy to upkeep the playing field which, under his work, was the best in south Georgia as far as beautiful grass.

His little diner sat across from the Osceola Motel. You could get a full-course meal and short orders such as sandwiches, and it was the place to catch up on and spread the gossip. The cash register sat on a glass case that displayed candy and cigars for sale. The wall on the left side as you walked in had hundreds, maybe thousands, of pennies glued to it along with black-and-white photographs Johnny had acquired of Irwin County football stars.

In the fall, Johnny also kept a blackboard in the restaurant for football stats from the previous Indian game. Any Indian boy who passed Johnny on the street or came to his place to eat or get a cold drink was made to feel like somebody.

According to the accident report the *Star* on January 30, 1969, King was driving alone in a 1961 Ford about 8:00 p.m., two miles north of Ocilla on US Highway 129, when his car rounded a curve on the wrong side of the road and collided head-on with a car driven by L. D. Phillips of Tifton. Phillips and his wife were killed in the collision.

We always heard that King's last words were, "Go, Big Red."

In May of '69 there was another blow to the family although it did not involve a literal death - Coach Elliott was out.

"I did not have that desire…I had fulfilled the desire that I had," Kermit says, looking back on his decision to resign as head coach. "I was tired of the attitude of some…They really…I just felt like my hands were tied." He did not elaborate.

Popular in the community, Kermit remained in Ocilla. He took a banking job here, and the good people were glad that he stayed – and he never coached again.

"The community, more or less, had accepted me, and I was offered the job at First State Bank," Kermit says almost half a century later and still in the Ocilla banking business.

In the summer of '69, with Kermit out, the door to the teepee swung open and in stepped a fellow on slightly bowed legs. A new day in Irwin football had arrived. A smallish man, he had a funny name, close-cropped hair and a chaw.

The "Red Man" man was here.

Part V

41

Red Man!

Irwin County and Fitzgerald will meet head on Friday night in Ocilla's Lanny Roberts Memorial Stadium. Although nothing is really at stake as far as Region records are concerned...this is the game both teams point for, sometimes too much.

Actually both have more important games coming up in playoff competition but it would be hard to convince the players and the die-hard fans from each city.

Sometimes the teams point so hard for this contest that they hurt themselves in the playoffs, as with the Indians of 1964.

Although this is billed as a grudge match, it is really not as important as the playoffs coming up. As badly as all the fans want to win, they should remember that the players want to win even more. One of the teams must lose, unless it's a tie, and as badly as we'll feel if our team loses, remember the boys will feel worse. Each boy will give 100 percent, win or lose....There are times when we all fall short, not because of lack of effort...So win or lose let's have the right mental attitude, realizing that they are just boys, giving it all they have, capable of great heights and dismal failures, tremendous happiness and deep hurt.

Let's stick with the boys and give them 100 percent too. Win or lose, they're still ours.

—Charlie Ridgeway, *Ocilla Star*, November 13, 1969

Our new coach was known to friends as Buzzy, a nickname he says he picked up in elementary school for talking in class. Anyway, that's how the tobacco chewer who took over for Kermit Elliott in the summer of 1969 signed his name: Buzzy McMillan.

John McMillan at birth, he grew up in Augusta, Georgia, got into coaching at Wade Hampton in South Carolina and was an assistant coach in Macon when he heard that Kermit was out in Ocilla. Buzzy jumped at the opening. He drove down to Ocilla, interviewed and ultimately got the work.

Kermit, who knew Buzzy from college, says that while he did not twist any arms to get Buzzy the Ocilla job, "I didn't do anything to hurt his chances."

The boosters were fond of the new coach and the boys liked a lot of what he did and bought into his scheme. Like Buzzy, several boys on the team chewed tobacco, so they felt right at home with Buzzy, who didn't seem to mind the boys chewing but they could not smoke.

Certainly, Buzzy made a mark on the program and was his own man.

Buzzy McMillan, center, in 1969 with assistants Weyman Vickers, L, and Jett Beckhum. *Courtesy ICHS 1969-70 yearbook / copied by David Pierce*

Before the start of the 1969 season, among his first peculiar acts as chief, in addition to taking the boys to a coastal camp, Buzzy fitted the Indians into white helmets. He also made them yell *Red Man!* with a clap of their hands when they broke the huddle. The boys had to bark it out loudly in unison*, Red Man!,* and charge the scrimmage line or else Buzzy would be sore at them for not hustling. And the boys all wanted to hustle for Buzzy because he was such a great guy and fun to play for.

Some fans frowned. It was too much change and so sudden, particularly about the helmets. Traditionalists liked the old color – red, our crowning glory – and did not see the need for new headgear to start with.

But a lot was overlooked, if not forgiven, in Red Territory when Buzzy's boys of 1969 spent a lot of time ranked No. 1 in Class B.

After being whipped into shape at Camp Viking, the gnat-bitten Indians took nine scalps in a row on the way to 10–2 finish and brought home another region crown. While it hurt to lose Oscar Roberts and them to graduation, there were some good athletes on the 1969 squad who made a difference. Lamar Howell stepped in at quarterback with mean ability. The wheel horse, Al Dorminy, who later signed with the University of Florida Gators, was as hard to tackle as any man in cleats and his sidekick, Bob Roland, was fast as anyone.

"I didn't leave Buzzy without any material," Kermit Elliott remembers.

And Buzzy knew how to work it.

Ronnie Barrs, L, in 1969, with teammates Al Dorminey, Lamar Howell, Bob Roland and Gerald "Head" Hunter. *Courtesy of ICHS Library / copied from 1969-70 yearbook by Lucy Pierce*

Though a loss at Vidalia kept us from going to state again—and earlier we were beaten down by Fitzgerald—10 wins and just a couple of losses made the best first-year record for any coach in Irwin County history.

For his good work in 1969, Buzzy was named the Class B Coach of the Year, the second year in a row that an Irwin County coach had won the award.

No doubt about it; Buzzy was a keeper in the year of 1969. But you know how it is in coaching.

Before moving on, let's back up to the white helmets.

Why white?

Well, Buzzy says, it was nothing he had against the red ones. But he wanted a new look: white helmets over red jerseys and gray pants. Besides, white was cheaper than ones of color. He says helmet makers had the base white; colored hats from the company he dealt with cost more. Going with the standard white was softer on the budget and easier to get one replaced if it broke. "It was an economic reason," Buzzy says.

The new helmets that featured cage-style facemask for the linemen had a sticker over the ear hole. You had to put the stickers on yourself. The sticker design that Buzzy imagined was not a number but a logo in the likeness of a charging Indian brave. On each logo were the words *Red Man*, which happened to be Buzzy's chaw of choice that came in a green-and-white pouch.

"I did chew Red Man," the old coach says. But he says that wasn't the reason for the Red Man sticker or making the boys bark Red Man when they broke the huddle. "I was looking for something that would sound good coming out of the huddle and that was a snappy name for it: *Red Man!*"

Also, summer camp changed when Buzzy hit town. Gone were the days of holding camp in Ocilla. Instead, the week-long work was conducted in mid-August near the Georgia coast at

Camp Viking, which Buzzy knew about from his days at Hinesville. The private camp in Liberty County hosted high school athletic teams and somebody told our boys that it was named after the NFL's Minnesota Vikings.

Buzzy told the *Star* in August 1969 that our first trip to Viking was for a period of shaping up and to get acquainted with the coaching staff far from the distractions of home. And Viking was about as far away from Ocilla as outer space, or roughly 125 miles.

That summer, which began the long and loyal career of Indian assistant coach Weyman Vickers, there were cabins for sleeping and a dining hall. The cabins faced a large, open field like a cow pasture where the drills were conducted. It never rained and was always very hot and humid.

There was no air-conditioning in the cabins, just a fan, and you never saw anyone from back home like you were in the Army. If you ran away homesick or sick of football it'd take two days to find civilization. You were pretty well out of luck, and for many an Indian boy, Viking was the first encounter with sand fleas.

"It was a hell hole is all I remember," says Derrell Young, who played an end position. "It was rough." Looking at back now at old Viking, "We enjoyed it. It was fun."

42
Integration

While Fitzgerald's team had been integrated for a couple of years already, Irwin County got its first black players into football in 1970 and it worked out fine. These pioneers from the "black school" across town in the poor district of Ocilla called "the Hill" were a natural fit because for many years, friendships among the kids had crossed racial lines.

The new boys in football was just one aspect of the integration movement that had been winding through the schools.

Nobody says there wasn't a Civil Rights issue in Ocilla. We were told that some white men came here from Cook County with baseball bats to make trouble. But as for football, the kids were all right. To us, there was always room in the Big Red teepee for new members to join the fight and help the Indians to win.

By this time the federal court order to desegregate public schools across America was working as well as it could in Irwin County. The order, which stemmed from a 1954 case in Kansas, was unpopular across Dixie and in Irwin, devising a plan to meet the mandate was not a bowl of cherries. But there's no record here that anyone threw sticks and stones or blocked the entrances when our public schools were opened to black pupils, and in the end there was more outrage over the killing of a dog.

"I remember it went pretty smooth; didn't have the trouble they had in other places," says Richard Fussell, who helped usher in the age of desegregation of Irwin County Hi as principal of the school from 1969-70.

Someone had killed a dog belonging to principal W.H. Adams of the high school that caused quite a row.

Fussell, now 82, who was a follower of segregationist George Wallace, doffs his cap to the courageous Alfonso Owens. Owens, who was the principal of now long-defunct Ocilla Hi & Industrial School, paved the way for court-ordered desegregation of schools to work in Irwin County where change was slow and never easy.

"Alfonso Owens did not put up with any racism in the public schools. He wanted kids to get an education," Fussell says.

Mr. Fussell, who passed out stickers for George Wallace and was traveling with the campaign when the presidential candidate was gunned down, came to Ocilla from Reidsville, Georgia, to replace principal Adams, who had resigned in May 1969.

"I wasn't all that concerned" about desegregation in Ocilla, Fussell says. "I'd been in the military in Korea and I had worked with every kind of people and I knew it could be handled."

Certainly, in the theater that was football in Ocilla integration worked. There was no tragedy on the team, no protests or quitting among the pale-faced boys when our first black players from Industrial took the field with the Indians. We were glad to have them. It was an interesting time – integrating the ball team. Before that, there's no telling how good we might've been with such men as the spectacular Loren Moses of Ocilla toting the pigskin for us.

"I wanted to play but … that's a long story," says Mr. Moses, hesitating. "There were just some things that occurred that I could not tolerate."

That's all Loren Moses would say.

Loren graduated from Irwin Hi in 1969 and recalls having many white friends in football, friends who wished he'd play. He went on to star in track at Fort Valley State where he ran the 100-yard dash in 9.6 seconds.

In the spring of 1970, after drilling the white boys, Buzzy worked closely with the in-coming black kids to teach them the ways of football they did not understand. The new players also had to have equipment, which Buzzy arranged for. We were told the new uniforms, pads and all Buzzy bought to equip a team were a strong lick against the budget. We heard grumblings that Buzzy spent more on the black players than the white ones. That did not concern the team very much. Like the rest of us, the newcomers reported for summer camp and we all made it work. The mixed-race team was helped to work by this being a small, rural community where a lot of our young men had friends of either race, partly from working side by side on the farms and knowing one another from being about town, and so the transition to a mixed-color squad came natural.

Kenny Moses, brother of Loren, was one who helped blaze the trail for black athletes at Irwin County Hi. Speedy at the time, although he was not as fast as Loren, Kenny Moses says now that he did not want to go to the white school.

"I liked it where I was at," Kenny says, referring to the Industrial School whose teams were the Wildcats. They did not have football at Industrial.

Now involved in a Jehovah's Witnesses ministry, Kenneth Moses remembers his father told him that integration was inevitable. Looking back, "It wasn't hard," he says of transferring to the formerly all-white Irwin County Hi where football players were big dogs on campus. "Everything went pretty smooth as far as I'm concerned. Didn't get any real friction from anyone. It was just all new."

When Kenny came out for football, we were happy to have the humble kid with speed enlist to fight for Big Red victories.

"Football wasn't even my sport," says Kenny with a chuckle, when reminded that he was about the fastest Indian footballer at that time. "I liked track and field. That's pretty much all we had at the black school."

Today, more so than for integration, former principal Fussell, who now resides in Americus, Georgia, fondly remembers the Ocilla community for its generous, hearty people. "I enjoyed it. It was a good town," he says, where folks routinely left treats on his doorstep, such as sweet potatoes and buttermilk, to make him and his family feel special.

"They found out I liked buttermilk. I'd open the door and there'd be some buttermilk."

As for the killing of the dog, Fussell says he put an end to the matter when he paddled three boy suspects who were named to him by principal's office secretary Martha Cook, wife of former coach Ralph Cook.

43

Playing to Win

Lamar Howell, who made the big plays for the Indians when they reeled off three straight victories to open the season before being injured, returned to action last Friday night and Irwin County returned to winning, dumping Pelham 27-12. Irwin had lost three in a row with Howell on the sidelines.

Ocilla Star, Oct. 29, 1970

This is definitely a rebuilding year for the Indians, Buzzy McMillan commented to the *Star* at the start of the 1970 season. *We have only four starters back from last year's team, and we've a long way to go.*

Filled with the spirit of winning, the boys thought Buzzy was sandbagging our foes, which was sort of cool. We'd sneak up on people, win region, go to state. Funnier things had happened. The whole Indian family wanted to believe this could be our year.

But Buzzy wasn't kidding and maybe too often the boys did not play very well. There were some crippling injuries during the season also. The key casualty was our best player, Lamar Howell, a farm boy who came from a long line of Howell brothers to play football in Ocilla. The first footballing Howell was Jimmy, whose nickname was *Peanut.* He graduated in 1964 and then came Sammy, followed by Lamar, Donnie and then Ronnie. Their dad, Jesse, was a farmer most famous for growing cantaloupe and watermelons.

The hard-driving Lamar was supposed to be our horse that year, having moved to halfback, passing to William Cook the quarterback duties, but Lamar battled a very nasty deep thigh bruise suffered at a scrimmage in Savannah during camp week that sidelined him a lot and in a small community where you don't have a groundswell of talent every year, if you lose your lead dog, like Lamar, and the other boys do not play up to their potential, you're not making the playoffs.

"A coach on the field," Buzzy once said of Lamar. "He was a great competitor and had a lot of talent."

The Indians stepped back up that year to Class A and appeared in silver-grayish helmets, which replaced the white ones. The new color harkened to the 1950s and early 1960s, which some found amusing, and they had a new peel-and-stick arrowhead on either side above the ear hole, and the boys also got new jerseys.

Teammates Robert Griffin, L, Troy Smith and Mike Brown at spring training 1970.
Courtesy ICHS 1970-71 yearbook / copied by David Pierce

We shot out of the gate fine, going 3–0, giving up only six points before heading to Fitzgerald on September 25. The AA Hurricane, under Jesse Dyess, was also undefeated and as usual was picked to beat the Class-A Indians, especially with Lamar unable to go.

Very early in the first quarter a feel of magic crept into the air just for an instant, like this night was destiny for Irwin to beat Fitz for the first time in seven years. The cool brush of hope on a warm evening was felt on our necks when hard-running James Griffin of Ocilla, a sophomore, cracked the line. Hardly any time had gone off the clock and most people were still standing when James ripped the defense at full gallop.

The Irwin side roared at the sight of James digging for the goal line.

James remembers that play. "It was a 22 trap," he says, then adds, "I was 10 yards out when somebody nailed me and I fumbled."

From another angle, it appeared as if James dropped the ball; that he wasn't hit; that the ball just came loose as he was chugging. Either way, it went as a fumble and there was a gasp of disbelief on our side of the field as ole Fitz, in those gold helmets like Notre Dame, pounced on the loose pigskin and they went on to beat our brains out.

Later on in a game we needed to win for playoff sake, the 1970 Indians hosted Seminole County, again without Lamar. It was a tough scrap and with only six seconds on the clock we made a touchdown on an eight–yard toss from William Cook to Art Davis to climax a 90–yard drive and move Irwin to within a point of tying it up at 14. Buzzy said to go for two. So we set up to go for broke but the run play we attempted was stopped short and there went our ponies.

> *Because Seminole won they are still in a position to win the region championship,"* Ronnie Wheeler wrote for the *Star*. *"However, losing the game does not eliminate Irwin. There is still a chance, a good chance, for Coach McMillan to pull the Indians out of the fire. Finally, to clarify something: Many people have accused Coach McMillan of not doing his job because he called a PAT play and chose to run instead of kick for a tie. The reason for this is plain and simple: Irwin County plays to win, not to tie.*

Irwin did not survive the fire, losing a shot at the playoffs when Turner County held us to a 13–13 tie, giving the unbeaten Rebels from Ashburn the region title.

It was the first time that Irwin had not made the playoffs since 1966 and so the season of 1970 was checked in the disappointment column.

After the season, and despite his injury, Lamar made all-state. East Laurens, a team we defeated 21–6 in the final game, presented Lamar with a plaque as the Most Outstanding Opponent. The unusual award was given at Dublin during the East Laurens sports banquet. The *Star* carried a page one photo of Lamar and Buzzy with the small plaque between them. *Lamar is the best all-around back I have coached in nine years,* Buzzy was quoted as saying.

Lamar signed to play college football at Southern Mississippi and became a corporate accountant.

In 1971, spring training went very well for the Indians. There were 63 of us out for ball. Leading the way on the line would be senior guard and linebacker Mike Brown, the hard-cut younger brother of former Indian star Ricky Brown, with Derrell Young and Anthony "Preach" Jenkins at ends; two powerful juniors, James Griffin and Tommy Benson, would key the backfield along with Kenny Moses. As spring practice under Buzzy closed, everyone was looking forward to school letting out for the summer and, come fall, we felt we'd be really strong and win back the region and, maybe, take a little more.

Then the reservation was hit by a bomb. There was no team meeting about it or anything. There was just smoke and fumes and the rotten smell of rumor.

Boys were extremely anxious. It was really quite a shock to lose Buzzy.

Team captains Derrell Young, l, Mike Brown and David Pierce in spring training 1971. *Courtesy Ocilla Star / copied by David Pierce*

44

'Wasn't All My Idea'

Coach Buzzy McMillan has assumed duties as athletic director and head football and track coach at Murray County High School in Chatsworth, Georgia. Murray County is in Region 5–A.

Coach McMillan...resigned at ICHS early this year and recently announced the acceptance of the Murray County post....

"This [ICHS athletes] is one of the finest groups of young men I have ever worked with," McMillan said recently. "Every one of them put their whole heart into the game and that is what it takes to make a winner."

Coach McMillan also expressed appreciation to the boys' parents and "all other Irwin Countians for their help and support in the last two years."

Local citizens have extended best wishes to Coach McMillan for success in his new position at Murray County, and appreciation to him for his work at ICHS.

~ *Ocilla Star,* July 1, 1971

"Buzzy was a good man. I liked him," says Bobby Dix, a strong Booster Club member in the 1960s and '70s.

"I thought he was a good coach," says Lamar Howell, who now resides in Tifton. "I'd loved for him to have stayed on in Irwin County for a long time."

But like an old ball coach from Dublin, Georgia, Ben Snipes, used to say about coaching: "You get on the wrong side of the right people and they've got enough power to put you in the road."

And Buzzy had gotten on someone's wrong side.

While on the surface it appeared to be a case of a man ready for a change, maybe to a bigger school, "it wasn't all my idea," Buzzy says now, adding that he's not sure why the powers did not bring him back for a third season. "It sort of caught me off guard but those things happen in life."

Boys returning for the 1971 season who liked Buzzy and thought we could do great things with him as coach were angry and mystified. Many at first felt betrayed by the coach for leaving. But then it was decided there must be something behind the whole affair that Buzzy could not control that caused him to be thrown overboard.

"I appreciate that," Buzzy says when informed that some boys he'd coached in Ocilla tried to save his job.

Boys in his corner had only pieces of the story and did not understand many things. The Buzzy affair in 1971 was not played out in the *Star* and he did not address the team.

"They fired Buzzy," says James Griffin, one of our half backs at the time.

Boys took it from the fruits of the gossip tree that Buzzy was sacked for his handling of black players, particularly for spending so much to equip the new athletes; failure to make the playoff; failure to keep up the new gym, especially the sinks, and for being absent too often needlessly.

The rumors were all very confusing to the hearts of the youth who didn't have the whole story. A few boys and parents loyal to Buzzy begged school officials in the summer of 1971 to let Buzzy come back. The board, meeting at the Courthouse, would not discuss the matter with them. Later, an article appeared in the *Star* that implied Buzzy's departure was a done deal as early as spring.

Few who had the inside scoop are alive now to talk about it. Harry Mixon, an Ocilla attorney whose son, Warren, was our center on the 1970 team, says the problem with Buzzy was, "he spent too much money." Mixon did not offer a figure. One sum ginned up at the rumor mill was $13,000 owed to two equipment companies for purchases the school board had not authorized. Somebody said the equippers froze the school's credit for nonpayment; that the booster club, with whom Buzzy had been close, would have to help pay off the debt.

"Buzzy bought what he wanted to and charged it to the Board of Education (and) they couldn't pay for it," Bobby Dix says. Mr. Dix remembers the school board called Buzzy onto the carpet to remind him that "they were his boss; that the booster club was not his boss." A retired postman and farmer, Dix says Buzzy visited him and another booster asking for their help to save his job. "He came out here and talked to me and I said, *Buzzy, it's too late. You gotta go.*"

According to Harry Mixon, after Buzzy had gone, a stash of green jerseys in boxes was found in a basement somewhere in Ocilla, suggesting the coach had bought the outrageous tops for the boys to wear instead of the traditional reds, which would have been blasphemous.

"Green jerseys?" Buzzy says with a laugh when told of the discovery. "I don't know anything about that."

Before Buzzy left Ocilla, while he was still in the packing phase, Ben Snipes and Phil Jones, who were in town to interview for his job, visited the beleaguered coach at his home. Snipes says he had heard of board members in Ocilla "putting Buzzy down." He and Jones wanted to get Buzzy's side of the story.

Snipes would not divulge Buzzy's reply.

After coaching in Murray County for two years, he worked for a little while at a carpet plant but a good deal of his life after coaching was spent in banking.

"I still have fond memories," of Ocilla where, he says, "the community spirit" made football special.

His son coaches high school football in North Carolina. Buzzy, now reported to be bald, portly and living in Calhoun, says to say hello to his old friends back in Ocilla, and yes, Buzzy says, he still chews Red Man. Although he admits he could lose a little weight, he says he feels good.

"I'm 75 years old and I don't need a walker."

45

A Hard Transition

The Irwin County High School Indians opening their 1971 grid season in Alma last Friday night put on an offense show that shut out the Red Raiders from Bacon County 34–0. The Big Red, led by junior James Griffin, ran up more than 300 yards total offense in the effort while the Indian defensive unit held the Raiders to less than 25 yards. It was definitely a show of power by the Indians and likely a salute to new ICHS head coach Conrad Nix.

~ *Ocilla Star*, September 9, 1971

There were many qualities Irwin County school officials were looking for in a new coach to replace Buzzy. Certainly, he'd have to win. Maybe take some hall duty. And, obviously, the new bonnet-wearer must know who was his boss; the school board ruled, not the Booster Club. So, feelers went out. Calls were made. One call went to a residence in Lincoln, Alabama.

"They just got my name," says Conrad Nix. "I had coached in Warner Robins for a couple of years, and they called me right at the end of the school year."

That was in the summer of 1971, when Buzzy's old job was up for grabs, and because he had coached in Georgia before, Nix had knowledge of our program.

He remembers discussing the Ocilla opportunity with his wife, Patsy. "We came down for a visit and things materialized from there."

Nix put in a call to one of his Lincoln assistants. "When I took the job at Ocilla, I called him up and said: *Mike, we're going to Ocilla, Georgia*, and he said, *All right*."

Mike Battles had never heard of Ocilla or the Big Red.

"I told him it was going to be okay," Nix adds.

Battles, then 23, could not get to Ocilla right away; he was in summer school at Southern Mississippi finishing classes for a teaching certificate. But that did not delay Mr. Nix any. After moving here, Conrad and a crew collected Battles' things from Alabama, loaded them onto a truck and transported the load 290 miles to Ocilla. They dropped off his belongings at the front of the gymnasium on Sixth Street at the high school.

When Mike arrived, he drove straight to Douglas, Georgia, where the team was in summer camp, and was put in charge of the defense. He lived that summer in the gym at Ocilla before he and his wife, Carolyn, moved into a house.

Nix says life as a coach in Ocilla took some getting used to.

Coach Nix, L, in 1971 with assistants, L-r: Mike Battles, Weyman Vickers, Ronnie Burgamy and Tim Rankin. *Courtesy ICHS 1971-72 yearbook / copied by David Pierce*

"When I went there, I don't know why, but I had to go the board meetings and the board would meet til about eight or nine o'clock and then we sat on the steps of the courthouse til one o'clock in the morning talking." Nix recalls. "They had a vision of winning and wanted to win."

Straight-laced with a military-style persona, Nix failed to connect with some of the older players who'd been loyal to Buzzy. But that did not deter Nix, who came bearing the whip—not milk and a warm blanket for a pity party.

"It was a hard transition" from the Buzzy days, says Richard Williamson, who was the high school principal. Although "as a coach he cared about kids and was probably the best motivational coach that I ever saw … Nix came on strong,"

And some boys bucked who didn't like Nix's attitude or his game.

"I think that's pretty common," says Mike Battles. "Every time a coach comes in you have those who liked the old coach and those who are looking for a change. You just have to go in and fit with the community. You go in and do your thing and hope it works."

The first time he met with the boys in the gym on a hot summer afternoon in 1971, Nix, sporting gold shorts, the color of Fitzgerald, which was a mark against him, told the players that Jesus should come first in their lives. Later he introduced the team to the Jericho Road, a hard conditioning drill. Although eventually he found gray shorts to wear, Nix left little doubt that he wasn't Buzzy.

Camp that year was conducted at South Georgia College in Douglas, 25 miles away, and it was tougher in many ways even than Buzzy camps, except you were not as gnat-bitten as at Camp Viking.

Nix had us run the Wishbone offense, which was new to the region, and after a week of Camp Nix, Christmas came early with the arrival of new uniforms. Although he had restored Irwin to red helmets, which was a feather in his bonnet, Nix had put away the red-and-gray jerseys and pants of the past. In their place were new white, skin-tight knit pants for the boys to wear with lightweight, modern, mesh-type red jerseys you could see through that looked almost pink over white t-shirts. Not every boy was appreciative.

Nix also introduced the club to girdle pads. Some boys howled, reported to feel naked and sissy in the new-style outfit and wondering to themselves what was so wrong with the old-style uniforms that prior Indians had worn in our playoff years?

It was a tough season. Certainly, the boys were not the team they wanted to be, or what some had thought they would be, if Buzzy had stayed, and probably a few of the older boys did not play up to their ability.

We got off to a blazing start, though. After wiping out Bacon County at Alma in the opener, the boys made a tremendous goal line stand at Nashville to beat the Rebels of AA Berrien County 6–0 in the final seconds as the big crowd on both sides stood. In week three, the first home game, the boys got over on 1–A South foe Miller County, 15–8, and prepared to lick Fitzgerald for the first time since 1964.

The game was rated a toss-up, with a nod to Fitz, and in the end the statistics were close. But reality was cold and the Canes broke our tomahawk. Basically, the Indians had no answer for Fitz quarterback Eddie Luke. Eddie Mac Dix of Ocilla, who was 5-feet, 5 inches, had a tough night trying to cover receivers almost a foot taller.

Then later in the season of 1971 star lineman and linebacker Mike Brown, who'd played football since he was small, a natural athlete, hard and rugged, quit the club after a closed-door powwow in the field house with Coach Nix. Losing Mike for reasons that were not made known to the team by Coach Nix was huge and there were key injuries and instability at quarterback that affected the outcome of certain games as well. Some boys on the 1971 squad were benched in favor of younger players as Nix was evidently positioning a team to make a run in 1972.

On September 1, 1971, we took a hard loss at Donalsonville, falling to Seminole County 13–7 in a crucial region game in which our two workhorse backs—juniors James Griffin and Tommy Benson—were injured in the first quarter. It was a tough night and then after the game Nix did not endear himself to the deflated tribe. Some mamas of the Indian players had prepared sack meals of fried chicken for the team to eat on the bus ride back to Ocilla. But Coach Nix, disgusted with our poor play and all, said no chicken. It was a sick kind of lousy night and everyone was upset.

"The first year was sort of okay," Conrad Nix says of the 7–3 record, "but it wasn't up to the expectations or whatever."

Certainly, 1971 wasn't what the seniors had been hoping for their whole life.

Mike Brown, never a fan of Nix, says, "I believe if we'd had Buzzy we'd have won the state championship."

46

Rude Awakening

Coach Conrad Nix and his Indians will be in Camilla Friday and indications are that most of Irwin county's folks will be there too. There is still a question hovering over Eddie Mac Dix who received a knee injury in the Vidalia game. He may not get to play or may see limited action. Walter Hudson, who missed the Vidalia game because of an injury, likely will return to the line-up Friday. Meanwhile, folks in Ocilla are grooming their 'boys' for the contest. Activity will reach a peak tonight with a community-wide pep rally at the high school. Contests scheduled will pit local fans, in male and female categories, for 'Big Mouth' awards. The rally is expected to bring out all the 'Go' signs. There has been no word on a motorcade from Ocilla going to Camilla,

> *but from reports, the route to Camilla is going to be bumper-to-bumper with Irwin vehicles anyway.*
>
> —*Ocilla Star*, November 31, 1972

Finally, in 1972, the Big Red was smoking. Nix's wishbone attack produced one of the most potent offenses in Georgia that year. Defensively, despite the loss of top Nix assistant Mike Battles, who went back to Alabama to coach, the boys held most foes in check. Six victories were shutouts as the boys of 1972 went 10–0 for the first time since Walter Sumner's team did it for us in '64, which was also the last time we'd stopped the Hurricane, and beating Fitzgerald was always a good sign for Irwin County.

"We had a great football team," recalls Richard Williamson, who was in his second year as principal of the high school.

James Griffin, one of many seniors on the squad, did a yeoman's work for us that year. When healthy, there wasn't a better back you'd want on your team than No. 23. The hard-charging Indian set the Georgia record in 1972 for single-game rushing with more than 400 yards, and it held for many years. While Kenny Moses was probably faster on a dead run, James was more of a cutter, a slasher, ripping defenses like a belt saw through a piece of pine.

"James was ultra-talented," says Eddie Mac Dix, a former teammate. "He could run sideways and backward as fast as he could forward. I called him 'running scared.' He was jumpy quick, had big thighs…and he would see things out of the corner of his eye and he would react. You couldn't get your hands on him."

Not bad for a kid who never wanted to play football.

"I played for my daddy," James says.

Growing up the youngest of three children born to Vincent and Virginia Griffin, James was content to check oil and tires, wash windshields and pump gas at his father's service station on Irwin Avenue.

The elder Griffin never played ball but wanted to see James play. "I just didn't want to play," James recalls.

Seeing his friends pass by the station going to and from football practice did not faze James. Then one morning, he and his father were sitting at the Osceola restaurant, having biscuits and sausage. James remembers Johnny King came over to their table and asked if James was going out for football like the other boys.

Mr. Griffin, somewhat forlornly, spoke up and said no, James was not going to participate.

Hearing this, James—who loved his father very much and knew how much the game meant to him and to the community—said to his old man, *Okay, I'll play; I'll play for you.* His parents never missed a game together.

James recalls those good ole days when football was king in Ocilla. "Every time we played out of town, we had more people in the stands than the other side did."

Going to Camilla that year, 1972, for round two of the Class A playoffs with Mitchell County, after beating Vidalia in round one, Irwin was 11–0 for the first time since 1953 and was the first team in our history to be 11–0 in a season that included a win over Fitzgerald.

Just one win away from going to state, they'd made a tremendous run to get the opportunity. The Indian exploits had given fans many thrills and to get one over on Fitzgerald, 39-14, was a feat few ICHS alums could relate to.

How Sweet It Is, crowed the headline in the Star after the Big Red calmed the storm in game 4. And if you've never been on an Ocilla team that beat Fitzgerald—and that's a majority of old Irwin County boys—take if from Eddie Mac Dix: "It was exhilarating; one of those high school moments."

Dix says Coach Nix made beating Fitzgerald a priority that year.

The boys, going to and from practice on the field, were made to run under the goal posts, tap the bar and yell, "Ten and 0, beat Fitzgerald."

"We just refused to lose," Eddie Mac explains. "The coach had us to where we were invincible."

The Indians ended the regular season that year as Region 2–A champs by bouncing Blackshear, 47–0, and drew Vidalia in the first round of the playoffs on Thanksgiving Eve in Ocilla. Anticipating an overflow crowd at Lanny Roberts Memorial Stadium, Irwin mailed more than 1,500 tickets to Vidalia. The 8-2 tribe was no joke to us. After we jumped out to a big lead, and it seemed like we had them subdued, they came back and the outcome was in doubt until Carlton Fletcher intercepted for Irwin at the very last to preserve the victory.

> Reported the *Star*, *The Irwin County High Indians moved another step up the ladder toward a state football championship last Wednesday night as they held off a determined Vidalia high team 28–21 in a playoff-chiller.*

Well, speaking of chill, it was cold that night in Camilla where the unbeaten Indians met the 11–1 Mitchell County Eagles for the right to go to state.

We want Irwin!...We want Irwin! was the chant that had come out of the Eagle camp the week of the game. The Indians thought that was funny and hit the Eagles in the teeth. Unfortunately, it did not have much of an effect. And before long, our boys found themselves on the butt end of a good ole country smack-down, and it was back to reality for the Big Red nation. Irwin fans spent most of the game sitting on their hands, shivering, stunned, disappointed.

The game unraveled early and we couldn't get it together.

In the first half, the Big Red defense was mauled, giving the fired-up Eagles two scores, each on long drives, and the offense soft-served them a third score by allowing a 78-yard run back of an interception that put the birds up 21–0 at halftime. Then on the first series of the third quarter, with Irwin backed up to punt, the ball sailed over Mike Clayton's head and rolled into the end zone where an Eagle pounced on it for another touchdown. They went for two and made it.

The Indians scored on a 92-yard drive and actually ended up with more total yardage than the Camilla team, but the Eagles easily took the night.

> *Nothing cools title fever quicker than a loss,* the *Star* bawled, *and Irwin County's high hopes for a state class A football crown were snuffed 29–6 in Camilla last Friday night.*

Eddie Mac Dix sums it up: "They blocked a few punts, it was a hometown crowd, and you talk about Big Mo? Big Mo got on their side and they beat the heck out of us."

Ronnie Howell, who played some that night as a receiver, remembers a few whipped Indians crying in the huddle.

"They had a good team and they just won the game," Coach Nix says now when asked what went wrong in Camilla. He believed cold and adverse conditions were contributing factors. "If we'd have played it at our place …."

James Griffin believes the problem in Camilla was not the weather but a case of the Indians taking Mitchell County lightly due to poor mental preparation by the coaches. He says the Indians were made overconfident by Nix showing them a game film between Mitchell County and lousy Cochran. On film, Cochran was "the sorriest team I ever saw and Mitchell County barely beat them," James Griffin says.

"We underestimated Mitchell County," Williamson says. "There seemed like there was no way we could lose to them."

While it wasn't Irwin's time to take it all, it wasn't Mitchell's, either. The high-flying Eagles got fried, 34–15, in Camilla by Carrollton for the state championship.

Nix conducted spring training in 1973 and after school let out for the summer, he left for Northside of Warner Robins, where he became a coaching icon.

The old coach says now that he and his wife, Patsy, really enjoyed their two years in Ocilla and made many long-time friends here. He says he left for what he saw as a better opportunity at a bigger school.

James remembers his old coach was a driven man. He believes Nix "was working in Ocilla to get to Warner Robins. That's what he wanted."

As far as a coach, James will tell you, none was better than Conrad Nix. "But as far as player relations, he didn't give a crap about us. He just cared about winning. Winning was his number one deal. He could've had some compassion and love for the players."

Nix has never wavered on his philosophy toward high school football.

"Obviously, you want to win but my basic philosophy is that high school is some of the greatest experience for athletes. I wanted our guys to have good memories of high school and to be successful adults, people, and provide for their family and somewhere in the mix, they learned a little bit about Jesus."

47

Impossible Dream

It is time for a very important season in Irwin County football history to begin. We have the opportunity and responsibility to defend the Region 2–A Football Championship. This will require a 100 percent effort from all of us and this should be our goal for the coming year. Football practice will begin Monday night, August 6, 1973, at 6:30 PM at the field house. We will work in shorts for two weeks at approximately this time each evening (Mon.-Fri.) Camp will be the week of August 19–24 at South Georgia College in Douglas. We open our season with Bacon County on Friday night, August 31, 1973. Looking forward to seeing you August 6, 1973. Sincerely, Coach Snipes."

—*Ocilla Star*, Aug 2, 1973

The next man in the Big Red saddle was hyper and hard to read. But give him a few good men who wanted to play some football, and if you could follow his calls, then Ben Snipes, as he proved in 1973, could hang the Ws.

Snipes really was excitable. Before one game in 1973, the former Georgia Bulldog was so hyped at school that principal Richard Williamson sent Snipes to the field house to chill out, get a hold of himself.

"That's just me," Ben Snipes says now when asked about his old reputation for being so intense. "I can't keep it all inside. If I do, I blow up."

Strapped like a Marine, with a haircut to match, Americus native Snipes was a good guy and fun to play for, according to some of his former charges. But it was often a struggle. Snipes would get so caught up in the game that he couldn't clearly spit out the play he wanted the boys to run.

Nobody questioned the new coach's passion; his heart was in the right place. And Snipes enforced strict rules, such as hair length; he liked the cleaner cut. Not so surprising, he had a spot of temper, too. It came out once when some kids were picking up roots in a lot. The boys were clearing the ground near Lanny Roberts stadium for use as a practice field when Snipes slugged one of the school boys.

"We had a situation," Snipes explains, "where some people were not working like I thought they were supposed to and one kid took a cut at me, and to be honest, I don't know what happened."

Police were called.

Otherwise, the clean-shaven Ben Snipes was the nicest guy and one of the best football men you'd ever come across.

People remembered Snipes when he was in town in 1971 interviewing for Buzzy's job, which went to Nix. When Nix left, Snipes brought an updated résumé to the hiring body in

Ocilla. Having coached with Nix earlier in his career gave Snipes a leg up on the field.

"He knew me a little bit," Snipes says of Nix, "and he recommended me to Williamson. Out of that came my offer to be the head coach. They wanted to win and I wanted to win and we got together on that."

That year, 1973, we had lost 15 men to graduation and had just five seniors, but nobody wanted to hear any excuses, so when Snipes lost the opener, which was to his old team, Bacon County, the Indian family was sore. "They were ready to run me out of town." Then on the following Friday, the Big Red got hammered in Ocilla by AA Cook County. His feet to the fire, Snipes stuck to his guns, and in game 3 redeemed himself with a nice victory over Wilcox County at Rochelle. This gave the Indians a mark of 1–1 in the single A region before facing Joe Compton's Hurricane of 1–AA.

Fitzgerald had hired Joe back that year to coach. "He got more out of his players than anybody," Snipes says of his hero, Joe Compton.

Under Joe, Fitzgerald was winless that year facing Irwin. But it was a riveting affair down to the wire in the old rivalry. Though fumble-prone, the Indians hung in, kept it close, and with just little time on the clock, Kenny Fletcher tossed short to Carlton Fletcher who caught the ball, spun, and under a fevered assault, pitched back to Charles Paschal, who dashed 49 yards for a touchdown to make it 20–18. On the two-point try to tie it, Snipes called for a pass. So, the boys set it up. Kenny Fletcher threw to Charles Collins but the ball was tipped away by a 'Cane defender in the end zone and time ran out on the Indians.

"We didn't quite know how to take Coach Snipes at first and that was reflected in our start to the season," explains Carlton Fletcher. "We only had five or six seniors…and there was a lot of grumbling about the way Snipes ran things. I remember he was hesitant with his play calling; he had to talk himself into some plays on the fly, which was confusing to us. … But in the fifth week of the season something clicked. We won and just kept winning."

In fact, after losing to Fitzgerald, the boys sacked their next six opponents by a combined score of 196–40, including upsets of Jeff Davis and Berrien, and claimed a share of the Region 2–A title by crushing Blackshear in the final game.

Because Irwin and Jeff Davis ended the regular season tied with one region loss apiece, a playoff, called a "regional final," was necessary. It did not matter that Irwin had beaten Jeff Davis already; the rule required a tiebreaker. The game was conducted on a neutral field at Douglas on November 16, 1973. Hundreds of whooping Indian fans watched Irwin steam the favored Jackets, 29–0.

> *They've Done It Again,* screamed the page 1 headline in the *Ocilla Star*, referring to the Big Red capturing the region title for the second season in a row and fifth out of the last seven.

> The *Star* reported: *Irwin's biggest play of the half ... was made by the defense. Early in the second quarter Jeff Davis had a first down at the Irwin one-yard line. On the first play, Mike Rutherford met the Yellow Jacket runner at the line of scrimmage with a savage tackle that jarred the ball loose. Ronnie Jones fell on the ball in the end zone to give the Indians possession at the 20. Many people feel that this was the play that turned the game around for the Big Red machine.*

The next Friday, ahead of a motorcade of ramped-up Indian fans in buses and cars, the boys traveled over the back roads into Toombs County for a showdown with the Bulldogs of nemesis Lyons in the quarterfinal, which also was known as the "area championship."

With only 2:22 left, and Irwin up by one, anxious Irwin fans gasped when a Bulldog broke loose toward the goal line with the ball. It looked like he might score and maybe they'd win the game. But Ronnie Jones of Ocilla ran down the streaking back and ripped the ball loose. Theodis McLain fell on the fumble and Irwin won the crown, 14–13, and we all went home happy.

Remarkably, Irwin was just a win away from going to state. Standing in our way was a booger-bear, one of the best teams in all of Georgia that year.

They called it Mount de Sales. Founded in 1876 by the Sisters of Mercy, Mount de Sales had more talent than the Indians, surely, and outweighed our boys by a ton. Their best back was Johnny Henderson. Their big dog was Zambiasi. You pronounced it "Zam-beezy" and everybody who knows football remembers Ben Zambiasi. He went on to set all kinds of tackling marks at the University of Georgia at linebacker and later was a star in the Canadian Football League.

After the game with Mount de Sales was delayed a half hour for a statewide address by Governor Jimmy Carter on the energy crisis, the boys battled the Cavaliers on even terms for a while. In fact, we had a one-point lead after the third stanza. But the Indians ran out of gas and the Henderson boy cut us to shreds.

"They put two guys on me," Carlton Fletcher says, remembering Henderson's punt return, "and they abused me all the way down the field. I remember watching Henderson run by on his way to the end zone from flat on my back."

Once the Cavaliers got the lead, their talent and size kicked in and they stuck a sword in us.

> *Dream Comes to End,* squalled the *Ocilla Star* headline after the loss to Mount de Sales. The story read, in part: *The Impossible Dream, as many Irwin fans called this year's Big Red Machine's chances of a winning season, came to an end Friday night as Mount de Sales downed the Tribe 28–7.*
>
> *...Facing a larger, quicker and more experienced team, the Big Red...showed determination that brought them from a 1–3 record to the semi-finals of the state championship.*

After the game, some disgruntled men were overheard on their CB radios, accusing Mount de Sales of cheating.

But that wasn't it, says Carlton Fletcher, who made the North-South all-star squad that season. "They had better athletes at almost every position."

"They were better than us," acknowledges Coach Snipes, repeating the remarks he made in 1973. "Zambiasi, Johnny Henderson—they beat our butt."

48

Frustration

It was a sweltering Monday afternoon when this interview was made, and it was obvious that our ICHS Indians were ready for a cold shower and some home cooking. Despite the heat, however, they were gracious enough to comment on the football camp and prospects for the upcoming season.

Bruce Giddens told me, "We had the best football camp that I've ever been to. Our spirit was good; our morale was great. We feel we're going all the way this time."

Lewis Hall echoed Bruce's sentiments, saying, "It was a great camp and we feel that we've accomplished a great deal. We're pointing to the great '1' at the end of the season.'

The rigors of practice were noted by David Zorn, "Sure, it was tough at camp, but I feel it was worth it. We all want the big 1."

Indian Mentor Ben Snipes expressed his views on the team's situation as this: "Physical-wise, we feel we're in real good shape and we're ready to play. ...The weather has been fair up until today. It was a real burner this afternoon. But we're much further along that we were at this time last year."

—*Ocilla Star*, August 1974

The Indians of 1974 broke from hard days at camp in August and soared to No. 1 in the Class A polls after whipping Fitzgerald for the second time in three years and we all looked forward to adding some serious hardware to the trophy case in the school lobby.

A good number of the boys who'd helped win the region for us in 1973 were back in the lineup. Charles Paschal led the class of returning aces. A senior, fast and 180 pounds, Charlie made his mark in 1973 as one of the region's best backs. He brought speed and agility while 220-pound junior strongman farm boy Carlton Jones was put at fullback to block and to grind out the really tough yards.

The hot bid for quarterback between senior Ronnie Howell and junior Wesley Walters had gone to Ronnie, the little brother of former Indian star Lamar Howell, and we were stout across the defensive front where big boys Tony Hayes and Terry Warren held the fort.

It was a tight Region 2–A. Besides Irwin, the contenders promised to be Bacon County, Jeff Davis and the new kid on the block, Southeast Bulloch. These three were last on our schedule.

The slate makers set Irwin up with three AA teams—Berrien County, Perry and Fitzgerald—to open the season and the Big

Red knocked them all out in securing their hold on the top slot in Class A.

> *The kids deserve this honor,* Ben Snipes told Harmon Roberts of the *Star* after the poll came out with Irwin County No. 1 in Class A. *They have worked for it, but their feelings are as mine. We'd rather be on top at the end of the year than any other time.*

The game with Fitzgerald was wonderfully exhausting.

Snipes' favorite coach, Joe Compton, was 1–1 that year when the Indians came calling.

Midway the fourth quarter, Snipes was standing on the sideline next to assistant Irwin coach Marion Roberts, watching Fitzgerald try to move against the rugged Indian defense.

"I looked over at Marion and I said, *This game is going to wind up zero to zero*, and then they fumbled and we scored real quick."

Later on Henry Mercer fell on a 'Cane fumble in the end zone and we went on to beat our oldest rival.

After Fitzgerald, the Indians had a bye week. For some reason, during the bye, we got voted out of the No. 1 slot. *Star* writer Harmon Roberts predicted pollsters would slide Irwin back on top if we were to beat Claxton the following week in the kickoff of regional play. That was the last word from Roberts in the paper about polls.

Fuming over not being No. 1 anymore, the Indians stomped Claxton of fruitcake fame and three others by a combined 149–12 to be 7–0 headed to Statesboro on November 1 for what was billed as the state's game of the week between us and Southeast Bulloch.

> *Two buses have been chartered to transport Irwin*

fans to Statesboro so a large following can be expected, the *Star* reported.

Located in the community of Brooklet just outside Statesboro, 120 miles from Ocilla over mostly backroads, Southeast Bulloch began football in 1966. Always a power in Class B, the Yellow Jackets of Larry Freeman moved up to Class A in '74 and brought with them a scary record.

> *They're a bunch of players,* long-time Irwin assistant coach Weyman Vickers said to the *Star* the week of the big game. *And we're going to have to be on our toes to stay on the field with them.*

Bulloch had won 31 games in taking two state titles when the Big Red rolled into Statesboro, and our boys were tight as a new pair of dungarees. We fumbled four times, possibly from the jitters. Bulloch also had butter fingers. We scored when Ronnie Howell outwitted defenders on a 76-yard romp and Charles Paschal ran back an 84-yard punt for another but the Lord let Bulloch take the night, 16–14.

"Maybe we were just a tad too confident," says Ronnie Howell, looking at it now. "We had the team to beat them." Ronnie remembers fullback Carlton Jones suffered a concussion. "I sent him out of the game and they sent him back in and he was just as lost in that huddle as a goat."

The ride back to Ocilla was awful, like we all needed surgery. Everyone was sick and the boys felt lousy.

> *The Big Red played well and have nothing to be ashamed of,* Harmon Roberts cried in his *Star* write-up. *The team, even in defeat, proved they were not quitters and the game was not decided until the waning seconds*

of the contest. This reporter said the Indians played as champions and if the breaks had been a little different, the score would likely have been in favor of the Big Red.

While the loss brought rain to our heart, there was football left. The show had to go on. Just win out and maybe Bulloch stumbles so the Big Red gets a turn at them again in a playoff. The boys slammed Jeff Davis and Bacon but Bulloch got the region anyway and the Indians turned in their broken tomahawks with nine wins and just the one loss. They did not get any hardware.

Roberts wrote that while most teams would be *delighted with a 9–1 record, the Irwin County Indians would gladly swap theirs for a 6–4 record, giving up four victories over Class AA schools, for a win over Southeast Bulloch and a trip to the region playoffs. Therefore, the season has actually been one of frustration for the Indians.*

Bulloch by the way got stoned in the first round by No. 1 Carrollton in Statesboro.

Forty years have washed under the bridge now but Ben Snipes still relives the Bulloch game. "We fumbled four times and they fumbled three times and they got all seven," Snipes remembers, adding: "You ever heard of, when the Lord don't intend for you to win?"

49

‘Movie Stars’

Ocilla—Irwin County kept its perfect record intact here Friday thanks to the Dix brothers.

Robby and Alex Dix came up with a pair of key turnovers for the Indians, who converted with a 13–6 victory over Region 2–A opponent Jenkins County.

Jenkins, a stubborn defensive team, gave up its first touchdown with only six seconds left in the first half when Irwin’s Michael Cummings cracked across from the five.

Irwin is now 5–0 and meets Cook at home next Friday night.

—*Tifton Gazette*, October 9, 1975

Then we got Mike back. Everybody in Indian land remembered Mr. Battles from when he was here in 1971 and although we hated to see Snipes go, the Big Red family was glad Mike Battles agreed to return to Ocilla as head football coach in 1975.

The experts said we might win five games. Our line overall was a runt, with a defensive end at 150 pounds, and some were green and there was a hole to fill at quarterback, not to mention a new coach. And we'd lost a lot to graduation.

We thought maybe give Mike some time to build a team and, in a year or two, we'd go places. You never knew with kids, though. The boys that year were looking at the Big Dipper. Snipes had left Battles a dangerous bunch. They make movies out of teams like that. "Our offensive line was small, but good God they were gutsy," says Lewis Hall, who starred on the 1975 team as a 135-pound halfback. In fact, that year, ten days before Christmas, despite what all the prognosticators had said at the start of the season, the Big Red stood at the threshold of history.

When Snipes left, there was some sentiment in the community that assistant coach Marion Roberts get the job. Mike Battles already topped the most lists of prospects, though. "He had a lot of energy and was a fun kind of guy," says Richard Williamson, the former principal. "We just knew that he was very capable and got in contact with him."

A Mississippi boy, good with kids, Mike was in Alabama coaching when his phone rang in Anniston. "They called me about the job," Mike remembers. "I went down and talked to them and the rest is history."

His wife, Carolyn, also made the trip. Friendships they'd

formed here in 1971 played a big part in their decision to move back to Ocilla in 1975.

"We just had the greatest friends there. It was just a special time, and when I see those old movies like *Fried Green Tomatoes*...that was Ocilla and that was our time there," Carolyn says. "It was more than community; it was total family."

Lewis Hall remembers the team was hardened by Snipes, fearless and eager to win, and so when Battles took over, "he walked into a sweet thing."

Battles employed the wishbone, which fit with our size and abilities. Nix had run the same offense when he was here. With the wishbone, "we just clicked and had fun," Hall says.

The quarterback job that year went to wiry senior Wesley Walters. A farm boy and a natural athlete, Wesley became one of the best who ever played in Ocilla at reading what the defense threw at him, and as the season wore on, "They couldn't figure Wesley out," says the old postman, Bobby Dix, a longtime Indian fan and father of three Dix boys.

A key to the wishbone's success was fullback and at that position the boys of 1975 were well set with Carlton Jones. A beast and one of the biggest boys on the club, the Jones kid was a top college prospect at 225 pounds. Carlton also played linebacker and could lift the front of a farm tractor with his bare hands.

The Indians of Class A opened the season of 1975 with three games against AA schools, including Fitzgerald, and stuffed them. They got over on Berrien County and then Perry before taking down ole Fitz. The Hurricanes were having a dumpy season, but when they came to Ocilla on September 19, they put up a good exchange as one might expect of a rival. "A lot of guys on the team had girlfriends from Fitzgerald, so we had a rivalry going on and off the field," says Robbie Dix, who played a 150-pound defensive end.

Late in the fourth quarter, there was no score. Fitzgerald was driving, however, and things looked bleak for the Indians. Then Larry Washington, a linebacker whose nickname was Bear, came up big, picking off a pass at the Fitz 37. On the first play after the interception, William Lampkin dashed 33 yards to the four. Carlton Jones bulled his way over the goal from the one, Tony Tucker made good on the PAT and that was all the scoring for the night.

We hadn't beaten Fitzgerald in back-to-back seasons since the 1920s.

Later, against AA Cook County, in a game marred by cheap shots by the Hornets that infuriated Indian fans and almost caused a fracas, the boys struck for four TDs in the first quarter and easily took the contest.

"The efforts of the whole community just got centered around that football team," Richard Williamson recalls. "We were mowing people down pretty regularly."

The boys fed off the energy and the Booster Club treated them to large, juicy steaks as reward for each victory. "We got tired of steak," says Robbie Dix.

September 31 the region lead was up for grabs when Southeast Bulloch came to Ocilla unbeaten. The boys remembered what Bulloch did to us in '74 and vowed revenge. The first points went to Irwin on a 15-yard toss from Wesley Walters to his favorite target, Henry Mercer, and then in the third, with Irwin down a point, Wesley engineered a 69-yard drive, made a TD on a run play and ran the ball in for the two-point conversion to close the scoring and knock Bulloch out of the playoff picture, 14–6.

Finally getting some respect from the pollsters, the Big Red hammered Jeff Davis to capture the region crown on the way to a perfect regular season.

"We were pretty good but we got lucky on several occasions," says Lewis Hall. "The good Lord looked down on us … and we were just good enough to hold our own."

For the Indians, the 1975 Class A playoffs began at powerhouse Carrollton, the defending state champ, and it was supposed to be too close to call but our boys played with their hair on fire and made it look easy. They jumped out to a 13–0 halftime advantage over the home-standing Trojans, and during halftime festivities, Carrollton boosters presented their head coach, Charles Grisham, a new car. The Indians went on to smash the Trojans, 29–6, and moved to No. 1 in the polls.

Then came probably one of the hottest games in any class that year. The battle between our boys and No. 2 Mary Persons out of Forsyth was called the South Georgia championship with the winner going to state. It was technically the semi-final, and no finer game was ever witnessed in Ocilla. The Indians made two TDs in the first half and the Eagles got two in the second half to make it a tie at the end of regulation. Because there was no overtime or sudden death, officials huddled to go over the yardage. The team with the most yards would be declared the winner.

"I thought we'd lost," says Robbie Dix. "We stood on the sidelines for a long time before they figured out who won the game."

When the tallying was done, officials said that Irwin County had won, 16–15, based on the penetration rule. Irwin fans

Wesley Walters #10 and Carlton Jones #40 celebrate a victory in 1975. *Courtesy ICHS 1975-76 yearbook / copied by David Pierce*

stormed the field. Our boys had pulled victory out of the fire by a clever play partly devised in the huddle by Wesley Walters.

It was fourth and two with just a few ticks left on the clock and we were trailing by four yards in penetration, so the game basically came down to this one play. Taking the snap, Wesley turned and made a nice fake to Carlton Jones, who was being keyed on, and then he slid down the line with the ball, reading the defensive end. When he noticed the end go with Michael Cummings, Wesley darted inside, picking up ten yards and sending the Big Red to state for the first time since before these boys of ours were born.

When this team has had to suck it up and go this year, that's just what they've done, Mike Battles told reporters after the game with Mary Persons. *They love this game, and it shows. They have a lot of character.*

And so, it came down to one.

These boys of ours, who were supposed to be home by now, shooting at deer or rabbits and saying *wait 'til next year,* were loose but many were serious as they boarded yellow school buses waiting at Lanny Roberts Memorial Stadium. Destination: a place called Jefferson. The papers said there were about 40 boys leaving that day. The town was on fire. Storefronts were painted red.

That was December 15, 1975, a cool Saturday morning. The peanuts and cotton were over. The Big Red was supposed to be finished by now, too, if you believed the prognosticators back in August. Yes, it'd been a charmed fall, the way the fall needs to be lucky your way if you're going to be special, and there was just one piece of business left before Christmas came and the Ocilla community would settle in for whatever winter brought.

The buses rolled away from the field house, made a left turn onto US Highway 129 at Willett's Truck Stop and proceeded to Fitzgerald and parts north trailed by a decorated motorcade.

Before long, the streets would be deserted as if it were Sunday.

"We were a football town," says Lewis Hall who, like his battle mates, had come of age in Ocilla hearing stories of former Indians like Danny Paulk, Walter Sumner, Oscar Roberts and all our greats of the past. And yet those old warriors, as good as they had been, never won the big one, so partly this ride was for them.

There were no cell phones then or iPhones or Kindles to play with. Along the way, the boys on this storybook ride amused themselves with song. They had great camaraderie, and they'd listen to and sing anything—rock, country, gospel. They were from Ocilla, Irwin County, peanut country, home of Walter Sumner, and proud of it. They loved to hunt, fish, play football, and have a little fun. Growing up together in a farming community where thrills were hard to find, the boys were close and dullness was a matter of perspective.

As little boys, many grew up playing tackle in the backyards of Ocilla and working on farms pulling weeds, cropping tobacco and handling sweet potatoes and corn. They had become lifelong pals and confidants. They'd played in the midget league together and later in the junior high program, so they had come up a tight bunch, savvy in football in a football-savvy community. You couldn't pull them apart with two tractors.

So, this was their big moment and the community's, as the caravan coursed through south Georgia, bearing the hopes and dreams of so many. The pride of Ocilla, Irwin County, saw from their windows all the posters on the roadside saying things like "Big Red," and the fire in their gut went higher.

The boys were already on edge. Someone had created a monster. A newspaper article out of Athens the week of the big game implied that the Irwin boys were overrated. The defense was ripped and Wesley Walters was cited as no more than a figurehead. Carlton Jones, our big fullback who'd gained a thousand yards, was called out as just a dive runner. It had also excited the Indians when coaches whispered into their ears some trash talk out of the Jefferson camp in north Georgia.

Along the way, they saw south Georgia people emerge from businesses when the caravan passed by, standing on sidewalks and on the side of the road, waving at the undefeated Indians and yelling well-wishes at them to bring it home.

"We were movie stars," Carolyn Battles recalls with a laugh.

50

Our Time

After 230 miles, the buses bearing the Big Red crossed the city limits sign of Jefferson and stopped outside the stadium. The boys were quietly intense as they disembarked. A party of Indian fans who had arrived early whooped and hollered at the sight of the boys.

"Our confidence level when we got there was so high we didn't think about the possibility of losing that game," says Robbie Dix.

The boys walked onto the field and later, after they had rested, began to put on their gear. The ones who wanted it were taped, one ankle then another, and a little more time passed. When they were finished with the warm-ups, the boys in white outfits with red helmets jogged back to the field house to get the final word from Mike Battles.

There wasn't much left for the coach to say.

Then just a little prior to eight o'clock in the mill town of Jefferson, in the cold air of north Georgia, the Irwin County Indians charged onto the field as their side roared and the Big Red band played that old familiar fight song.

Everybody there to root for Irwin wore their best game attire and many had on something in red.

A number of fans with Ocilla ties who lived in Atlanta or Athens had driven to see the Big Red play. The faithful who could not be there were with the boys in spirit, and the departed who had been loyal to the end, like Johnny King and Lanny Roberts, were also there somehow.

Back home, red-streaked Ocilla was a ghost town. Police, teachers, storekeepers, farmers, plumbers…everybody was in Jefferson. Altogether it was like a big family reunion on the red side of the field.

Around the Jefferson field were a track and a fence. A host of Indian fans stood behind the fence line on the track, so large was the Indian crowd, larger, even, than the assemblage across the way.

We got the ball first – and, well, it really wasn't much of a game after that.

On the first play, our big boy, Jones, made a nice run. And then on the third play from the 34-yard line, before anyone had set down, Michael Cummings of Ocilla sprinted 66 yards along our side of the field, and we all became loons; the rout was on.

Somehow, it wasn't all about beating Jefferson; it was deeper than that. This was our show, our season that we'd waited for in long-suffering.

They were called the Dragons, by the way, those Jefferson High boys in blue. They played well and were to be commended for a fair game. But it was our night. Anyone we played would've lost.

> *These kids have had a rough road to come and just made up their minds to do it,* Battles—dubbed St. Mike in the *Gazette*—explained to reporters after the game. *I know some people picked us to go 5–5 but they couldn't measure what was inside of these players. They're bluebloods. They don't like to lose whether it's throwing to the line, football or whatever.*

Wesley Walters acquitted himself superbly, answering his critics with a big night running, throwing, tackling, and Carlton Jones was his normal, beastly self; strong and hard to put down.

The defense played a natural game.

Irwin was up 25–7 at the half. A lot of our younger kids coming along saw action in the fourth quarter when the starters were pulled against their wishes.

"We wanted to score more," Robbie Dix recalls. "We just wanted to beat the snot out of them."

When the final whistle blew, with the score 39–13, a flash of Big Red fans, seizing the history of the moment, rushed onto the field where the happy Indians hoisted their awesome red helmets as we made magic that night. The boys of Irwin County High celebrated not only a state football title for themselves and their little school, but for the farming community from which they hailed. Somehow, in filling out the 1975 slate with 13 Ws and no Ls, the kids paid homage to every boy, big or small, fast or slow, who'd ever put on the pads in Ocilla, even going back to the old school-yard days of the early Terrapins, and for the countless fans who'd lived through the boys so long, this was their night too, and it was for all the coaches who'd come and gone through without winning the big one.

"We were just a very fortunate group of guys that stuck together," explains Alex Dix, a junior that year and younger brother of Robbie Dix.

Lewis Hall remembers 1975 was a season when "everything fell in place. The right people were in the right spots, and the little people played over their heads and did a real good job of it."

Decades later, Mike Battles calls 1975 "a special season; it was our time." He adds, "It all bounced right. Everything that was supposed to happen happened. It was just one of those special times. We had great kids and in a small town kids cycle through and … it takes a lot of luck" to go unbeaten.

No football season in the history of Ocilla, Irwin County, Georgia, had ever ended on this high of a note. All others had in some way ended in disappointment. That night the victors were feted like kings to supper at a restaurant before returning to Ocilla. Ocilla merchant Charles Harris rented a room for the affair with his own money. The celebration was one of those where everybody stands and applauds when the coaches, their wives and the heroes of the evening enter the room ten-feet tall, and people usually get up and say a few words. The supper was going to be held if our boys won or lost, but winning made it a grand, historic occasion.

"Just really felt like on top of the world," says Carolyn Battles, trying to explain what it was like to be state champ in Ocilla.

About three o'clock in the morning the boys got home where they were welcomed by a multitude of cheering fans, some of whom had not made the trip but waited up for them to arrive.

"When we got back, they had painted the town red. They had 'Mike Battles for President,'Alex Dix remembers with a chuckle. "I think the community enjoyed it just as much as we did."

So how was it, winning state after so many years of trying and crying?

"Oh, man," Alex's father, Bobby, exclaims, "it was a tremendous boost to the community. Every store in town had a sign in the window … A state title will bring a lot of people together in a small town. The people grouped together just like the players did."

In a small community such as Ocilla, he adds, "There ain't nothing like it."

Georgia's 1975 Class A State champions coached by Mike Battles, third row far right. The team, led by quarterback Wesley Walters, #10, and fullback Carlton Jones, #40, went unbeaten. *Courtesy the Sandy McClurd collection*

PART VI

51

Playoff Ban

It's early yet—much too early to really tell anything—and there are all of those young, inexperienced players. But talking with Irwin County High head coach Ed Blount and watching the young Indians go through practice in preparation for the 1982 season, one can't help form feel the excitement that is building in the Irwin Camp.

The past few seasons have been promising ones for the Indians. Irwin fans, longing for a return to that heritage that was their football team for so long, have seen players who seemed destined to bring that return.

But injuries, a bad play here and there, and more than an abundance of bad luck have left the Indians a point or two shy of the coveted playoffs the past couple of seasons.

—*Carlton Fletcher Ocilla Star*, September, 1982

And so, we finally won that state title in football and the fire can't go any higher than that. We haven't been on the golden perch since, although we've gotten very close the last couple of years so maybe we'll cross the river before long.

This year, 2015, men who played on that historic 1975 team as boys assembled around a tent anchored at the Irwin-Fitzgerald game in Ocilla. Naturally, we lost to Fitz – those guys have really been eating our lunch - but it was good to see the old Indians again at their reunion, which went well, according to Reggie Miller and some others who were there for the occasion. Regretfully, some figures from the milestone season of 1975 were absent. The quarterback, Wesley Walters, is dead. Carlton Jones, the brutal fullback on that incredible band of over-achievers, who went on the play at Florida State, also left us too soon, electrocuted at a job site. Wesley, who played football for the University of Georgia, once intercepting a Georgia Tech pass, died in 2004 of heart failure. Indian fan extraordinaire Harmon Roberts is dead. Charles Harris, whose love for the Indians spanned decades, is also deceased; his old department store on Fourth Street where you were always made to feel special is now a fitness center. There are just too many to name who've gone on. But football in Ocilla still works, and even though the railroad has long taken up the tracks to Ocilla, as nothing here is worth shipping, nobody can take away that title.

In 1976 we hunkered down with a cherished desire for a

repeat. Certainly, we had the athletes and the momentum to make another big run at state. The program was operating at a high level. But the boys got busted for an illegal scrimmage and there went our hope of two state titles in a row. It was in all the papers, really hot, and smacked of politics. We were told that Battles put the Indians into an illegal drill with the Tift County Blue Devils and somebody snitched to the Georgia High School Association, which was often criticized for lack of effort and oversight. The committee slapped Irwin County with probation, a fine of $500 and no playoffs for 1976. Irwin County's side howled in protest. Lawyers got involved. It was really a stink, lots of emotion. Reeling from the upheaval, the boys lost their first two games that year, one to defending AA state winner Americus. But after falling to 0–2, the Indians came alive, determined to play out the string and not quit. In a show of strong character—and as a swipe at their detractors—the Big Red ran the table, including a 9–7 win over Fitzgerald, to finish the season 8-2. Although unbeaten in the region, the boys could not go back to the playoffs because of the ban.

The Star said in a commentary:

> *Coach Battles admitted he was wrong and asked the Association to punish him, not his team. Instead...the GHSA rules that he, along with his team, would suffer severe consequences. Perhaps the executive committee decided, since Irwin had been reported for fighting the year before, that the little Class A school was supported by a bunch of people who only caused trouble and played by their own rules. So they made the ruling without really finding out what the team was like...Irwin played teams that, instead of trying to play better football, tried to start fights. Teams like Clinch County, Brantley county and Berrien county took cheap shots all*

during the games with Irwin. This would have caused any person to be angry, but Coach Battles had prepared his team and they just took the cheap shots in stride. There were instances of opposing players throwing elbows, hitting when a player had already scored a touchdown, hitting late and one case where a Brantley player had the gall to spit into the helmet of one of the Irwin players.

Four new Indians initiated into summer camp 1980 with bad haircuts; standing l-r: Kim Paul, Jeff Smith, Andy Paulk; in stance William Hudson *Courtesy Ocilla Star / copied by David Pierce*

But life had to go on and Battles stayed with us just a little longer. In 1977 the boys put six in the win column and tied Fitzgerald but we did not make the playoffs. And in 1978 we got moved up into to a harder division, AA, and finished 3–7, including a 35–12 beat-down by Fitzgerald, and after the spring of 1979 Mr. Battles bowed out and went back to Alabama, where he coached his way into the Alabama high school football Hall of Fame.

Needing a good coach to lead us back to glory, we gave the bonnet to Ed Blount. But he never did really get it to work. His first year, 1979, as members of 2-AA South, we lost every game for the first time since the 1930 Ocilla Hi Terrapins. In 1980, we improved to 6-3-1 then retreated in '81 with a 5-4-1 mark. During his time in Ocilla, Mr. Blount complained a lot about a lack of talent and leadership. "We just don't have the athletes," Blount cried to the *Tifton Gazette*. "We don't have the depth we need." The boys made the playoffs in 1982 under Blount with a pretty good 6-4 mark but got knocked out in the first round by Claxton, 22-7, and Mr. Blount was ready for his check.

A point of pride in the Blount era was All-State tackle Keith Johnson, who signed to play football at the University of Georgia in 1982. Keith lettered all four years at Georgia while playing on the offensive line. At guard, he saw a lot of action as a freshman on UGA's SEC championship team before he was moved to center in 1983 when the Bulldogs went 10-1-1 and won the Cotton Bowl 10-9 over Texas.

Johnson, who was plagued by injury through much of his college career, died in Athens in 2013.

Keith Johnson, with trophy in 1982, played for the University of Georgia. *Courtesy ICHS Library / copied from 1982-83 yearbook by Lucy Pierce*

52

Compton Takes Over

The Irwin County High Indians went into last Friday night's big sub-region battle in Waycross with high hopes of emerging as victors over the Bulldogs and claiming their second straight sub-region 2-AA south title. But it wasn't to be and their hopes were dashed as Waycross, aided by five Irwin fumbles, won the game 31-7.

Anyone in attendance—and there was a host of Indian fans at the game—can tell you that Waycross won the game. They could also tell you that Irwin County beat itself on the field as four Waycross scores resulted from three Indian fumbles and had a bad snap from center on an Irwin punt attempt...it could have been that the Indians were too anxious in the beginning and the tensions resulted in the miscues....The Irwin team grew tired in the second half as fresh Waycross troops were poured onto the field.

—Steve Carter, *Ocilla Star*, Nov. 15, 1984

An Army veteran and old farm boy who loved to fish and drive an old truck, a master of the old-time "Box" offense, former Irwin nemesis Joe Compton was well-profiled for the Ocilla job if he'd take it and help us be a winner again.

His "mad man" reputation aside, nobody knew more about kids and football than Joe Compton, who grew up in Alabama and was retired, living in Fitzgerald, when Irwin got in touch with him. Spectacled, a student of government, economics and history, Joe was best at home in T-shirts and a cap, and maybe you heard that he agreed to take our boys in hand if part of his compensation was a calf.

Joe needed little indoctrination, or introduction to football, in Ocilla, when he took over for Ed Blount. Everybody remembered the bald man with Popeye arms and his famous Notre Dame Box from his coaching days at rival Fitzgerald. Joe was only fifty-three—young yet, and although he had never won state with the Hurricane, he conducted Thomson to the crown in 1968 and later won a title in North Carolina. And so with Joe in the saddle, Irwin figured to do great things, and we don't say this in a pouting spirit, but there's no telling how far we might have gone in '84 and '85 if not for Waycross.

Joe was respected across the coaching world and he put the fun back in football for us. The boys all thought it was cool playing for a legend.

"I learned more in one practice under Coach Compton than

I did the previous coach for three years," says rotund Ocilla auctioneer and radio broadcaster Andy Paulk, whose frame when he played on the line for Compton was 6-feet, 1 inch and 196-pounds. "There were two kinds of people: those who liked him and those who didn't. He was a good coach and you worked hard...If you played for him, you were in the program. If you were a rebel, you were out."

Says Chad Sumner, who played some at quarterback for Compton in Ocilla, "He was hard, but he was fair and fun to play for."

One of Joe's signatures was to find a play that worked and beat you to death with it. If it worked, Joe called the play time and again, marching the boys up and down the field until you stopped us; and while in Ocilla, he got much mileage out of Stanley Hall, a bruising halfback who signed to play college ball at Florida State.

"It was fun, man," Hall says of playing for Compton. "We played as a team. We played as a family."

Joe's presence made games with Fitzgerald more interesting than usual, and it was a little weird seeing the old 'Cane in a Big Red cap.

> *The game is big in these communities,* Coach Compton told reporters in 1984, *but in reality, it is just another game. I have stressed, and the kids know, that the games that count are the games in the subregion.*

Joe whipped Fitzgerald twice in his six seasons as chief.

The Compton years in Ocilla are probably best remembered for four classic scraps with Waycross—two in 1984 and two more in 1985—when both schools were AA. Those games still bug Stanley Hall. He remembers thinking there was no way the Bulldogs should've been in the league with the Indians under the average daily attendance rule.

"They cheated," says Hall, adding that Waycross High was too big to be in AA. "They caught them years later."

Three of the games with Irwin were played in Waycross at Memorial Stadium.

> *I said before the season started that they should not even be in this region, and I still feel that way,* Compton told reporters in '84 prior to the Region 2-AA title game with the Bulldogs, winners of the AAA state championship just three years earlier. *"They dress out from sixty to seventy folks, and the sheer numbers give them a distinct advantage. According to our ADA figures now, we qualify as a Class A school. If we were Class A, we'd stand a strong chance of winning the state championship. I feel we're four touchdowns better than all of the other teams but Waycross.*

That year, 1984, the outmanned Indians went down hard to the Bulldogs, 31–7. A week later, Irwin rebounded in round one of the playoffs by stuffing Swainsboro, 25–0, to win the sub-region title. Then Joe's boys met Waycross again the next week for the Region crown. That night the Bulldogs of Dale Williams got it, 19–0. A similar scenario was played out in 1985.

Joe Compton's six years in Ocilla did not end as happily as we had hoped and we brought in Scott Swafford, who had won state for Villa Rica in 1986, so maybe he could do the same in Ocilla, but he didn't, and Chip Stuart after him could not get the machine in gear either. By 1994, the boys were a mess. Somehow, they had forgotten how to win.

53
New's Era

OCILLA—Irwin County head football coach Ross New had a solid idea what to expect when he took the reins of the Indians program last year.

"We came in here knowing it was going to be a hard year," said New, entering his second season at the Ocilla school. "We started nine freshmen and sophomores on offense and eight on defense. We kind of knew what to expect."

New likes what he's seen in preseason drills, listing the team's strengths as its work habits and overall team speed.

"These kids are from a farming community," he said. "They'll do anything you ask of them."

—*Tifton Gazette*, Aug. 25, 1995

> Look out Fitzgerald! *It's a New Era at Irwin County,* declared a headline in the *Tifton Gazette*'s August 24, 1994 edition after Irwin school bosses hired Ross New out of AAAA Bradwell Institute to do big things in Ocilla.
>
> New told the paper: *Bradwell is a big area and a big school that has a great winning tradition. But I wanted to take on the challenge of turning a losing program around. I also felt that Irwin County would provide my family with more of a community setting.*

At the risk of copying Charlton County, New passed out black jerseys for the boys to wear in their home games. The young Indian defense became known as the Black Death. New's first troop, the '95 team, was not very impressive. Seemed so much losing in the past had gotten into the boys' psyche.

> New got on the stump. *Our biggest key will be having the kids believe they can win,* New told reporters in the summer of 1995. *Just having that attitude makes a huge difference. They haven't won here in six or seven years, and the idea starts creeping in of 'What's going to go wrong?'...The biggest thing I'm preaching is just because you're a sophomore or junior, don't let that stop you from stepping up and being a leader.*

Miraculously that year, 1995, the team, which included New's son, Josh, stunned Fitzgerald, 28–0. In 1996 we skunked Fitzgerald again. In fact, New seemed to have their number. But with an early loss that year to Charlton County, which New referred to as the "University of Charlton," and dropping games to Clinch County and Hawkinsville, our boys did not make the playoffs. But New's plan was working and in 1997, all those kids from three and four years ago appeared now as veterans—strong and heavy across the line, and ready to win.

Jake Walters, a junior, was the quarterback that year. Although he grew up wanting to be a halfback, coaches felt Jake was better as signal caller, like his dad, Wesley, an Indian star from 1975.

"He never put any pressure on me to play football," Jake says of his father. "It was something that I enjoyed doing. It came pretty natural."

The alternative to football, he says, was driving a tractor for his grandpa, Lorie Walters, on the farm.

That year, 1997, prior to the game with Fitzgerald, some ugliness crept into the rivalry; both stadiums and the Ocilla Country club were vandalized with spray paint. Spots on the grass at Lanny Roberts were set on fire with gasoline. Irwin, playing in Ocilla, rolled Fitzgerald for the third season in a row, which had never happened. The next week we got our brains beaten out in Folkston in a region matchup with UGA-bound Boss Bailey and his cohorts of No.1 Charlton County. Two weeks later Irwin did not look much like a playoff squad when the boys took another drubbing, this time at Homerville to the state's No. 3 team, Clinch County. But in game six, the Big Red held off Hawkinsville in a game that Jake Walters would remember as the turning point of the 1997 season.

"It just felt like we couldn't be beat again."

The boys played with their hair on fire the rest of the way and made the playoffs as the No. 4 seed.

Making their first trip to post season in eight years, the Indians traveled to Twin City to battle the Bulldogs of Emanuel

County Institute. Jake Walters remembers ECI had this one boy, a back, who'd committed to Notre Dame.

"They were just going to beat the stew out of us," Jake says, recalling the pregame hype. Irwin pulled the upset, 14–6, for our first playoff victory in ten years. Then we ran into some luck when, in the second round, on a night when Jake and the boys downed Dooly County, two powers in our region, Charlton and Clinch, both got whipped. A week later New's savages knocked out Macon County, the perennial Class A power of the '90s, setting the stage for a matchup between Irwin and Crawford County for the right to go to state. Boys on the team were not born the last time we made state.

The semi-final game would be played at Georgia Dome.

The Dome?

Oh, Mama. Crank the truck and feed the dog. We're going to "Hot-lanta."

This is an unbelievable feeling, Irwin fullback and future Georgia Bulldog Shane Hudson told reporters about playing in the Dome.

That was the first year high school football was played in the Dome. Folks in the Ocilla community never got to Atlanta very often, and to go up to watch our boys was like country come to town. Atlanta had never seen so many peanut pickers. And to be on TV, what a rush, and good exposure, for this small rural community that had slept through the Industrial Revolution. All games in each class were shown on Georgia Public Television.

And with crazy Indian fans filling a decent little portion of the giant facility, we're happy to say that our boys took care of business, partly with a little luck on a bad snap and a missed extra point by Crawford County. The Big Red got its points on a Hudson plunge and a point after and by golly we wound up going on to state.

Shane says now that playing in the Dome was like " … the

biggest thing in anyone's life ever. We all got new shoes."

Irwin boosters had bought the boys special shoes to wear on the artificial turf.

> *Just call it destiny,* Kevin Taylor of the *Tifton Gazette* wrote the week of the state title game. *For years the Indians have been the doormat for many schools in Class A.*

Of course, Manchester had their own vision of destiny.

If you want to get the hell knocked out of you, come to Manchester and take a left turn, barked Blue Devil head coach Greg Oglesby the week of the game with our boys for state.

Everybody went who mattered. It'd been 22 years, a long time between drinks of water.

Manchester was 150 miles from Ocilla and you couldn't get there from here. You had to go up I-75 and take a left on the backroads to reach Manchester and maybe some of us got lost but we still managed to fill our side of the stadium with more fans than the Devils had on their side.

It was a good night for football, starry and chilly, and we fired up the scoreboard when Jake Walters threw into the end zone to a diving Kendrick Wallace for the game's first points.

Manchester in western Georgia 40 miles from LaGrange was as good as advertised. The contest was tied at seven at the half but we had lost the momentum when we blew a scoring chance right before the intermission.

"I fumbled the ball going into half time and that kind of changed the tide," Shane Hudson remembers. "In the second half, they just whipped us."

The final was 28–7.

It was sad and sort of humbling to get beat after all this time but you had to give it to Manchester. The better team won. We still loved our boys and greeted them on the field. At least we could say we'd made it to the big dance by way of the Dome and only a few teams had been so privileged. It was very good to be at state in Manchester playing for the high honors while showing off our peanut-picking pride and our good-looking mamas in a clean way but it was still hard to lose.

In 1998 the fire started up again. The boys got their act back together. Certainly, Coach New, in his fifth season, had the program at a high level now. The Indians hammered Fitzgerald and finished 10–0 for the first time since 1975, and we won the region. But making state two years in a row was a little too much to ask as here came Crawford, paying us back with a first-round knockout.

In 1999, for the fifth time in as many years, the Big Red beat down Fitzgerald and in the playoffs drubbed Hawkinsville before the roll of the dice went against us and the drums fell silent in Folkston against Charlton County and that was all she wrote in Ocilla for Mr. New. There was the spring practice, and when school let out for the summer, 2000, Ross New took off his bonnet and went to AAA Carrollton, leaving the Indian family a little spoiled with a 32–5 record over his last three seasons.

In the decade after New left, the Indians did not kick down any doors. In fact, we lost something close to half of our games and never won more than seven games in a season. Four times our boys had a losing record and twice finished .500 and there wasn't much talk anymore about the Dome where champions played. But each season we kept hoping would be better than the last. The first five seasons of the decade were spent in AA, where the competition was tougher, and while the record says we made the playoffs seven times out of ten in the 2000s, four times under Jute Wilson, we never had a sensational team that was a threat to go all the way and Fitzgerald began to whip us again on a regular basis.

In 2000, Tommy Dopson led the boys to a 6-6 record, including a AA playoff win over Turner County, before losing to Toombs in round two, and that was the year Verondre Barnes of Ocilla broke Stanley Hall's Indian mark for career rushing with 4,886 yards over four years.

In 2002, the Indians under Jute Wilson, who coached our boys from 2001 through 2006, surprised AAAA Bainbridge in Bainbridge, and went on to win a playoff game over Southeast Bulloch. Another highlight of the decade, although it did not go Irwin's way, was the renewal of the Cornbread Bowl. Somebody decided it'd be awesome to relive the mid-1960s games with Tift County, without the melee, of course, and so Coach Wilson conducted his AA Indians to Tifton on September 3, 2004 for a game with the AAAAA Blue Devils. Our boys lost a tough one, 14–0. The next year, again in Tifton, the gesture was repeated, 33–0, in favor of Tift.

Somewhat solemnly, 2006 marked the end of football in the pines north of town by the golf course. That 60-year-old reservation was replaced by new digs, Indian Field, on the south end of town in August 2007. Although it was sort of sad to leave Lanny Roberts, the new Big Red village was inaugurated with much hoopla and suspense generated by the Irwin booster club.

Indian Field on first night of football 2007. *Courtesy Sandy McClurd collection*

On the surface, by cutting ties with the golf course that was part of our football heritage, it appeared school officials could not stand anymore tradition. For as long as most people could remember, many a boy spilt blood there. There'd been a lot of hollering and groaning, wonderful pageantry and fellowship on those special fall Friday nights, and we'd had some great fun and sometimes it wasn't so much fun but we looked back and it was all good and entertaining. There was just a lot of history at that old field where football began in 1946 with the Terrapins and it was home to our one and only title team. We'd seen a lot of boys become great athletes on the plain in the pines next to where the golfers played and there wasn't really anything wrong with the grass. It was what it was and it was full of memories. But the old problem with parking, with so many cars and trucks ripping the fairways, had gotten too big, and the field house had not been updated since the 1970s. So, a new reservation on old farm land was located off Georgia Highway 90 south of Ocilla by the new school.

Former Indian great Walter Sumner said a few words at a ceremony marking the end of football at the golf course field on a night when feelings were mixed.

Certainly, emotions were high at the first game played at the new field and it was Fitzgerald.

Marty Roberts wrote in the *Star*:

> *Friday night was the start of another high school football season in Georgia, but it is highly doubtful that an opening night will be remembered like the one Irwin County had on Aug. 31, 2007. The all new Indian Field opened and there was a standing room only crowd there to remember it. It was every Irwin County fan's dream to have a stadium to be proud of, and Irwin County now has one of the finest facilities in the state. The new stadium even took some of the sting out the 16–0 loss that the Indians suffered to the visiting Fitzgerald Hurricanes. The Indians took the field to a standing ovation from the overflow crowd, with fireworks piercing the sky.*

Anna Daniels of Ocilla in 2007 shows her spirit before the first game at Indian Field. *Courtesy David Pierce*

54

A Man Called Bean

The Indian Touchdown Club hosted the 5th annual "Meet the Indians" dinner last Thursday night. The touchdown club furnished the meat, while parents of the players and cheerleaders supplied the fixings. "This is the biggest crowd we've had since we started this in 2001," said Coach Jute Wilson. "With support from our community, we can be as successful as any other school in our area. It takes a total community effort for a small town like ours to compete with the larger schools in our region, but if the support we received tonight is any indication, we are well on our way to becoming the club we dream of being," said Touchdown Club President Marty Roberts.

—*Ocilla Star*. Sept. 5, 2005

There is something sad about this story but you need to hear it, especially a growing boy hoping to be a famous football player.

"I regret that I didn't plan for life after football mentally."

That's the word from Justin Anderson, who played at Irwin High and then for the University of Georgia before being drafted by the Indianapolis Colts of the NFL where he was cut due to injury and ended up back in Ocilla, trusting in the Holy Spirit to make a way for him back to pros, if not the pros again then please, God, show him a way to something else.

"There's not any jobs, no money, no opportunity in Ocilla," Justin says during a workout at the local fitness center, sporting red shorts, a Georgia Bulldog T-shirt and size 15 shoes. "I wake up every day trying to wrap my brain around what I have to do."

Friends call him "Bean" and Justin's fine with that. As a child, he was nicknamed "Bean Head" by his grandfather. The name was later shortened.

No wonder Justin played football. He was big enough to pancake a bear. But there were other things that drove him to the gridiron. Our biggest warrior of the 2000s, in fact one of the heaviest and the most decorated Indians of all time, Justin remembers there wasn't much good for kids like him to look forward to in Ocilla. Football was his ticket out.

"The only thing for black people, people on my side of town, was drugs," he says. As a child, Justin struggled with attention deficient disorder; he also stuttered and was teased by other kids. "I wasn't a very popular guy growing up in school."

But he used those factors as motivation.

With his mom, Loretta White, and father, Tony White, Justin Anderson poses during 2011 Senior Day in Athens with then-Bulldog head coach Mark Richt. *Courtesy Justin Anderson*

When Justin was ten, he struggled to make sense of the death of his grandfather, John O. Anderson, a key figure in his development."God blessed me with football in my life," Justin says. "I was going down a dark road...By the eighth grade, I had NFL dreams because I knew there was no opportunity here. It was kind of my way out of Ocilla."

If not for football, Justin says he would have probably ended up "in jail or dead."

Justin's football awards and recognitions make a list as long as his arm: three time All-State selection, USA Today's All USA first team, invited to play in the US Army All-American game. After graduating from Irwin County High in 2006, Justin played football at Hargrave Military School, where he was named a Super Southern 100 and a rivals.com prep school top fifty.

At 6-feet, 5 inches tall, 330-pound Justin K. Anderson manhandled boys in high school. At Georgia, a bad toe kept him out of action a lot before the Colts drafted him but he suffered a shoulder injury and they cut him during his rehab. Justin has never played a down in a pro game.

"It was a shock to get that phone call. They said they were letting me go...They asked me if I had any questions, and I said, *No*."

After being released by Indianapolis, Justin played in the Canadian Football League and then in arena ball in Orlando, Florida. But he was unhappy, so the Ocilla giant returned home, where he began to work himself back into NFL shape.

Although he could not have foreseen or prevented the injuries that have plagued his career, he admits, "I sort of feel like I let everybody down, let myself down. I had that mentality of being a hometown hero."

Justin earned a degree in consumer economics at Georgia but was never sure how to apply it. In late 2015, Justin was just hoping for a call from his agent in Birmingham, Alabama, about a return to the pro ball, but also praying that if he couldn't play football, God would open another door.

Because of injuries that hampered his play, "People still don't know how good a player I really am," says Justin, a godson of former Indian great Stanley Hall.

"I've talked with him," Hall said, "and told him not to worry about being a disappointment to anyone. He's just got to make up his mind what to do."

By December of 2015, Justin was healthy again, the shoulder good enough to pound on defensive men. But he didn't have any NFL work. To stay in shape, he was running and pumping iron – and going to church.

His workout routine included grass drills at old Lanny Roberts Memorial Stadium. Justin was one of the last of our boys to play at the old field in the pines where many great athletes, like Walter Sumner, had trod. He says he was sorry the preserve was abandoned and when invited by coaches to work out at Indian Field, he declined, preferring the solitude of the old stadium where his dreams of playing in the NFL were molded.

"In my heart and mind, it ain't over yet," he says. "I just want to be back in the trenches."

55
Dome Bound

An incredible performance by DJ Pollard and a stifling defense propelled the Irwin County Indians football team into the second round of the state playoffs. Friday, the Indians (8-2-1) held the Wilkinson County Warriors to 8 second-half yards and won, 30-13. The No. 3 seed Indians move on to face the No. 11 Trion Bulldogs Friday night at 7:30 p.m. at Indian Field in Ocilla. Pollard was a force for Irwin, as usual. For the second season in a row, Irwin advances to the state quarterfinals and its opponent is a familiar one. In three of the past four years, Irwin and Trion have met in the playoffs...Irwin Head Coach Buddy Nobles said he thought the defense did a great job and the offense controlled the ball well. He said the team never let itself get too high, kept fighting and got the job done, signs of an experienced team.... Trion used trick plays and forced turnovers to beat Turner. Nobles said the Bulldogs are very well disciplined, tough on both lines and are well coached. "Man, these guys are good," he said....He loved the crowd Friday and hopes to see another big crowd for the Black Friday contests. "What better way to finish Thanksgiving weekend than to come out and watch the Indians?" he said.

—*Ocilla Star*, Nov. 25, 2015

They started playing the state championship games at the Georgia Dome in 2007. There was pride and prestige that went along with playing at the Dome for all the marbles in your class. If you made it to the Dome, you had hit the daily double; you made State. That was very good. You were a top dog. Playing at the Dome was your bonus; being in Atlanta on the biggest of Georgia stages playing for the title with all the TV people there, the bright lights and that artificial turf where the Falcons played was tall cotton but the Indians in 2007 were not in that class of folks.

In 2010, when we thought we should be on the right track by now, the boys backslid to 2-8 for the second time in three years. That didn't cut the ice and after four seasons at the helm, John Gamble was let go as coach with two first-round playoff losses woven into a deficit record.

Looking for a man to restore the dream and to charm discouraged fans, school leaders called on Jon Lindsey. Lindsey came to us from over at AAAAA power Camden County, where he had been an assistant for defense under long-time head coach Jeff Herron, who'd won a state title in 2008.

Lindsey brought to Ocilla more than a screwdriver.

"The program was down in 2011," Lindsey says now from his home in Paulding County where he is coaching. "I felt it needed a complete overhaul. The players were weak and didn't have much football IQ. The coaches didn't believe in the program which was understandable at the time. I brought the same approach we used at Camden. Outwork and outcoach your opponents. We ran the wing-T and three-five defense. I changed some things to fit Irwin County but 80 percent of the program was the Camden program. Lifting a lot of weights, attending summer football camps and taking the Irwin County coaches to football clinics sped up the process."

Sometimes it's a big victory that jumpstarts a program. In our case, it was the agony of a defeat. The year was 2012. Irwin strolled into the playoffs and got ambushed. Trion came to Ocilla in the first round and knocked the Indians out, 31-6. It was a jarring blow to Jon Lindsey and everybody was sore. That was good for Ocilla football, however. There was a lot of soul-searching on the reservation because of what Trion did to us. We woke and saw the light. The boys rallied and we got back to the playoffs in 2013. Lindsey's mad-rushing tribe was going for broke. In the first round, they stomped Trion, then rolled Johnson County before coming within an eyelash of going to state, losing by a point in the semi-final round to rugged region foe Charlton County.

"I felt like we should have beat them in 2012," Lindsey says of Trion. "We had to change the mind-set in 2013. Just getting to the playoffs was not good enough. Our kids were hungry in 2013, and we learned and matured from the 2012 loss to Trion."

In 2014, Lindsey left the door open for a clever coach to succeed in his place. Boys were excited about playing football again. They crawled out of the woodwork to be part of the Indians' winning ways. Lindsey also had inspired the return of flag football and tackle football to the recreation league. "The recreational program is vital to high school sports and I was glad we got it back in Irwin County," says Lindsey, who moved on to coach at AA Cook County.

Buddy Nobles took over what Lindsey had built in Ocilla. His job with our boys was clear.

It's not about rebuilding the program, Coach Nobles told news people in the summer of 2014 when he put on the bonnet.

It's about keeping in on track.

And make no mistake; it was also about going to the Dome, and winning, which was the best cure of all for our temperament.

Nobles needed no indoctrination. After a successful coaching stint in Florida, he was an assistant at Fitzgerald, which gave him a unique perspective on Irwin County football. Later, he was the offensive coordinator for Coffee High in nearby Douglas when our school bosses tapped him to take over the Indians.

Perhaps no coach in Ocilla history ever entered his first season with more expectation than did Mr. Nobles. But he hung in doggedly and he's done a real nice job for us.

That year, 2014, the boys were perfect in the region. In the playoffs, led by dynamo D. J. Pollard, Irwin crushed Atkinson County and out-scored Dooly County before wiping out Commerce, setting the stage for a showdown with Hawkinsville for the state title in the grand Dome.

One win away from the crown, the community was dreaming that our time had come again to take it. Store fronts were streaked in red. It'd been 39 years since we last won state and

Head coach Buddy Nobles with Jakyron Young in the 2014 playoffs against Commerce. *Courtesy South Georgia Sports Network*

everyone you met would talk football with you, while in a vacant lot where a gas station used to be at Fourth Street and Irwin Avenue was parked an old yellow school bus with a sign stretched across the side that read "Dome Bound" for all see. Someone joked that we needed the National Guard to come watch over the town while everybody was gone to the Dome; it'd be a good day to rob and loot in Ocilla.

So, the hearty faithful got their cars and trucks lubed, got prayed up with Jesus, loaded up the mamas and them and everybody went to see our boys play the Red Devils of Hawkinsville at the Dome on the afternoon of Dec. 12. It was a great getaway for some football, maybe a good time to do some shopping, and Big Red fans, proud to be from Ocilla, Irwin County, were anxious also to see familiar faces on the big screen and wave at everybody back home watching the Indians on television.

By the way, we were supposed to beat Hawkinsville handedly. But when a high snap sailed over our punter's head, which led to a quick six, we gasped, and when an Indian misplayed the second-half kickoff and the Devils stuck a horn in us for another easy six, we threw up our hands. It was a high-caliber contest on the biggest of stages with all the pomp, and maybe the boys of Buddy Nobles were nervous, but we did not play our natural game and the Devils made it out of Atlanta with the 2014 Class A title. The final in the scorebook was 15-6.

The Indian family was in a grievous state, feeling we had given the game away.

Later, a billboard put up on Hwy 319 in Ocilla courtesy of a local bank patted the Indians on the back for a "great season." For a year thereafter, the boys had to look at that sign. And it was good. Nobody argued that. But maybe for some the sign was a source of frustration—and motivation.

We had to go back.

56

Unfinished Business

In today's age of technology and Internet, the State game will be one that is gone over and over and picked apart. Please know I replayed many things in different games over and over in my mind and in my heart this season and over the years of my career. The 'Play' near the goal line is one that I will live with forever. It is a call if it works then it works, if it doesn't you take the brunt reality and go on. I take full responsibility. Please make sure as we 'talk' on the Internet that it is easy to go over a decision with plenty of time to analyze and say, 'I would have done this and that.' In the game the 25-second clock means everything! Funny how life is like that also! I still take full responsibility...Last but not least thank you to my family! Tammy, Kasey, Kaleb and Kenley! We are a football family. We live and die by this crazy game of football!!! We are now part of Indian Nation and what a great thing to be a part of!...I love you with all my heart and I thank God each day for all of you !!! Please everyone have a Merry Christmas and a Great New Year! Indian Nation will rise again!!!

—Coach Buddy Nobles, Facebook, Dec. 13, 2015

And so we went back to get the prize. Just making the playoffs wouldn't have been quite enough redemption. Determined, the boys of 2015 defeated Turner County 34-24 for the 400th victory in school history: they won the region for the second time in as many years, which had not happened here since the 1970s, and in the playoffs we beat up Wilkinson County, topped Trion and held off Emmanuel County Institute to reach the Dome again–on a mission.

Irwin was in elite company. Not everybody's taken their ambitions to state, let alone two years in a row.

"I was not shocked," says former Indian coach Jon Lindsey, referring to Irwin's back-to-back appearances in the Class A title game. "Looking back now, I feel like we set the bar high and the kids that were in the program after I left only knew winning."

And it seemed like the Big Red might have a little destiny or karma on its side going back to the Dome that year, what with 2015 being the fortieth anniversary of our one and only title team.

Everybody for the Indians was sober about the task ahead, and Fitzgerald was there, too, at the Dome, in 2015, playing for their first title since 1948. How cool was that, us and Fitz both playing for a state title in the same year at the same facility? Even some Indian fans said they were rooting for the Hurricanes. Somebody with their own perspective on the old rivalry from the timber days made up T-shirts that said, "Rivals at home, friends at the Dome" to mark the unique occasion.

Certainly, Fitzgerald was due. So was Irwin County about due after coughing it up in 2014.

The theme among the Indians and fans on their return to the Dome was *"Unfinished Business."* The words were spelled out on store windows and across the top of the *Star.* Students at the school held a send-off rally for the team on Thursday, the day before the title game.

By the way, we were playing an ole south Georgia foe, Clinch County, whom we'd socked in the regular season.

On game day, business was especially slow at an Ocilla tire and lube center. "It looks like Sunday," observed a man who was spraying for bugs along the interior edges. "Fitzgerald will be like this tomorrow," he said, referring to the Hurricane's game on Saturday.

A portly man of some thirty years with beefy arms, a half-bald head and greasy hands burst into the center about some tire trouble, saying there wasn't much else for him to do; his boss was off to the Dome to see the Indians play.

"They'd better win," bawled the desk clerk. "They choked last year."

But there again, you need some luck, and while we didn't choke, we weren't very charmed, either, and Clinch handed us our hats.

"It is what it is," Indian announcer Andy Paulk cried on the radio as the curtain came down on yet another season with no title.

The Big Red did not give up any easy points like in the heartbreaker of 2014. Still, they fell short of the dream. We had a bad snap. We had a bad pass. But nobody wanted to say the best team lost. Clinch beat us up pretty good, if you want the truth, and fans were sort of humbled by it and wondering if we were Dome-jinxed. Even though our boys had raked Clinch in the regular season, 28-12, the Panthers were missing their two best men in that game, played in Ocilla, and as fate would have it, that pair of skilled players was back for the Dome game and the cats mauled us, 24–7.

And that's where we stand.

It'd be nice to end this book by saying our boys are state champs again but we cannot find the bridge, even though we love them and they are champions in our minds. There is a bridge you must cross over to football glory and among us only the Indians of 1975 have found it. Maybe next year. We all cherish the hope of doing it in 2016. Our coach calls it *beating down the door*.

Speaking of the coach, this year's game with Clinch was another hard one on Buddy Nobles, which is common in football towns where coaches are constantly under scrutiny, and after the loss he was moved to react on social media.

Business consultant and a thinking man's man, Walter Hudson of Ocilla, who played here in the 1970s under Conrad Nix, says coaching "reminds me of being real successful in business. Everybody can tell you how to run your business. Everybody can tell the coach how he ought to coach."

After the game with Clinch, and before the coach put out his Facebook message, the Indians on their yellow buses stopped at a restaurant along Interstate 75 south of Atlanta. A number of Indian fans also dined at the popular, red-sided eatery; many had come and gone before our boys arrived.

"I just told the boys they got to keep their chins up, keep fighting. We're going to beat that door down some day," Coach Nobles said in an interview as the boys filed into Buckner's to eat at the lazy-Susan tables where the specialty is always fried chicken. "We're proud to say we made it to state again but our hearts are hurting right now. We'll get back on the horse in January and get it going. We've got a good team coming back. We've got six or seven on defense and seven or eight on offense. I know I've got to do a better job as head coach. Our coaches do a great job so we'll pick it up."

Around town on Monday after the loss at State there was no angst or fever, none of the sick, irritable feeling like there was after the 2014 defeat, just licking our wounds and a faint buzz about Nobles' post on Facebook that sounded to some like an apology.

"I'm not going to say a whole lot," remarked Ocilla merchant Hazel McCranie about the play calling. "I go along with Coach Nobles."

On Facebook, the coach mentioned *the play.* Followers assumed Nobles was referring to the pass that was intercepted at Clinch's 7-yard line after the Indians had driven about the length of the field with a strong ground attack led by D.J. Pollard. Radio announcer Andy Paulk says the pass play did not have a history of working. Looking at it now, instead of passing so close to the goal, "I'd have had to go with D.J. two more times," Paulk says, and he believes had we scored, "it would have made a difference" in the tenor of the game.

Paulk, son of 1953 Indian great Danny Paulk, admits, however, the 2014 loss to Hawkinsville bothers him more than getting beat by Clinch. Either way, "I'm not really a Buddy Nobles fan," he growls.

Members of the 1953 team that went to state against Model and lost huddled at Max Alford's restaurant on Fourth Street to swap stories and watch the Irwin-Clinch game on TV.

"You know, last year we beat ourselves with all the fumbles

and centering the ball over the head a couple of times. We gave that team their points," Max cried. "This year we didn't beat ourselves. [Clinch] took it to us real hard, in my opinion."

On Monday afternoon, the mood around the field house seemed light. The silver helmets were all lined in rows on the floor by the back door. A coach was washing the shirts and there wasn't the feeling of doom but a confident vibe heading into 2016, a sign that the program is operating at a high level.

Several players were in the locker room. One emerged, accompanied by another, to shed some light on the Clinch game from the players' point of view. Said speedy back Cartavion Benyard: "Just playing in the Dome was a great experience and a great honor to go back two years in a row. We had to work hard to get back there. I wish it would've turned out better than it did."

Senior defensive end Drake Gaines added, "I hate that we didn't win but I guess it wasn't our time."

"They're still winners," commented Gwen Mike at her florist shop on Fourth Street.

By the way, Fitzgerald also lost at the Dome. Of course, that's their problem. We have our own business to take care of, kids to love and raise and to root for, and victories to go after in this community bounded by fields of cotton and peanuts where there isn't a lot to crow about but victory in Jesus.

"What just an unbelievable community," Buddy Nobles said after the Clinch game. "I mean, they've done so much for the kids. Our kids play hard for the community. I want to win state so much for the community of Ocilla because they've been so good to me and so good to my family and they've been so good to these kids.

"That's the thing that I love; how good they treat these kids."

Epilogue

Waiting for the artist to design a cover for this book gives me time for a couple of updates. Irwin County made it back to State this year, 2017, and guess who we lost to: Clinch. We've got to stop that. Critics say Irwin is getting out-coached at State by those guys. If you recall, the Panthers topped us in 2015 for State and just now clobbered us once more after the Indians rolled them in the regular season in which we finished 12-2. Our other loss this year, as one might imagine, was to Fitzgerald. The fame for the Class A marbles was supposed to be played in Atlanta at Mercedes-Benz, but organizers cancelled many contests due to snow. So, we played Clinch in Ocilla at Indian Field. There was a sign across the front of the fieldhouse that read: "Welcome to Irwin County." Ocilla had never hosted a state title game before and it was a super affair, except for the outcome, which was 21-12 for Clinch. Indian fans raised donations to help pay for the signs that were made and put up around town in support of the Big Red. By the way, if you remember "Bean," you will be glad to know that he has a job now. The former Indian giant, Justin Anderson, is working for Rhett Royal, who played for the Indians in the '60s, in the land surveying business. It's not football and Justin's heart still is set on a return to the NFL but the big man from Ocilla sounds happy and we wish him all the best.

Moving on to what I wanted to talk about. There's a chief's head painted on the Ocilla water tank. That is our city seal, which suits us well since our town was probably named for Chief Osceola and this is "Indian Territory." In football, while we've certainly had our ups and down, our head is above water in the record. Since 1952, with the opening of Irwin County High School, our boys have won about 60 percent of their games. That isn't too shabby when you consider all things and although we haven't won State in forty something years, some teams in this area have never won it and we look up at Fitzgerald which hasn't won state in almost 70 years. Certainly, the distraction that is football has done its job for us in Ocilla, Irwin County, going back to the Terrapins of the 1920s. We've had a lot of fun with the sport, seen many good boys come and go, laughed and cried, lived and died through the boys of our ball team and you don't have to be a psychologist to explain why it matters to a community like Ocilla if the Indians are victorious.

"The Irwin County school system is important to the community and the people of Ocilla," says former coach Jon Lindsey. "I believe a successful athletic program brings confidence and pride to communities, especially small towns like Ocilla."

Jake Walters, our quarterback in 1997 who became a banker,

said when the boys are going good, the town rallies and you can feel the spirit.

"I think it brings the community together especially in the playoffs. People will paint their windows. Even people who don't go to high school football games start pulling for them."

With some exceptions.

"I just ain't never cared for football," growls Earl Bagley, a one-man band at an Ocilla auto repair shop. "I reckon I've been around cars too long."

But the Big Red faithful can't imagine not having football to cheer over, and Lisa Hudson, a member of the Irwin band's drill team when she was in high school, says the sport has helped put Ocilla, Irwin County, on the map in a positive way. Lisa, wife of Walter Hudson and keeper of L's shop on Fourth Street, says she and Walter do not go to the games like they used to when their two girls were in school but they feel better when the boys win.

"In a small town, you don't have a lot of good things to happen," Lisa says.

Maybe the best reason of all as to why the community of Ocilla likes so much to win is summed up by one so wise Tifton lawyer Shane Hudson.

"It sure beats losing," says Shane, the fullback on our 1997 team that went to state. "It's a pride thing," he adds. "One of the things about our class was, we beat Fitzgerald all four years."

That's something else we need to get a handle on besides our economic situation. The Indians haven't stopped Fitz this century. Although we've tied them, our last victorious evening against the Hurricane was in 1999. Maybe we're jinxed when it comes to our nearest neighbor. Or does it go deeper? "The rivalry has lost a little bit of its luster," admits radio spotter Bill Barrs, a Fitzgerald police detective who last played for Irwin County in 1991 as a tight end on a team that finished 4–6 but beat Fitzgerald 18–10. "When you talk about this new generation, they don't see the rivalry like we saw it—blood, sweat, and tears, get after 'em. But I think the gap is beginning to close back up."

The Indian family wishes that were so. Speaking of this new generation of Irwin County boys that has discovered football, the battlers in red are not their fathers, who were mostly low-tech farm boys. Today, they're bigger, for one thing, and some are faster and stronger than boys of yore.

"I think it's all those steroid chickens or something," Andy Paulk quipps.

Certainly, they are more numerous than ever, with upwards of 60 boys dressed out for games, and pipeline is full of ones eager to take their turn on the Big Red.

That's what winning does. Marty Roberts of the Booster Club says the recent success of the program has attracted more players and more fans and drawn more attention to the school system. "Everybody wants to be a part of it now."

It's for sure that on game night our boys will battle with all their heart and the good folks of the community, however many are encouraged to do so, will be rooting them on. Nothing else can expose the heart and soul of a small community like Ocilla the way football does. And the fact that fans know many of the players by name is further testimony to life in a small town where football is a tie that binds the generations together.

No doubt the game has never solved anything for us economically. Yet we yearn for these boys of ours to do well in sport and in life because they are products of our families and our own little piece of society. They reflect who we are as people, our values, hopes, and dreams, and if the boys win, somehow it's a victory for all of us in the Ocilla vicinity because we all seem to be in the fight together and if they lose, Saturdays in Indian country cannot be very crisp and blue.

As Ocilla continues the economic struggle, keeps searching for ways to attract and retain young people in the modern age, we watch our boys grow up to be Indians and in a perfect world, their own sons and grandsons will be Indians to carry the torch of this fine old tradition. Of course, it is not perfect. But come fall, on those special Friday nights in Ocilla, you will find an eagerness and anticipation over football among fans that cannot be replicated in church and politics.

"Family," says Walter Hudson, alluding to the nature of football is the Ocilla community. "It's all about family."

And if you've ever played football in Ocilla or coached here, then you know that you are a part of it for life.

The End